MOTOR OMNIBUS
BETWEEN
HANLEY AND [LEE]K.
TIME TABLE
July 13th, 1914, and until further notice.

HANLEY TO LEEK.

	WEEK DAYS						SUNDAYS						
	a.m.	a.m.	p.m.	p.m.	p.m.	p.m.	a.m.	p.m.	p.m.	p.m.	p.m.	p.m.	p.m.
Hanley (Crown Bank) ...	9 5	11 35	2 5	4 10	6 15	7 35	11 10	2 5	2 45	3 35	5 20	6 30	7 45
Cobridge (Elder Road ...	9 11	11 41	2 11	4 16	6 21	7 41	11 16	2 11	2 51	3 41	5 26	6 36	7 51
Milton Station	9 22	11 52	2 22	4 27	6 32	7 52	11 27	2 22	3 2	3 52	5 37	6 47	8 2
Stockton Brook ...	9 30	12 0	2 30	4 35	6 40	8 0	11 35	2 30	3 10	4 0	5 45	6 55	8 10
Endon	9 34	12 4	2 34	4 39	6 44 Stop	8 4	11 39	2 34 Stop	3 14	4 4	5 49	6 59	8 14
Longsdon	9 51	12 21	2 51	4 56		8 21	11 56		3 31	4 21	6 6	7 16	8 31
Leek Market	10 3	12 33	3 3	5 8		8 33	12 8		3 43	4 33	6 18	7 28	8 43

LEEK TO HANLEY.

	WEEK DAYS						SUNDAYS					
	a.m.	p.m.	p.m.	p.m.	p.m.	p.m.	p.m.	p.m.	p.m.	p.m.	p.m.	p.m.
Leek Market	10 15	12 45	3 5	5 10		8 45	12 15		3 55	4 55	6 30	9 0
Longsdon	10 27	12 57	3 17	5 22		8 57	12 27		4 7	5 7	6 42	9 12
Endon	10 44	1 14	3 34	5 39	6 55	9 14	12 44	2 45	4 24	5 24	6 59	9 29
Stockton Brook ...	10 48	1 18	3 38	5 43	6 59	9 18	12 48	2 49	4 28	5 28	7 3	9 33
Milton Station ...	10 56	1 26	3 46	5 51	7 7	9 26	12 56	2 57	4 36	5 36	7 11	9 41
Cobridge	11 7	1 37	3 57	6 2	7 18	9 37	1 7	3 8	4 47	5 47	7 22	9 52
Hanley	11 13	1 43	4 3	6 8	7 24	9 43	1 13	3 14	4 53	5 53	7 28	9 58

FARES.

	Leek	Longsdon		Dunwood	Endon (Plough Hotel)	Stockton Brook	Baddeley Green Post Office	Milton Station	Holden Bridge
		Post Office	New Inns						
Hanley	11d.	9d.	8d.	7d.	6d.	5d.	4d.	3d.	2d.
Holden Bridge	9d.	7d.	6d.	5d.	4d.	3d.	2d.	1d.	
Milton Station ...	8d.	6d.	5d.	4d.	3d.	2d.	1d.		
Baddeley Green Post Office	7d.	5d.	4d.	3d.	2d.	1d.			
Stockton Brook ...	6d.	4d.	3d.	2d.	1d.				
Endon (Plough Hotel) ...	5d.	3d.	2d.	1d.					
Dunwood	4d.	2d.	1d.						
Longsdon (New Inns) ...	3d.								

The 'Buses will stop to set down or take up Passengers at any point.

Tickets are available on the day of issue only, and on the 'Bus upon which they are issued.

Passengers are requested to see that a Ticket is punched in their presence, representing the value of the fare paid, and showing the Section to be travelled over.

Half-price Tickets are not issued. Two Children under twelve years will be allowed to travel as one fare. All children over three years of age must be paid for.

The Company give notice that, while every effort will be made to keep correct time, they will not be responsible for any loss or injury which may arise from delay ; and the Company also reserve to themselves the right to make any alteration in the fares or Time-tables without notice.

All Parcels must be paid for, except those carried by hand, and not occupying a seat or part of a gangway.

The Company is prepared, on application, to run later 'Buses for parties of guaranteed numbers.

General Manager's Office,
Stoke-on-Trent,
Telephone 801 Central.

C. H. Vyse, The Royal Printing Works, Stoke.

THE POTTERIES

MOTOR TRACTION CO. LTD.

a retrospect . . . by Geoffrey K Smith

Venture *publications*

Computer Origination, Design and Layout by John A Senior

This busy scene at Longton Bus Station captured the flavour of PMT when the Author's earlier book on the history of the Company was published in 1977. Centre stage is one of the Eastern Coach Works-bodied Bristol VRs, with an Alexander-bodied Daimler Fleetline standing behind it. Moving towards the camera is a former Wigan Corporation Massey-bodied Leyland Titan, by then with Berresfords, whilst the single-decker AEC Reliance from the same fleet carries a Willowbrook body. Only one of these manufacturers survives – Alexanders – but in a very different reincarnation. Nothing remains of any of the once-thriving factories where all these vehicles were built. *(John A Senior)*

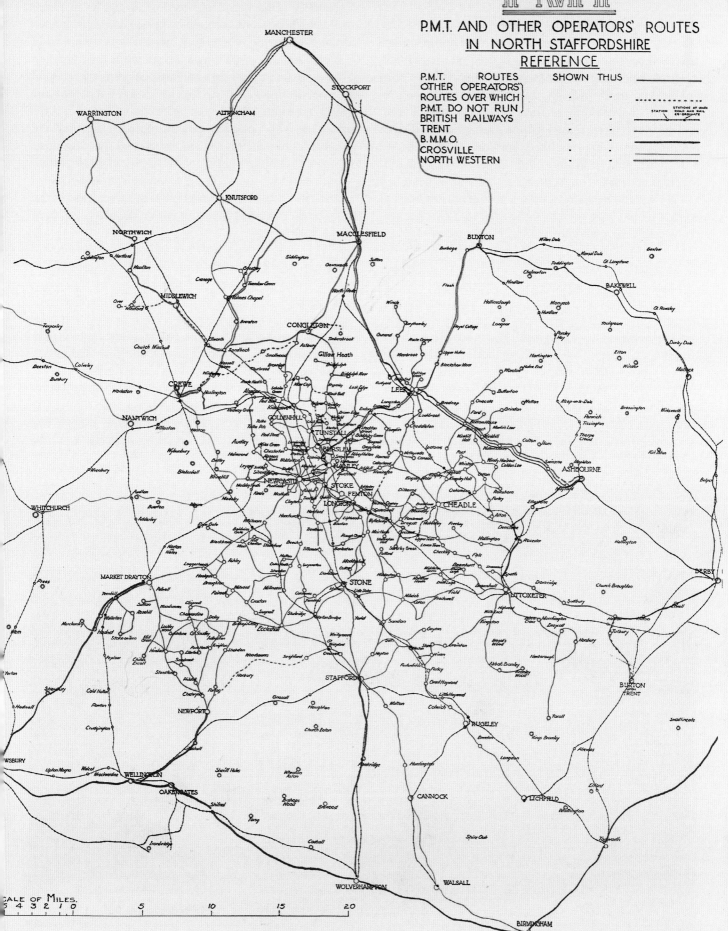

P.M.T. AND OTHER OPERATORS' ROUTES IN NORTH STAFFORDSHIRE

REFERENCE

P.M.T. ROUTES	SHOWN THUS
OTHER OPERATORS' ROUTES OVER WHICH P.M.T. DO NOT RUN	
BRITISH RAILWAYS	
TRENT	
B.M.M.O.	
CROSVILLE	
NORTH WESTERN	

STATIONS AT which STATION ROAD AND RAIL CO-ORDINATE

SCALE OF MILES.
5 4 3 2 1 0   5   10   15   20

Introduction

It is now over 30 years since the publication of *PMT – A National Bus Company* and now approaching 78 years since the formation of the Potteries Motor Traction Company Limited on 1st June 1933 – and double that time since the first horse tram ran in the Potteries, the creation of one George Francis Train, in 1860. For these reasons I am most grateful to the publisher for giving me this opportunity to mark these milestones with a second book on the PMT Co. Ltd together with notes on its predecessors and successors.

If I were to be asked what my favourite 'bus books' were, I would have to say *The Sowing and the Harvest* and *State Owned without Tears* by WJ Crosland-Taylor, *Wheels to the West* by Clem Preece and Walter Womar's autobiographical notes in his *Turning Points – a lifetime in Transport*. There are others, of course, but all these books were written by 'busmen' of vast experience about their own careers and companies. As such they have an authenticity which it is difficult for the outsider to emulate. They also have a wonderful store of 'in-house' stories and anecdotes which an enthusiast such as myself would find difficult to copy. I can only claim to have worked at PMT as a 'temp' in the Traffic Office on summer vacations from Theological College.

So, in writing this book, I have not made any attempt to offer anything more than an enthusiast's view of PMT using such historical material and personal memory as I could come across from a great deal of careful research. Some of this 'research', done in schooldays, included frequent cycle rides to Stoke, Vale Place or Burslem garages, occasionally being given the chance, especially at Stoke, to go inside and talk to different people. There were evenings, when I should have been doing homework, when I took myself 'bus riding' and I can still remember the shock when I made the transition from half-fare to full-fare and my pocket money did not rise accordingly! Money still had to be left to buy the latest Ian Allan ABC. I even produced my own for PMT complete with Company history, route list, fleet list and pictures, obviously never published and long ago lost! Since the publication of my first book in 1977 further information has come to light, much from the Kithead Trust, and the PMT photographic archive, now in the care of the Potteries Museum and Art Gallery, has been made available.

This is in no way a definitive publication and so it will not be a book containing lots of bus numbers or route lists except where the text makes this necessary. No attempt will be made to go into the minutia of company records or accounts. Neither will there be any cataloguing of changes to the route system over the years which, I suspect, would become tedious to most readers. This book will give but a glimpse of the colourful story of bus operation in North Staffordshire.

Both publisher and author hope that enough is contained within these pages to interest, inform and entertain the reader. So, sit back, read, look at the pictures and enjoy.

Geoffrey K Smith
Stafford
March 2011

Smart and shining, in traditional PMT livery.

Part 1 – The PMT Story

Early Years – Horses and Steam

The year was 1755. An ironmaster and engineer, James Outram, built a colliery line in Sheffield using L-shaped rails. This became known as 'Outram's Way' and hence 'Tramway'. Yet it would be another hundred years before George Francis Train, an extrovert and clever American from Boston, brought his tramway to North Staffordshire.

However, the first provision of a public passenger service in North Staffordshire was not concerned with the operation of tramways at all. It was made in 1848 when the North Staffordshire Railway Company opened its line from Stoke-on-Trent to Norton Bridge, a tiny hamlet between Stone and Stafford. A further 14 years were to elapse before the advent of the trams.

Train had already pioneered horse trams in Birkenhead, London and Darlington before he arrived in the Potteries where work commenced on his line from Burslem to Hanley when 'the first sod' was turned in Waterloo Road on 25th November 1861. Thus was The Staffordshire Potteries Street Railway born.

Some may consider this a pretentious title for a mere two and a half miles of track, and in the early days it was even necessary to change cars at the toll-gate in Cobridge! Trams ran from Burslem Town Hall to Foundry Square in Hanley every hour or half hour for 3d.

George Francis Train's horse tram, a 'People's Carriage' or 'the ludicrous horse tram'? Above is a tram 'The People' in London in the early days whilst below is 'Queen' in the Potteries after the take over by GB Bradford. *(PMus)*

George Francis Train – 1829-1904

Exuberant, eccentric, entrepreneur, are just some of the words that have been used to describe this American orphan, for George was born in Boston, Massachusetts, but orphaned at the age of four after a plague of yellow fever killed his family. He was brought up by his strict Methodist grandparents who hoped he would become a minister of the church.

The ministerial life, however, was not for Train who became involved in the mercantile business life of Boston and Australia before coming to England in 1860 where he hoped to make his fortune out of street tramways or 'Peoples Carriages' as he would refer to them. He pioneered systems in Birkenhead, Darlington, London and the Potteries, but in 1861 he was arrested for 'breaking and injuring' a London street! On leaving England he toured Europe and made round the world trips in 1870 and again in 1880.

On returning to America he referred to himself as "Citizen Train", becoming a shipping magnate and getting involved in the setting up of the Union Pacific Railway. He was a prolific writer, confidant of French and Australian revolutionaries and, in 1872, a Presidential candidate in the USA. He was offered the Presidency of a proposed Australian Republic but declined. Train became a very rich man, forming his own finance company trading in real estate and he was a slavish supporter of the temperance movement and a champion of women's rights.

In spite of all this he was jailed for obscenity and in 1873 was arrested and threatened with being sent to a lunatic asylum. His journeyings have suggested that he was the inspiration for Jules Vernes 'Around the World in Eighty Days' – Train actually accomplished it in 67! George became ill with smallpox whilst at the home of his daughter in 1903 and died in New York the following year, being proclaimed as 'one of the few sane men in a mad mad world'.

PMT's resident artist, Alf Fallows, created this drawing of a horse tram in Hope Street, Hanley outside the draper's shop of Enoch Bennett, Arnold Bennett's birthplace. It was used on the front cover of the PMT House Magazine of March 1967 to celebrate the 100th anniversary of Bennett's birth. *(AC)*

In Darlington, Train's horse tram company, The Darlington Street Railroad Company Ltd, was short-lived, the four-minute-ride line opening in January 1862 and closing at the end of 1864 – with the winding up of the company following in 1866.

Train never made any money from his Potteries venture, which threatened what was left of the coaching trade including the first horse-bus in the district which had commenced in 1842 and ran from Longton to Burslem, fare one shilling. The novelist Arnold Bennett offers a wonderful description of the horse-tram in his novel about life in North Staffordshire, *The Old Wives Tale*:

'Incredible as it may appear, there was nothing but a horse-tram running between Bursley and Hanbridge – and that only twice an hour, and between the other towns no stage of any kind ….

The ludicrous horse-car was typical of them. The driver rang a huge bell five minutes before the starting, that could be heard from the Wesleyan Chapel to the Cock Yard, and then after deliberations and hesitations the vehicle rolled off on its rails into unknown dangers whilst passengers shouted good-bye …. And this was regarded as the last word in traction'.

In a letter to the General Purposes Committee of Hanley Town Council in August 1861 Train wrote that he was 'desirous of constructing a line from Longton to Goldenhill', but this did not happen. Faced with insurmountable difficulties, debt, problems with his step-rail type of track and, in April 1862, a fatal accident, it all became too much for him.

In that fateful year a 16 year old boy, George Gater, stepped onto the driving platform of the tram to ride with the driver, Henry Brown. He attempted to jump from the car and run to his home in Pitt Street but his foot caught in the vehicle and he was thrown under the wheels. The lad died within 15 minutes. George Francis Train was forced to quit and leave the country disillusioned and in debt.

This was not to be the end of the horse trams, however. Train's company was leased to a local man, GP Bradford, believed to have been a Councillor, who continued with horse traction but promptly removed the step-rails and relaid the track with grooved rail, again to the standard gauge of 4ft 8½ins. Under George Bradford's management the company continued for almost 20 years, the loss-making shareholders being quite content with the idea of 'promoting the public benefit'. No extension to the horse tramway was ever made; this had to wait until after The Staffordshire Potteries Street Railway Company was wound up, which happened in 1880.

Henry Osborne O'Hagan was in charge when, later in 1881, the Street Railway Company was acquired by his 'North Staffordshire Tramways Company'. O'Hagan

The Staffordshire Potteries Street Railway Company Limited.

THE affairs of the above-named Company being now fully wound up, and the property of the Company disposed of, notice is hereby given, that an Extraordinary General Meeting of the Shareholders of the Staffordshire Potteries Street Railway Company Limited, will be held in the Townhall, Hanley, on Wednesday, the 15th day of December, 1880, at twelve o'clock at noon, for the purpose of having laid before them the accounts of the Liquidator, showing the manner in which the winding up has been conducted, and the property of the Company disposed of, and of hearing any explanation that may be given by the Liquidator.— Dated this 6th day of November, 1880.

Saml. J. Hooley, Tunstall, Liquidator of the Staffordshire Potteries Street Railway Company Limited.

was another flamboyant entrepreneur, but somewhat less scrupulous in his business dealings. Through his main company – The City of London Contract Corporation – he put in place a series of complicated and devious arrangements through subsidiary companies he owned or controlled, ensuring that the North Staffs Company would be financially hamstrung by having to make all arrangements for supply of rolling-stock, consumables, renewals and so on to be handled by one or another of O'Hagan's companies. The charges levied for such 'services' were apparently excessive, and whilst O'Hagan and his fellow Promoters did extremely well from the arrangements the North Staffs Company was milked of cash and slowly bled to death – and its ordinary shareholders were powerless to stop it. It perhaps goes without saying that those same shareholders received a poor return on their investment which was, apparently, a common theme in the 'management' of his other tramway companies, including those in Oldham and Darlington.

To the outside world, however, all appeared to be well, for Henry Osborne O'Hagan soon opened his first extension, a line from Stoke to Longton, but to the reduced gauge of 4ft; a second soon followed from Stoke to West End whereby almost seven miles of steam tramway were now in operation. A further extension was constructed from Longton to Normacot but the Board of Trade would not allow it to be used for steam trams because they considered the roads to be too narrow. The line fell into disuse and later became the property of Longton Corporation.

The steam trams were extraordinary vehicles, being Manning-Wardle locomotives hauling large double-deck trailers, the only double-deck tramcars ever to run in the Potteries. The first steam tram driver was Mr Edwin Edwards who died at his home in Fenton in 1910. He had been one of the first employees of the company and drove his tram on its trial run for inspection by the Local Government Board.

There were 14 of these offensive vehicles in use by 1882 when an interesting experimental car was built by the Beyer, Peacock Company of Gorton in Manchester for operation by the North Staffordshire Company. It was a self-contained tram requiring no separate trailer for the passengers. The steam trams proved themselves to be unpopular, people cursing them for 'showering dust and ashes' and for 'smothering the place with soot, smuts, sparks and smoke'.

At the end of seven years working an appeal was made by the Local Authorities to the Board of Trade to refuse the renewal of the licence. The Board acceded to this request and the Potteries towns became tramless.

A classic view of one of O'Hagan's double-deck steam trams which plied the route between Stoke and Longton during 1881/2. The locomotive was one of four built by Manning-Wardle. The driver-fireman stands proudly in the entrance doorway to his engine. It has been suggested that the two youths were 'coal boys' employed to fetch coal to the tramway termini in order to refuel the 'beasts' during the working day but they seem to be far too clean and smart for such duties – is one the conductor with his cash bag? *(PMus)*

This action, however, enabled petitioners and public alike to realise the value of the steam tramway service. The routes were gradually reinstated, for in reality the hated steam trams were better than none at all.

Arnold Bennett, constantly fascinated by the trams, wrote in his novel *Clayhanger*:

'A house stood on a hill, and that hill was Bleakridge, the summit of the little billow of land between Bursley and Hanbridge.

'.... People were now talking of the advantages of living 'up at Bleakridge', 'above' the smoke and 'out' of town. The 'new steam cars would pull you up there in three minutes or so, every quarter of an hour.

'It was really the new steam cars that were the making of Bleakridge as a residential suburb .... Land was changing owners at Bleakridge, and rising in price .... Cottage property in the centre of the town depreciating.'

The line of which Bennett wrote was the original horse tram route from Burslem to Hanley.

Twenty more Beyer, Peacock trams were placed into service in 1884. They had Wilkinson engines and eight-wheeled single-deck trailers. Such was the success of these cars that O'Hagan's company continued to operate for another twelve years. Average receipts for the final three years of operation were 14.15 pence per car mile. 360,156 car miles were operated each year carrying 3,913,746 passengers. There were 6.75 miles of route.

There were many incidents on the tramway over the years but a particularly unfortunate tragedy occurred

in Stoke on 13th April 1894 at four o'clock in the afternoon. A three year old child, Jane Ridgeway, fell into the canal adjacent to the tramway. Timothy Trow, a steam tram conductor, leapt from his tram and plunged into the canal in an attempt to rescue little Jane. Whilst in the cold water Timothy suffered an attack of cramp and drowned. The heroism of Timothy Trow is marked by a small monument which still stands opposite the end of James Street in the West End of Stoke. Jane was later rescued by John Forrester from Shelton. The present writer was invited to conduct a Memorial Service at the monument on 13th April 1994 to commemorate the centenary of the tragedy.

The last steam tram was driven by Charge Engineer Mr W Eardley as late as 1902, going to the scrapyard, a site adjacent to Park Avenue in Shelton, perhaps with not too many regrets from the local populace. Better things were in store.

How many readers have seen this memorial to Timothy Trow which stands by the long-since abandoned Newcastle canal?

Steam tramway men posed in front of a Manning-Wardle locomotive at the opening of the system in 1881. *(PMus)*

The scene at the closure of the steam tramway in May 1899 at the resting place in Shelton adjoining Hanley Park. *(PMus)*

Surviving documentation from the Kithead Archive showing the Light Railway Order which authorised construction to begin under The Potteries Light Railways Order of 1897, and, right, a letter from the Board of Trade to Sidney Morse, the BET Solicitor, granting an extension of time before work must begin. *(Kithead)*

THE LIGHT RAILWAYS ACT 1896.

POTTERIES LIGHT RAILWAYS

ORDER OF THE LIGHT RAILWAY COMMISSIONERS

Authorising the construction of Light Railways in the Potteries District of Staffordshire.

Preliminary.

1. This Order may be cited as "The Potteries Light Railways Short title. Order 1897" and shall come into force on the day when the same is confirmed by the Board of Trade which day is hereinafter referred 5 to as "the commencement of this Order."

2. Words and expressions to which by the principal Act or Interpretation. any Acts in whole or in part incorporated with this Order meanings are assigned have in this Order (unless the context otherwise requires) the same respective meanings and in this 10 Order—

The expression "the Company" means the British Electric Traction Company Limited;

The expression "the principal Act" means the Light Railways Act 1896;

15 The expressions "the railway" "the railways" mean the railways and works by this Order authorised and the

III.   A   B

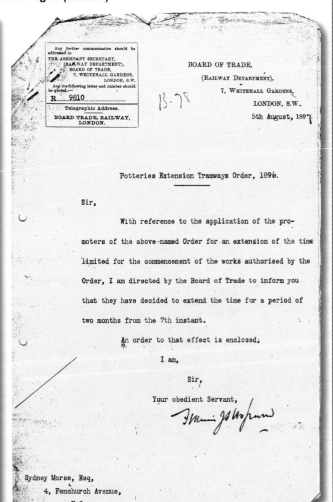

Any *further* communication should be addressed to
THE ASSISTANT SECRETARY,
(RAILWAY DEPARTMENT),
BOARD OF TRADE,
7, WHITEHALL GARDENS,
LONDON, S.W.
And the following letter and number should be quoted —
R   9810
Telegraphic Address.
BOARD TRADE, RAILWAY,
LONDON.

BOARD OF TRADE,
(RAILWAY DEPARTMENT),
7, WHITEHALL GARDENS,
LONDON, S.W.,
5th August, 1897.

B.78

Potteries Extension Tramways Order, 1896.

Sir,

With reference to the application of the promoters of the above-named Order for an extension of the time limited for the commencement of the works authorised by the Order, I am directed by the Board of Trade to inform you that they have decided to extend the time for a period of two months from the 7th instant.

An order to that effect is enclosed.

I am,

Sir,

Your obedient Servant,

Sydney Morse, Esq,
4, Fenchurch Avenue,
E.C.

Into the Twentieth Century – Electric Traction

The first electric trams in North Staffordshire ran on a Wednesday afternoon in April 1899 when a number of the new cars were used in order to familiarise the drivers with the control and operation of the new vehicles. It is quite possible that the first run was over the original horse tram route between Burslem and Hanley. But before any of this could happen a great deal of work needed to be done.

Not least was the formation of the company which was to operate them, the newly formed British Electric Traction Company Ltd, which, following the demise of O'Hagan's venture, leased the lines of the North Staffordshire Company.

It was in 1897 that work commenced to relay the whole of the tramway with new heavier track retaining the 4ft gauge of the steam tramway. With the exception of the double-tracked section between Hanley and Stoke, the whole system was single-track with passing loops. The generating station was at Stoke, feeding the current by overhead wires to the electric motors beneath the cars. Work progressed rapidly and the inaugural ceremony took place in the power house at Stoke on 16th May 1899 by which time the whole of the 'Main Line' from Longton to Goldenhill was completed as well as a spur from Burslem to Smallthorne. The ceremony was followed by a tour of the system using three of the new electric cars and a Directors' lunch took place in the Victoria Hall in Hanley. Great crowds of people turned out to inspect the new tramcars.

Arnold Bennett, again from *The Old Wives Tale*: 'You could not foresee the hundred and twenty electric cars that now rush madly bumping and thundering at twenty miles an hour through the main streets of the district!'

The British Electric Traction Company had acquired a controlling interest in the North Staffordshire Tramway and on 28th June 1898 a new Company was incorporated and registered as The Potteries Electric Traction Co. Ltd. The BET grew quickly so that by 1901 some 124 miles of tramway were being operated by 36 companies of which PET was considered the flagship. So much so that at one time the Potteries Electric Traction Company was described as 'the largest and finest tramway system in the world'. Its Chairman in 1901 was able to tell shareholders:

'We must consider that the electric traction industry has now established a firm hold on the country and I think I may justly say this – that our Company may be looked upon as the leading representatives of the industry.'

The electric tram arrives in Newcastle – an impressive selection of dignitaries including BET Directors and local councillors pose proudly for the photographer on 16th May 1899 after the Official Inspection. It seems that passengers had been carried free of charge the previous day. *(PMus)*

A second generating station was opened at May Bank in 1900 and a new tram depot was built at Goldenhill. No further extensions were completed until 1904 when the system was extended to the mining villages to the north and west of Newcastle-under-Lyme which town was also further linked to the main network with lines to Stoke and Burslem. The PET parcels service (Prompt-Economical-Transit) was started in 1901 carrying, after only six weeks, some 3,000 parcels a week with twenty offices in the district where parcels could be left and collected. Later on messenger boys and vans were employed to extend the service beyond the tramway network. The service continued until 1942 when wartime restrictions curtailed its activities.

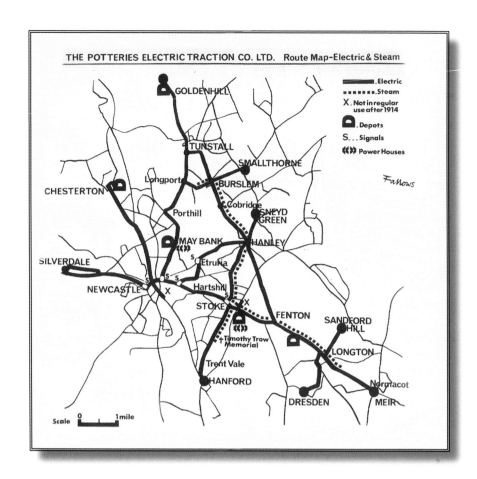

Once the various official inspections had been satisfactorily completed, operation could begin. Brush-built 24-seat car 67 is seen outside Longton Park Gates whilst working between Hanley and Dresden.

Arnold Bennett

1867-1931

Novelist, playwright, essayist, and journalist, Bennett was, like Train, too big a man to be contained within his home town. He was born in Hope Street, Hanley where his father was a draper and pawnbroker who bettered himself to become a Solicitor. After attending school in Newcastle-under-Lyme, Arnold failed his university entrance examination and became a solicitors clerk in London in 1889.

Bennett showed early promise as a writer and had won a writing competition in the *Staffordshire Evening Sentinel* whilst still at school. He went on to become editor of *Woman* magazine and in 1907 married a French actress, Marguerite Soulie. He never returned to North Staffordshire and died from typhoid fever on 27th March 1931 after a visit to France. Following his cremation service in London his ashes were buried in the family plot in a church in Burslem.

Arnold Bennett never lost his love for the Potteries or the North Staffordshire scenery, though he was sometimes critical of the people. In his novel *The Old Wives Tale* he refers to them as 'a poor, blind, complacent people'. The area gave him his inspiration for his finest novels, those set in the Potteries of which there were nine, including *Anna of the Five Towns*, *Clayhanger* and perhaps less well known *Grim Smile of the Five Towns*. Bennett watched the 'ludicrous horse-car' under the ownership of George Bradford and saw the introduction of the steam-trams, both of which he seemed fascinated with in his novels, but though he refers to them in *The Old Wives Tale* Arnold never saw the electric trams of the PET Company.

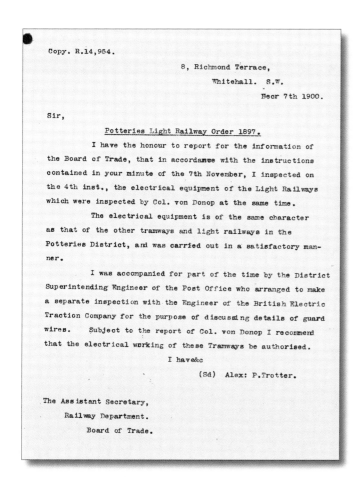

Copy. R.14,954.

8, Richmond Terrace,
Whitehall. S.W.
Becr 7th 1900.

Sir,

Potteries Light Railway Order 1897.

I have the honour to report for the information of the Board of Trade, that in accordance with the instructions contained in your minute of the 7th November, I inspected on the 4th inst., the electrical equipment of the Light Railways which were inspected by Col. von Donop at the same time.

The electrical equipment is of the same character as that of the other tramways and light railways in the Potteries District, and was carried out in a satisfactory manner.

I was accompanied for part of the time by the District Superintending Engineer of the Post Office who arranged to make a separate inspection with the Engineer of the British Electric Traction Company for the purpose of discussing details of guard wires. Subject to the report of Col. von Donop I recommend that the electrical working of these Tramways be authorised.

I have&c

(Sd) Alex: P.Trotter.

The Assistant Secretary,
Railway Department.
Board of Trade.

Mr Alexander P Trotter confirms to the Board of Trade that his inspection of the PET lines was satisfactory. *(Kithead)*

The Trams

To operate this system a fleet of almost 120 trams was built up. They were purchased at various times, the first acquisition being of 17 cars with Brush bodies on four-wheeled Peckham trucks, seating 24 passengers on longitudinal benches. These soon proved to have insufficient capacity for the heavy traffic building up on the 'Main Line'. Augmentation was provided in the form of ten 24-seat trailers built by Brush to match the original cars. The trailers, however, were soon put into store owing to the high cost of having to provide two conductors but were rebuilt as motor-cars in 1906. In spite of their small capacity a further 12 Peckham-Brush 24-seat cars arrived in 1899.

As route extensions were opened further trams were required and 30 were purchased in 1900, this time on Brill trucks but still four-wheeled and having seats for only 24 passengers. A fleet of 60 24-seat trams had been built up before the first of the larger cars arrived in 1901. These had eight-wheeled Brill trucks on double bogies; the first batch of 15, seating 40, was built by the Midland Carriage and Wagon Company and was followed by a second batch of 20, but built by Brush. A further batch of five Brush cars arrived in 1906, this time seating 44. Three similar cars which arrived in 1908 brought the total fleet to 103 and were to be the last new tramcars for PET.

Seen in leafy surroundings in Porthill in the charge of Driver W Kendrick is tram No. 52, a 24-seat car new in 1900. It was one of the large batch of 30 built by the Electric Railway and Tramway Carriage Works on Brill 21E trucks. The heavy greatcoat was an essential part of the driver's protection against the elements on the open-fronted tramcars. His right hand is holding the handbrake which would wind a chain to apply the brakes to the wheels whilst his left hand is on the controller which regulated the amount of current passing to the motor, and thus determined the speed. Above the lifeguard (situated under the front of the tram) the square projection from the collision fender is the access to the coupling socket used to attach the tram to its one-time trailer – or to tow it home in the event of a breakdown. The picture shows it making the last tram journey on the Tunstall, Burslem, and Newcastle route in 1928. *(PMus)*

What a glorious contraption! But what is it? In fact it is an early horse-drawn tower-wagon for the new electric trams. There appears to be no mention of PET, only the British Electric Traction Company with its head office in Norfolk Street off The Strand in London, and it proclaims itself to be Vehicle No. 1. It is possible that this photograph was actually taken before PET had been registered in 1898. The note on the back of the photograph confirms it was a locally-built edifice, by 'Hall Bros. Prize Builders, Burslem'. *(PMus)*

The small 24-seat Brush-built cars were clearly not going to cope with the demand met by double-deck steam tram trailers with a probable capacity approaching 100 when overloaded. Working them in coupled form went some small way to meet the problem but a crew of three was uneconomic. The lower view shows the piping for the air brakes, operated by the driver of the leading car but operating on both. The controller handles can be seen on the outer extremities of the photograph, confirming that operation from either end took place – the controllers in the centre have had their handles removed. *(PMus)*

Map from a PET Company brochure of 1925; there were four other depots as described in the text.

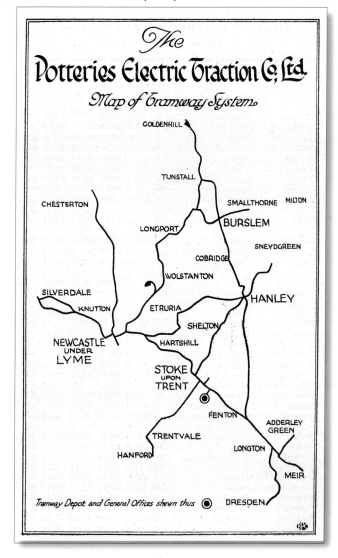

The Potteries Electric Traction Co; Ltd.
Map of Tramway System

GOLDENHILL
TUNSTALL
CHESTERTON
SMALLTHORNE   MILTON
LONGPORT
BURSLEM
SNEYDGREEN
COBRIDGE
WOLSTANTON
SILVERDALE
KNUTTON
ETRURIA
HANLEY
SHELTON
NEWCASTLE
UNDER
LYME
HARTSHILL
STOKE
UPON
TRENT
FENTON
ADDERLEY
GREEN
TRENTVALE
LONGTON
HANFORD
MEIR
Tramway Depot and General Offices shewn thus ◉   DRESDEN

All further purchases were to be of second-hand vehicles. The first arrived as early as 1907 when two Brush 40 seaters were acquired from the Middleton Electric Traction Co. Ltd, a BET subsidiary company outside Manchester. In 1920 three trams came from Sheffield Tramways, all 28-seaters. The last car to be purchased was in 1922 when No. 125 was acquired. Recent information from Peter Jaques at Kithead reveals it was purchased new for the sum of £800 (not as often quoted, second-hand from the Dudley, Stourbridge and District Electric Traction Company) and seated 32 passengers. It had been constructed by the Birmingham and Midland Tramway Co., another BET subsidiary, and was the only vestibuled car to be purchased thus demonstrating just how far the PET system had slipped behind. Realising this, the company rebuilt two of the 1900 cars with vestibules and doors. All three were painted bright scarlet and primrose. About this time car 50 was converted for use as a one-man-operated tram, with the driver collecting fares. How successful or otherwise this proved to be has not yet come to light.

The most significant occurrence in the mid-twenties, however, and again unearthed by Peter Jaques, was the decision to build (in-house) a low-height double-deck tram capable of passing below the low bridges. A pair of trucks were constructed and tested, but the project was abandoned and the use of the (patented) technology offered to other BET companies, though there seem to have been no takers. It seems possible that this and other tramway initiatives were sidelined by the on-going problems with the City of Stoke-on-Trent through congestion in the streets, resulting in the City Council taking the initiative to get rid of the trams.

Tram number 125 showing the enclosed driver's vestibule area, and looking smart in its primrose and cream livery. Note the position of the route board. (STA)

Early Motor Bus Services – before the First World War

In spite of the claims made about the successes of the tramway system at the start of the twentieth century, the PET Co. was quick to experiment with motor buses which were initially thought of as being useful feeders to the tram routes. In April 1901 the BET Co. purchased two Straker Squire steam buses which were sent to PET for experimental operation. It is interesting to speculate if this was done in view of the Company's not inconsiderable experience with steam trams. The buses were of the double-deck type with open seating on the upper deck, but were fitted with glass windscreens at the front to afford some protection to the intrepid passengers. They were first operated on a route between Burslem and Milton but were not powerful or reliable enough to cope with the hilly four mile journey. After a few months they were transferred to the flatter and shorter route between Newcastle and Trent Vale where they performed with no more success. The buses were losing 1.18d per bus mile and were sold in 1902.

Undaunted, more buses were purchased in 1904. There were three, registered EH1, 2 and 4, built by Brush – a BET associated company – and they had Mutel engines with a chain drive to the rear wheels. Again used as tram feeders, they were put to work on a route between Hanley and Bucknall but were no more successful than the Straker Squire buses and did not last long. Two were sold by 1906 and may have been used in the Trentham area; certainly a photograph exists depicting a bus in this district in that year.

The third vehicle EH 4 was rebodied, in fact it received two interchangeable bodies, one a 23-seat charabanc which could be exchanged for a tower-wagon body which was used for tramway maintenance and remained with the company until 1919.

EH I and 2 were the first petrol buses to be operated, albeit unsuccessfully, in the Potteries during 1905 and 1906. One wonders how the authorities permitted their use at all due to the front staircase almost obliterating the driver's nearside view, although had the PET operated double-deck trams, this type of staircase – 'reversed' in tramway parlance – would have been quite normal. *(STA)*

EH1 was originally registered EH 30 under the provisions of the Motor Car Act on 9th November 1904 but was re-registered EH1 under the Heavy Motor Car Act in 1905. EH 2 was not registered until 29th April 1905 so carried this number from the start.

Left is EH1 posed at the Brush works prior to delivery whilst EH 2 is shown overleaf demonstrating a well-patronised private hire, 1905 style. Many differences can be detected between these buses, such as the radiused upper corners to the windows in EH 2 and the curved panels between the side and the bulkhead behind the driver. Note also that all the wheels are the same size on EH 2.

Both were built at the Brush works in Loughborough with Mutel engines; EH 2 was exhibited at the 1905 Olympia Motor Show. *(STA)*

This is the third of the three PET vehicles, EH 4, which differed from the two double-deck machines as can be seen. It may originally have been a double-decker, but is seen here with a charabanc body which it is known to have carried, at least from 1905. Later it became a tower-wagon and was used until 1919. It is likely that the charabanc and tower-wagon bodies were interchangeable. *(STA)*

Four CD-type Daimler buses were acquired in 1913 to commence a somewhat adventurous route from Hanley to Leek via Endon and Longsdon, a distance of some 14 miles. This proved so successful that a further four similar buses were bought to commence a second regular bus service from Stoke to Stone also in 1913. Six more buses, this time Daimler B-types were purchased in 1914 for further expansion into the rural hinterland of the Potteries. All 14 buses were impounded by the War Department in 1915 and saw active service in France. Twelve second-hand machines were sourced to maintain services during the war, some running on coal gas carried in a large gas balloon on the roof.

The PET had built up its traffic on low fares and frequent services. One could travel from Longton to Burslem for 2d – just under 1p! Early morning and late night journeys for workers in the mines and pot-banks were run at half fare and the trams were operated for seven days a week throughout the year. Fifteen routes were operated covering 32 route miles with five tramway depots at Longton, Fenton and Stoke on the 'Main Line' and at May Bank and Chesterton within Newcastle-under-Lyme. However, in 1917 they were announcing fare increases on the buses due to the increased cost of petrol – it is not clear if the tram fares were also increased as other costs rose during the war.

In 1902 the PET company had carried 14,438,048 passengers. By 1919 the tramway mileage had increased to 2,459,553, whilst the number of passengers carried had risen to 31,586,966 or 12.74 per car-mile. The system had then reached its zenith, and the full route system was as listed on page 21.

The Potteries Electric Traction Company, Ltd.

MOTOR OMNIBUS SERVICES.

ALTERATION OF FARES.

Owing to the increased cost of Petrol and other Commodities, the Company is compelled to increase the Omnibus Fares. The increase will come into force on **THURSDAY, MARCH 1st, 1917,** and Fares will be as under:—

Hanley and Leek.

	Leek	Longsdon Post Office	New Inns	Dunwood	Endon	Stockton Brook	Baddeley Green	Milton	Holden Bridge	Cobridge
Hanley	1/1	11d.	10d.	9d.	7d.	6d.	5d.	4d.	2d.	2d.
Cobridge	1/-	10d.	9d.	8d.	6d.	5d.	4d.	3d.	2d.	
Holden Bridge	11d.	9d.	8d.	7d.	5d.	4d.	3d.	2d.		
Milton	9d.	8d.	7d.	6d.	4d.	3d.	2d.			
Baddeley Green	8d.	6d.	5d.	4d.	3d.	2d.				
Stockton Brook	7d.	5d.	4d.	3d.	2d.					
Endon	6d.	4d.	3d.	2d.						
Dunwood	4d.	3d.	2d.							
Longsdon, New Inns	3d.	2d.								

A comparison of fares before and after the 1917 increase, kept in the Traffic Office files, and now amongst the many surviving papers in the Kithead Archive. *(Kithead)*

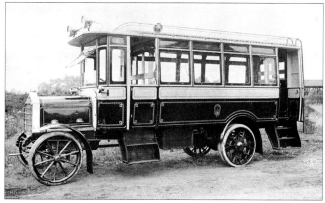

Two views taken by Brush near to its Loughborough works before the first of the Daimler CD-types were delivered to PET. Similar vehicles could be found in other BET fleets and the type was clearly intended to be a group standard.

Brush decided to withdraw from building chassis, following difficulties with Mutel, the engine producer, concentrating thereafter on bodybuilding alongside its core electrical work. BET then moved to Tilling-Stevens until purchases were first made from BMMO in 1924. *(STA)*

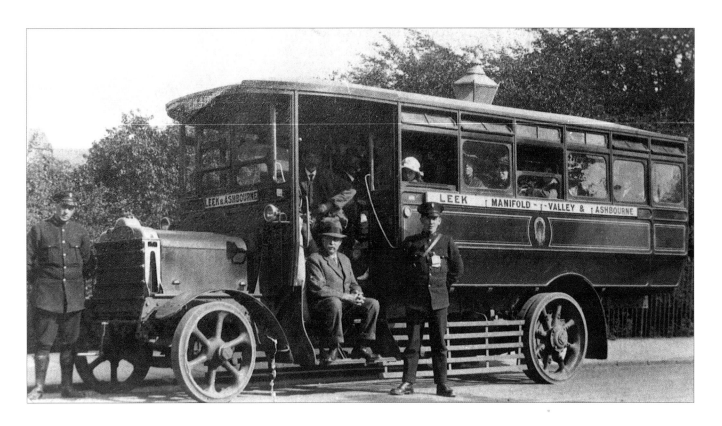

Above: The driver stands proudly by the radiator of his steed and his conductor, equally smartly turned out, is beside the very wide entrance door of this Birch-bodied Daimler Y-type. Elderly passengers seem quite happy sitting on the step but will soon move as the bus is about to embark on the lengthy and very rural journey between Leek and Ashbourne through the Manifold valley immediately after the First World War. *(PMus)*

Below: An unidentified Daimler, possibly one of the second-hand acquisitions made during the 1914-18 war after PET's own vehicles had been requisitioned by the War Department. It is seen at Fenton during the war years running on town gas, the gas bags being fitted on the roof and well boarded in, giving the appearance when empty, as here, of an open-top double-decker. *(PMus)*

Back in 1910 the six Potteries towns of Tunstall, Burslem, Hanley, Stoke, Fenton and Longton were federated into a single borough to be known as the Borough of Stoke-on-Trent. The adjacent Royal Borough of Newcastle-under-Lyme remained fiercely independent, however!

On the streets, despite the obvious benefits that changes from steam traction had brought, it soon became obvious that Arnold Bennett's love of trams was not going to last with the travelling public of North Staffordshire. Almost before the electric system reached its maximum extent the number of passengers being carried was certainly not increasing and very soon began to decline. In spite of operating 2,524,900 car-miles in 1924 only 25,489,636 passengers were carried or 10.09 passengers per car-mile. The decline can be attributed to many causes – some of which had of necessity been built into the system – such as the large mileage on single-tracked route because of the narrowness of the streets in all the Potteries towns. The number of low bridges in the area meant that the whole system had to be worked using single-deck trams.

Other vehicles using streets which formed the tram routes did not help the situation, and many heavily laden carts, lorries and wagons fitted with steel tyres and driven by horses, ran over the tram rails resulting in considerable delays to the electric trams. Yet the cost of building and maintaining the track fell entirely on the PET Co. which was additionally paying £10,000 a year in rates to the local authorities. Subsidence, causing roads to break up or sink, was also a major problem where track integrity was concerned.

Route	Year Opened	Route Length	Year Closed
Hanley-Goldenhill (Main Line)	1899	4.58	1927
Hanley-Longton (Main Line)	1899	4.03	1927
Stoke-Trent Vale	1899	2.11	1928
Hanley-Longton (Victoria Road)	1899	3.26	1927
Burslem-Smallthorne	1899	0.80	1928
Tunstall-Longport	1899	1.14	1928
Hanley-Newcastle	1900	2.75	1928
Longton-Meir	1900	1.29	1928
Longton-Dresden	1900	1.04	1928
Stoke-Newcastle	1904	2.07	1928
Burslem-Newcastle	1904	3.68	1928
Newcastle-Silverdale	1904	2.00	1927
Newcastle-Chesterton	1904	2.54	1927
Hanley-Sneyd Green	1905	0.81	1927
Longton-Adderley Green	1905	0.68	1928

The biggest threat, however, commenced in earnest soon after the end of the First World War when increasing numbers of motor buses were placed on the roads by numerous operators, most on the 'Main Line' and properly licensed by the Stoke-on-Trent Borough Council. In consequence of all of this the PET found itself in serious financial trouble. From 1922 onwards no dividends were paid on the Company's Ordinary Shares, and in some years no dividends at all were paid. In fact, the PET as such never again achieved financial stability. The people of the Potteries had shown an undoubted preference for bus travel. The situation became desperate and desperate measures were needed to mount a rescue operation. But in the event it was the

EO 579, No. 5, was a Daimler CD-type with 24-seat 'chara' body by an unknown coachbuilder. This vehicle was acquired in 1921 from the Sheerness Tramway Company, another BET group company but was new to Barrow-in-Furness in 1913. Note the two stout straps securing the front of the hood to the chassis. (JCC)

Inside Stoke No. 2 Garage in 1920. This was where the repair and maintenance was carried out whilst Stoke No. 1 merely garaged buses. Vehicles in evidence, all of which appear to be stored awaiting overhaul, are Daimler CDs new in 1914 and later commandeered by the War Office only to be returned to the Company after hostilities had ceased. The rear-entranced 29-seat bodies are possibly by Birch or, more likely, Brush. Note the large stack of solid tyres behind the bus in the centre, and the simple nature of the chassis frames in the right foreground. *(PMus)*

PET used local photographer J Templeman when it produced a guide to its services, and places to visit, in the late 1920s. He travelled widely across the Company's territory and produced some fascinating views. Sadly, the booklet was produced on cheap paper and we have not been able to find any of Mr Templeman's original prints. These three give a tantalising, if poor quality, taste of what he saw on his travels: first we see a bogie car turning in Tontine Square, Hanley, whilst an **SOS** bus waits to proceed and a lad on a bike nips in front of it; secondly, we see a tram about to pass beneath the low railway bridge at Longton railway station, with tracks also swinging off to the left; finally we see two trams and a bus at the crest of the brow in Newcastle Iron Market.

Below is an advert for Templeman's shop in Stoke; note that films would be processed and returned 'same day'. Notice also the emphasis on the newfangled wireless – still quite a novelty. *(AC)*

Stoke-on-Trent City Council which took the initiative, being determined to be rid of the clumsy trams. Buses, it seems, not needing rails and unsightly wires, were less of a nuisance than the trams in narrow streets. At the beginning of 1926 a special committee was set up by the Council to negotiate with PET for the removal of the tramways. This the company was not prepared to agree to without being granted permission to operate additional buses over all the tram routes, in addition to the routes for which licences were already endorsed. This seemed a perfectly reasonable request, especially when considered together with the large number of licences which the Corporation had granted to new operators running over the tram routes and whose services were taking a large part of the traffic carried by the slower trams. The City Council, however, refused PET's application for any licences to operate motor-buses over the tram routes.

An appeal was lodged by the company with the Minister of Transport. Sir Henry Maybury, Director General of Roads, was appointed to conduct an enquiry. The outcome of this was that the PET agreed to withdraw all 120 trams over a period of time in exchange for licences to operate 70 new buses over the tram routes. This was not an entirely satisfactory outcome but it was the best the company was going to get. Conversion was carried out over the next two years, except that, according to the Notice (reproduced on a later page) the route from Newcastle to Chesterton was abandoned in September 1925. However, among the first of the tram routes to go was the 'Main Line' from Longton to Goldenhill and by the end of 1927 over half of the

32 miles of tramway network had been replaced by motor bus operation. Finally, in 1928, the shorter spur routes, Stoke-Newcastle, Stoke-Trent Vale, Longton-Meir, Longton-Adderley Green, Hanley-Newcastle, Burslem–Smallthorne, Burslem-Newcastle and Tunstall to Longport were substituted for motor buses. The last tram ran on 11th July, 1928.

With the changeover from electric traction to motor traction completed the company began to put its financial affairs in order. This financial reconstruction was put through on 4th January 1932 when the PET wrote off £355,256 of capital. By this time the Road Traffic Act of 1930 had been enacted, ensuring the stability of the company. Naturally, a substantial financial loss to shareholders was involved, but it represented the true position of the company. The payment of dividends was resumed in 1933 and on 1st May the Potteries Electric Traction Company Limited became the Potteries Motor Traction Company Limited, thereby reflecting more accurately the activities in which it was now engaged. Mr PM Rossdale was its first Chairman.

The trams and other assets, including the depot at Chesterton and the power house at May Bank were sold. The depot at Stoke fell into disuse but remained company property whilst those at Fenton and Goldenhill were converted to motor bus operation. The face of North Staffordshire was about to change for ever.

The Company used various tactics to try to increase patronage during the 'twenties as its bus fleet was growing, including this coupon scheme to encourage people to use the new services. *(Kithead)*

POTTERIES
Electric Traction Company, Ltd.

HANLEY—ENDON—LEEK

SAVE MONEY by purchasing
POTTERIES Coupon Tickets

Special Cheap Returns with Coupons as under:—

Hanley—Leek	1/6
North Road—Leek	1/4
Hanley—Stockton Brook	6d.
North Road—Stockton Brook	5d.

General Offices,
Stoke-on-Trent.
3rd October, 1928.

J. LINDSAY WOOD,
Traffic Manager.

The balance swings to buses

Motor bus operation began in earnest in 1919 with the return of the Daimlers and the purchase of twelve Tilling-Stevens petrol-electric vehicles constructed by the Birmingham and Midland Motor Omnibus Co. Ltd from ex-War Department lorries. An insight into the use of these buses is given in the PET Drivers' Rule Book of 1922:

'In descending the following hills a dead stop must be made at the top and the transmission put into second gear:

LIMEKILN, IPSTONES TO FROGHALL, AND KINGSLEY HOLT TO FROGHALL.

'This regulation applies equally to similar hills met with elsewhere.

'With Tilling-Stevens machines, the dead stop must be made to ascertain if the brakes are in proper order before commencing the descent.

'Any infringement of the regulations with regard to ascending and descending hills means instant dismissal.'

During 1921 and 1922 further ex-War Department vehicles were purchased. These were AEC and Daimler Y-types carrying both Brush and Birch bus and charabanc bodywork, together with two small Garfords with Birch bodies. By the end of 1922 some 40 buses and charabancs were in service providing feeder services to the trams and offering Potteries people their first opportunity for trips into the countryside. Nineteen routes were in operation varying from the 1.9 miles from Hanley to Bucknall to the lengthy and very rural 35 mile journey from Longton to Gnosall via Stone, Eccleshall and Newport.

This was also the year, on the 25th July, that the Rectory House and grounds of St Peter Ad Vincula, Stoke-upon-Trent were purchased. These premises were adjacent to the old Stoke tramway depot, being separated only by Woodhouse Street. The rectory, built in 1852, became the General Offices of the PET Company. The tramway depot was brought back into use as Stoke No. 2 and a new bus garage, to be known as Stoke No. 1, was built in the rectory grounds.

Further new and second-hand Daimler and Tilling-Stevens machines were acquired amounting to 25 in all. Many were used to replace older buses. As yet all PET vehicles were of the single-deck type in deference to the large number of low bridges in the district.

In spite of the **AEC-B type radiator** this is a **Daimler Y-type (32, EH 3230) new in 1922. It carries a Brush 28-seat body. This splendidly posed picture has survived without any evidence of its origin, or reason for taking the photograph and so no information can be given about whom the dignitaries posed in front of the vehicle are, nor where the picture was taken. However, if the number of women on board is anything to go by it would more likely be a church trip than a pub outing!** *(PMus)*

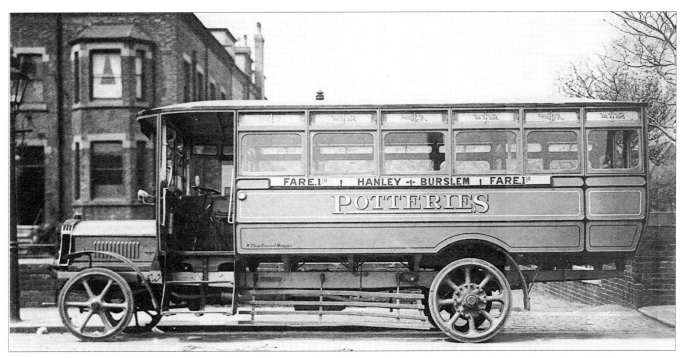

An unidentified early **TSM** (Tilling-Stevens) bus. The route board shows the fare from Hanley to Burslem to be 1½d, three ha'pence! (or about 1p) which is half of what George Francis Train charged for the same journey on his horse tram in 1861 some sixty years earlier! In the lower corner just behind the entrance door appear the words *W Thom General Manager.* Some of these buses were used as 'chasers' to chase the buses of the growing number of independents, both 'pirates' and licensed operators who were running over PET routes. It is known that a few of these vehicles were at first painted green. *(PMT)*

EH 2019, number 23 was a 1920-built **TSM3** with 29-seat Brush body. Amongst the plethora of information on the rear most significant is the **BET Magnet-and-Wheel** emblem. Above the registration number, painted on the rear window, are various licence and hackney carriage details. It is supposed that the number 45 above the door was the Hackney Carriage number for Stoke-on-Trent. It is repeated to the left of the door over the window. Each bus was required to carry a hackney carriage plate for each of the areas in which it operated, this bus having plates for Stoke-on-Trent and Stafford. If a bus broke down in service it could only be replaced with a vehicle carrying the correct Hackney Carriage plates for the whole route! *(PMT)*

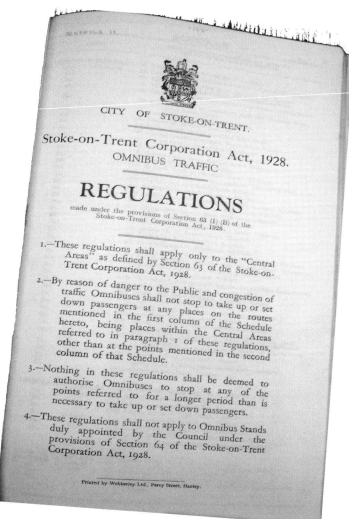

One of the more important events occurring after the demise of the trams in 1928 was the passing of the Road Traffic Act of 1930. It was to change the regulation of the bus industry for over half a century. Up to this time the industry was controlled by the Town Police Clauses Acts of 1847 and 1889. New legislation was clearly needed. This new act removed all licensing powers from the local authorities and placed them in the hands of 13 regional Traffic Areas covering England, Scotland and Wales. Each Traffic Area was empowered to control the operation of all Public Service Vehicles in its district. Had this legislation been enacted a few years earlier, PET's transition from trams to buses may have been very much easier. As it was Stoke-on-Trent Corporation Omnibus Sub-committee came to an end, PET coming under the jurisdiction of the West Midland Traffic Area.

By this time, with continued fleet expansion, more garage space was urgently needed especially to the west of the City. Accordingly, negotiations were entered into which resulted in the purchase of a property known as 'The Beeches' situated on the A34 half a mile north of Newcastle town centre. A new garage was built in the grounds to accommodate 70 buses. Building work was completed in 1932 when 50 PET and 12 Crosville buses moved in. The house, which was left standing, was converted into rest and refreshment facilities for the growing number of long distance coach passengers passing through Newcastle. The whole complex was extensively rebuilt and renamed 'The Four in Hand' in the late 1940s and remained open for a further 20 years until well after the opening of the M6 motorway.

On 1st June 1933, as already recorded, the Potteries Electric Traction Co. Ltd changed its name to the Potteries Motor Traction Co. Ltd to better reflect in its title the activities in which it was now involved.

At this time Mr W Thom, who had been General Manager since 1907, and a Director since 1928, handed over the reins to J Lindsay Wood, his Traffic Manager. Mr Thom remained a Director until his death.

In-house advertising from the Company Tour Guide. *(AC)*

EH 3873, number 42, a Daimler CB with Brush 24-seat body new in 1923. It was retained in the PET fleet until 1929 when it was transferred to W Proctor, a subsidiary company, with whom it remained until withdrawal in 1931. The mystery on this splendid full-frontal view is the destination board, 'Birmingham and Llandudno' which was clearly a Midland Red route, but even if this vehicle did do such a journey 'on hire to Midland Red' why use such a basic bus for what was then a considerable distance? *(STA)*

Left: EH 3228, No. 30, was the first of a batch of three Daimler Y-type 'charas' carrying Birch bodies. Yes, it is a Daimler, in spite of the AEC radiator. These Daimler and AEC radiators were swapped around almost at random. In fact, PET never had any AEC vehicles! *(AC)*

Below: Another Daimler 'chara' on a Private hire duty. There was obviously a second vehicle involved as there are members of the party standing on the offside running board, making more than a full load. Charabancs, to give them their full name, were delivered to PET between 1916 and 1924 but all had been withdrawn by 1930. Note that this vehicle has pneumatic tyres on the front and 'solids' on the rear, a common situation in the mid-twenties as tyre technology improved. Perhaps the cost of modifying the rear wheels and axle was not justified if the vehicle was nearing withdrawal.
(PMus)

The cover of the combined bus and tram timetable for 1926.

Below, and facing page lower: These two pictures, famous in PMT circles, were taken towards the time of the demise of the trams when competition between buses and trams was at its height. To the left (facing page) with car number 125, the last tram purchased by PET, is a Daimler Y-type bus, a War Department reconditioned chassis purchased from Samuelson of London in 1922 (XB 9997, 36) whilst below is the first of the SOS FS-type buses purchased by PET alongside tram 82, a 40-seat car dating from 1901. *(PMT both)*

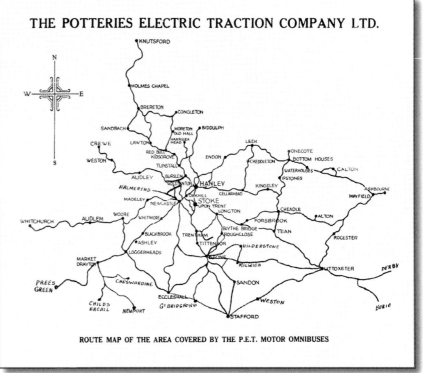

THE POTTERIES ELECTRIC TRACTION COMPANY LTD.

ROUTE MAP OF THE AREA COVERED BY THE P.E.T. MOTOR OMNIBUSES

The **POTTERIES** Official Touring Guide and its accompanying map seen above date from 1925. *(AC)*

Commercial advertising on **PET** buses dated from the earliest days even though this was an all saloon fleet. Roof boards had to be used as seen on this **SOS QL**-type bus. *(PMus)*

POTTERIES
Electric Traction Company, Ltd.

MOTOR OMNIBUS SERVICE between
NEWCASTLE AND CHESTERTON.

From MONDAY, SEPT. 28th, 1925, the Tramcar Services will be entirely replaced by Omnibus Services.

TIME TABLE.

Saturdays

	a.m.	a.m.	a.m.	and every	a.m.	a.m.	a.m.	a.m.	and every	a.m.	a.m.	a.m.	a.m.	a.m.	and every	p.m.	p.m.	p.m.	p.m.	and every	p.m.	p.m.	p.m.	p.m.
Newcastle dep.	5 30	5 40	5 50	10 minutes	7 0	7 15	7 30	7 45	15 minutes	11 0	11 10	11 20	11 30	11 40	10 minutes	1 0	1 9	1 18	1 27	9 minutes	10 36	10 45	10 54	11 3
Chesterton ,,	5 45	5 55	6 5	until	7 15	7 30	7 45	8 0	until	11 15	11 25	11 35	11 45	11 55	until	1 18	1 27	1 36	1 45	until	10 54	11 3	11 12	11 21

Sundays

	a.m.	a.m.	a m	a.m.	and every	p.m.	p.m.	p.m.	p.m	and every	p.m.	p.m	p.m.
Newcastle ... ... dep.	10 0	10 30	11 0	11 15	15 minutes until	5 45	6 0	6 10	6 20	10 minutes until	10 20	10 30	10 40
Chesterton ... ... ,,	10 15	10 45	11 15	11 30	until	6 0	6 15	6 25	6 35	until	10 35	10 45	10 55

Mondays and Fridays

	a m.	a.m.	a.m.	and every	a.m.	a.m.	a.m.	and every	p.m	p m.	p.m.	and every	p.m.	p.m.	and every	p.m.	p.m.
Newcastle ... dep.	5 30	5 40	5 50	10 minutes	7 0	7 15	7 30	15 minutes	12 0	12 10	12 20	10 minutes	9 0	9 15	15 minutes	10 30	10 45
Chesterton ... ,,	5 45	5 55	6 5	until	7 15	7 30	7 45	until	12 15	12 25	12 35	until	9 15	9 30	until	10 45	11 0

Tuesdays, Wednesdays and Thursdays

	a.m.	a.m.	a m	and every	a.m.	a.m.	a.m.	and every	p.m.	p.m.	p.m.	and every	p.m.	p.m.	and every	p.m.	p.m.
Newcastle ... dep	5 30	5 40	5 50	10 minutes	7 0	7 15	7 30	15 minutes	5 0	5 10	5 20	10 minutes	9 0	9 15	15 minutes	10 30	10 45
Chesterton ... ,,	5 45	5 55	6 5	until	7 15	7 30	7 45	until	5 15	5 25	5 35	until	9 15	9 30	until	10 45	11 0

General Manager's Office, Tramway Depot,
Stoke-on-Trent.
September, 1925.

BY ORDER.

C. H. Vyse, Printer, Stoke.

The above Notice shows the tramway replacement timetable for the Newcastle to Chesterton service as from 28th September 1925. Most routes remained with trams for a further couple of years. *(Kithead)*

Facing page lower: The tram replacement buses were a batch of 50 SOS QLs delivered in 1928, one of which is shown (VT 822 No. 123) with route boards for Stoke-Hartshill-Newcastle which was amongst the last of the tram services to go in 1928. *(PMus)*

A new development with the QL was the introduction of roller destination blinds, shown being demonstrated here at Stoke before the buses entered service. The very narrow driver's cab, a feature of the SOS buses, is seen to good advantage in this view. *(PMus)*

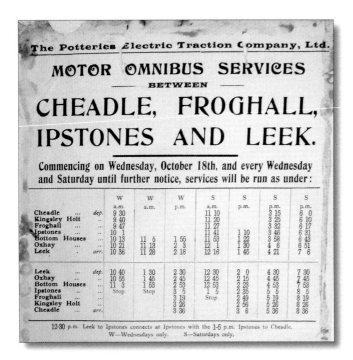

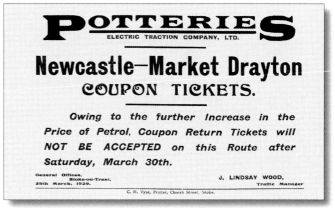

Increasing costs caused the withdrawal of Coupon Tickets on some services as shown above on March 30th 1929. CH Vyse along with JG Fenn remained the company printers until well into National Bus Company days.

Left: This service from Cheadle to Leek was typical of many which offered only a Market Day and Saturday service for shoppers. (Kithead both)

EH 3637, No. 40, was one of the small 20-seat Birch-bodied Garford 'charas' new in 1922 and retained in the fleet until 1929 when it went to Midland Motors in Birmingham for breaking up. What a pity the 'chara' on the right did not carry its registration number in the same position as the Garford! It is, however, a Daimler Y-type. The man in white is the Courier for the day, one Jess Redford. The Garfords were light and reputedly very fast so one wonders if the heavier Daimler was able to keep up with it. The picture is of a pub outing in 1924 or 1925 and was clearly taken at the start of the day – but of which pub was Thomas Marsh the licensee? (AC)

Number 17, EH 1860, was a TSM built in 1920 using the chassis of an ex-War Department lorry purchased by Midland Red and resold to BET. The body is thought to be a 28-seater with rear entrance by Jackson of Sandbach. Withdrawal came quickly, the bus only lasting until 1923. It is seen posed in Fenton Depot in green Chaser livery. (STA)

The 1930s – Extension by Acquisition

Almost co-incidentally with the abandonment of the trams came the advent of the BMMO SOS type vehicles. LG Wyndham-Shire, BMMO's Chief Engineer, was becoming less than satisfied with the performance of the Tilling-Stevens petrol-electric machines, and decided to design and build his own buses. He further decided that his new SOS creations were good enough to sell to other companies within the BET group. In the event only three, PET, Northern General and Trent, took advantage of this. Soon large numbers of SOS buses were seen on the streets of North Staffordshire. A batch of 30 S-type normal control saloons delivered in 1926 was followed by a mere four of its natural successor, the forward-control FS-type. These were the only FS buses exported from the Carlyle Works. The next development, the Q, was an attempt to increase the seating capacity of 34 on the FS to 37 which proved so successful that 37 remained the standard capacity of SOS saloons until production ceased in 1939. PET purchased ten Q-type buses in 1927 and followed these in 1928 with the successor the QL, similar but with smaller wheels and a body sitting lower to the road. Fifty of these were placed into service to be followed by

a further sixteen which came from Crosville in 1934. In the intervening five years various further additions were made to the fleet of SOS saloons including 25 M-types in 1929, the same number of CODs in 1930 and half a dozen IM4s in 1932. However, the big event was the introduction of the double-deck bus in that year when five REDD (Rear Entrance Double Deck) types were delivered. PET's SOS double-deckers were unique in being both of lowbridge, that is with a sunken side gangway on the upper saloon, and rear-entrance construction. All BMMO and Trent SOS double-deckers were of the highbridge variety and most had a front entrance. Fifteen more REDDs came in 1934.

The settlement with the City Council had permitted PET to operate a further 70 buses and it may be assumed these smart new vehicles appearing in large numbers frightened some of the less secure of the numerous independent operators who became ready to sell their businesses. Fortunately, PET were already looking to expand by acquiring competing operators.

Wilshaw of Cheadle operated under the title of 'Cheadle Express'. This Tilling-Stevens C60A2 was new in 1931 with a Lawton 32-seat body as seen awaiting passengers in Cheadle. The bus passed to PMT in 1933 becoming 196 (VT 7065). It was withdrawn in 1937. *(AC)*

Lewis of Cheswardine near Market Drayton operated this unidentified charabanc. Why, when so many of these popular 'chara trip' pictures were taken in the 1920s, did they so often chop off the front of the vehicle? The photo is printed on the reverse as a commercial postcard, and though never stamped or posted, on it is written:- Mrs Mary Stanley, c/o Mrs Mary Young, 16 Rigby Road, Blackpool and underneath *"Dear Mary. Glad you are keeping your ......"* But we shall never know the rest as the bottom of the card was cut off before it came into the writer's possession. Lewis sold out to PMT in 1936 possibly after this vehicle was scrapped. *(AC)*

This magnificent beast came to PMT in 1934 with the business of Knight of Hanley, who remained in business for many years as a furniture remover. Registered XJ 8930, it was new to Lancashire Motor Traders and had been exhibited at the 1932 Commercial Motor Show. Knight purchased the coach in 1933. It is a Leyland TS4 with Harrington 32-seat rear-entrance coach body. In spite of this unusual, for PMT, configuration it was absorbed into the fleet, becoming No. 195, remaining until 1949 when it saw further service with Fryer and Goodwin of Kidsgrove who kept it until about 1955. *(AC)*

This view was taken to show-off the immaculate signwriting on the rear of a new but unidentified, because yet to be registered, Cooke-Robinson vehicle which possibly has Lawton bodywork. Note the acetylene rear light beside the offside mudguard and solid tyres with twin rear wheels. Cooke-Robinson became part of Associated Bus Companies in 1936. *(AC)*

The first such acquisition took place as early as 1927 with the purchase of JM Roberts of Hanley who had only one route, but an important one, that from Stoke to Stafford. Four vehicles came into the PET fleet, three Daimlers and a Dennis, but none lasted longer than two years. Three more small operators were bought out in 1929. The first of these was Shufflebotham and Tipper from the small market town of Cheadle in Staffordshire; next came R James and Sons of Mobberley, a small village nearby and finally a more local company, that of SE Keeling at Blythe Bridge. Only seven vehicles were taken over of the dozen or so owned, the last of these

being withdrawn in 1936. They were a wonderfully mixed bunch and included buses of Bristol, Crossley, Daimler, Leyland and Tilling-Stevens manufacture.

As the effects of the tramway abandonment and the better regulation of bus services following the 1930 Road Traffic Act came to be felt it was inevitable that more of the weaker independent operators would give up, and many did. This came about in two ways, either by selling out to PET or by becoming a partner in one of the associations of independent operators which became a feature of bus operation in North Staffordshire in the 1930s. The Association of North Staffordshire Motor Bus Proprietors became a properly constituted company in 1929 when Associated Bus Companies was formed with offices and a garage at Vale Place in Hanley. The first chairman of ABC was Mr JG Leese who was also chairman of Stoke-on-Trent Motors. He was succeeded by a Mr Peake who later became a Director of PMT. The Managing Director of ABC was Mr A Beech.

Another major grouping of independent operators formed themselves into the Associated Trentham Omnibus Co. Ltd There were originally ten of them working their main route from Stoke to Trentham on a rota basis. Two of these operators, H Shaw of Hartshill and G Bailey of Hanley, were soon absorbed by J Hawthorne of Stoke. Tomlinson and Rigby acquired Hollins, also of Hartshill in 1927, whilst the shares of D and E Davies of Tunstall were sold to Baxter (Hanley) Ltd in 1933. The shares of Hawthorne and part of Baxters were absorbed in 1932 and 1933, but Associated Trentham was destined to be a short lived operation. PMT obtained control in 1934 operating it as a subsidiary until March 1935. Baxter (Hanley) Ltd continued to operate successfully on other routes. On final absorption of Associated Trentham by PMT only twelve vehicles were operated, mainly of Tilling-Stevens manufacture, but included two Gilfords, a couple of Vulcans and an SMC Pathan. All had been withdrawn by PMT by 1936.

In between 1928 and 1930 PET obtained a controlling interest in a number of independents which continued to operate as subsidiary companies until 1932. During these years a considerable number of buses both new and from the existing PET fleet were placed into the fleets of these operators, some 45 of which were re-acquired by PMT on their final demise. The companies concerned were

A & F Brookfield of Blythe Bridge; A Hayward and Son Ltd of Shelton; J Moreton and Son (Stoke) Ltd of Sneyd Green; P Prince of High Lane, Burslem; W. Procter and Co. Ltd of Longton and W & F Rogerson Ltd of Wharf Street, Burslem.

Between them they operated services within the whole of the North Staffordshire conurbation and going beyond from Longton to Stone (Brookfield) and Uttoxeter (Proctor). They operated over 80 vehicles, the largest operators being Rogerson

with 36 buses and Procter with 25. The smallest was Hayward whose business commenced in 1924 or 1925 when the partnership of Hayward and CM Dawson was dissolved. Charles Dawson continued to operate on his own account and was apparently more successful as he continued in business until acquired by PMT in 1960.

Also during this period a number of the smaller operators were purchased and taken directly into PMT ownership. This involved two further purchases in the Cheadle area, H Wilshaw trading as Cheadle Express with routes from his home town to Hanley, Leek and Uttoxeter and CR Kerry's Oakamoor Bus Service. Other 'prizes' included T Gee, Majestic, of Leek with a service from that town to Cheddleton and Mrs Williams from Stowe-by-Chartley who gave up routes from her home village to Stafford and Uttoxeter. After a lengthy period in the care of PMT this road became the preserve of Stevensons of Uttoxeter and latterly Arriva Midlands. A small operator in the Market

Upper: A standard SOS S-type bus of the first batch of SOS vehicles delivered to PET during 1925. It was one of 30 such buses which began the tram replacement programme. Note the pneumatic tyres. *(PMT)*

Lower: The SOS RR-type first came to North Staffordshire in 1930 when PET bought three for the daily Express Services to Birmingham and Manchester. They stayed in the fleet until 1948 and were joined by over 50 similar vehicles during the War years hired from Midland Red to help out with Works services to the newly established Royal Ordnance Factories at Swynnerton and Radway Green. *(PMus)*

Drayton area of Shropshire to succumb was Lewis of Cheswardine. The only ones with significant services in Stoke-on-Trent itself were the Norton Bus Company of A Lowe, Allen of Sneyd Green and C Knight of Hanley who continued in business as a furniture remover for many a year, and provided PMT with a magnificent Leyland coach with Harrington rear-entranced 32-seat coachwork which lasted until well after the end of the Second World War.

This Daimler trade advertisement features one of PMT's first batch of Daimler COG5 buses with Weymann Flexible patented bodywork, seating 35 and new in 1936. PMT were amongst the few BET companies taking this type of wooden-framed bodywork, City of Oxford and Devon General were two others. The body was designed with a degree of flex and claimed to give greater passenger comfort over uneven roads. *(STA)*

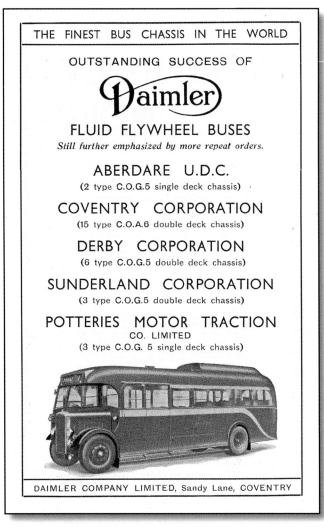

Mention should be made of Biddulph and District who had built up a small network of services radiating from Biddulph, a small town on the Staffordshire/ Cheshire border. This company was acquired in 1936 by the North Western Road Car Co. Ltd who gained the important route from Biddulph to Congleton and for the first time extended their operations into North Staffordshire. One other route, however, came to PMT, that to the outlying village of Biddulph Moor, together with three vehicles. It may have been that the split of this operation between the two BET companies was a direct result of the 1930 Road Traffic Act, Staffordshire and PMT being in the West Midlands Traffic Area whilst Cheshire and North Western were in the North Western area. Finally, before the outbreak of war in 1939, came the business of J Lymer of Blythe Bridge with routes from Longton to Hilderstone and Blythe Bridge. Eight vehicles were acquired by PMT including a Bedford WTB with Duple coach body which joined another Bedford, a WTL, which had come from Lewis of Cheswardine. Both were to remain in service until the end of the war. Mrs Lymer moved the remains of her business to new premises at Tean and continued in the Tours, Excursions and Private Hire sector under the name of Victoria Tours.

PMT expanded in another direction in 1937 by building a new wing of modern offices onto the rectory house in Stoke on land once occupied by the outbuildings and stables. By the outbreak of war on 3rd September 1939 PMT had either directly or indirectly acquired something over 40 small operators and increased the size of the fleet from the 55 buses and charabancs operated at the start of the tramway replacement programme in 1927 to some 270 buses and coaches. It must not be thought, however, that the 'battle of the independents' had been won for PMT still operated something under half of the buses on North Staffordshire roads, and may even have ceased to exist at all! Stoke-on-Trent is the largest British City never to have had a municipal transport system, though this is not to suggest that the city fathers have not made noises to that effect. Before 1930 Stoke-on-Trent Corporation, by virtue of a private Act had a greater degree of control over local bus services than many other towns had, and after the 1930 Road Traffic

This picture is one of a series of postcards produced in the 'thirties by PMT to promote its growing private hire business. The coach, a Leyland with Burlingham centre entrance body (CVT 35, 55) was nicknamed 'The camel' because of its roof luggage rack. It is shown when new, in 1936, and painted in full bus livery. This was the last new coach purchased by PMT for 15 years. It was originally fitted with a petrol engine, converted to run on producer gas during 1943 and 1944 before being fitted with a diesel engine in 1950 by which time it had been numbered 221. It was finally withdrawn in 1951. *(PMus)*

Upper: An early Leyland Titan purchased in 1934 with the typical Brush 'dog's leg' front of the period (AVT 551, 231). This, like all PMT double-deckers until the end of the war, was a lowbridge bus with sunken side gangway on the upper saloon. *(PMus)*

Middle: A later bus from the same stable, (FEH 803, 249). It is seen in Stoke operating on the 'Main Line' with a Stoke Motors vehicle behind. This bus was new in 1938 remaining in service until 1953. *(PMus)*

Lower: PMT was a regular purchaser of Daimler vehicles from 1913 until 1970. Seen here is a Weymann-bodied COG5 from 1939 (GVT 112, 52). The bus was photographed in Station Street, Birmingham about to depart for Dudley on Midland Red service 140, possibly to cope with the additional demands made on buses on Bank Holidays. PMT's service X1 from Hanley to Birmingham involved a long lay-over in Birmingham and so made vehicles available for such duties. *(AC)*

Act the council became critical of the control as exercised by the Traffic Commissioners. So, in 1937, with the support of neighbouring local authorities, it promoted a Bill to set up a passenger transport board controlled by itself and its associates. However, the proposal was rejected because, it was said, bus services in the Potteries compared favourably with those in other parts of the country. There was no justification for the Bill which should be rejected by Parliament. It was. This may also be the juncture to mention that PMT was unusual in another respect, namely that it was the only area agreement company in England in which there was no railway shareholding, and so there was no railway representation on the Board.

A Weymann-bodied bus heads t a least eight of these Brush-bodied Leyland TS7s paraded for a school outing when new in1935, though the photographer was clearly not interested in the front of the leading bus. Half-drop windows were ideal for looking out, something you would not be able to do when the later sliding types were introduced! *(STA)*

The same private hire in 1936, but this time using Weymann-bodied buses. The outing is going to New Brighton and the lead bus (CVT 27, 192) is showing 15, but from which school? One of the attractions in New Brighton in those days was its tower, as advertised below in the PMT Tours Handbook. *(STA)*

Below: The front cover of the PMT Handbook for 1934 depicts an artists impression of the only SOS LRR type coach PMT had. So far as is known, no photograph of it exists (AVT 567, 247). It was new in 1934 lasting until 1949. *(AC)*

Below: A 1940 built Daimler COG5, (HVT 272, 35), with Weymann lowbridge body illustrates just how smart and well proportioned bus design had become until wartime restrictions halted all bus production for almost two years. *(AC)*

Wartime again, a merger, then peace

With the war came a complete ban on leisure and holiday travel which did not affect PMT to any great extent. What did affect them was the need to transport ever greater numbers of workers, many of them women employed in industry for the first time, to such factories as English Electric in Stafford and Kidsgrove, Michelin Tyre Company in Stoke, the RAF at 16 MU (Maintenance Unit) in Stafford and to the newly established Royal Ordnance Factories (ROFs) at Radway Green and Swynnerton. Having few vehicles to divert from extensive holiday and leisure operations PMT soon found itself in desperate need of more buses. Midland Red came to the rescue by providing over 50 coaches surplus to their needs. They helped out in a crisis, performed well even though run into the ground by PMT, and were never returned to their owners. Wartime measures other than those connected with the blackout included the purchase of 44 producer gas trailers. These were fitted to petrol-engined vehicles, but were never entirely satisfactory resulting, as they did, in a great loss of engine power. They were abandoned as soon as conditions would allow. Many operators also tried perimeter seating, *ie* with the seats arranged around the sides of the bus facing inwards in order to widen the gangway to provide more room for standing passengers and so increase the legally allowed maximum capacity of the vehicle. PMT tried this, but Potteries people would have none of it. The story is told of the morning a bus so seated turned up to transport a crowd of women to work; they refused to board it, saying they were going nowhere until a 'proper bus' with 'right seating' could be provided! PMTs experiments with perimeter seating did not last long!

A further development to the Stoke complex came in 1940 with the building of the Sports and Social Club and the Staff Canteen in Woodhouse Street. In 1942 Mr CW Wroth became General Manager of PMT coming from the North Western Road Car Co. where he had been Chief Engineer. Cheadle Garage was enlarged in 1943 and the following year the Bus Station at Longton was opened on land bought from the Stoke-on-Trent City Council. New vehicles began to be made available again during 1942. All deliveries were now subject to Ministry of Supply sanction, and what a motley collection they proved to be! Twenty-three buses were received from no fewer than six chassis and four bodybuilders. All of the major manufacturers of psv chassis were turned over to the production of military vehicles and equipment more in keeping with the war effort, but the Government quickly realised that if bus operators were going even to maintain the minimum requirements of workpeople they would need some additional vehicles, though very few fleet replacements were allowed. From this time all new deliveries were allocated to operators by the Ministry in accordance with perceived need! All buses now received the mandatory white mudguards and platform edging, some buses receiving various amount of wartime 'drab' paint often on the roof, and in the case of some double-deckers the whole of the upper saloon received a camouflage treatment. All buses were fitted with headlamp masks and dimmed interior lighting, often provided by the simple expedient of removing half of the bulbs, though dimmer bulbs were also substituted.

More buses were hired, five 1930 Leyland TD1s came from East Kent staying in the Potteries until 1943 and eight Dennis Lancet saloons, new in 1934, were hired from Yorkshire Traction returning to their owners also in 1943 when PMTs first main batch of utility Guys arrived at Stoke.

CVT 9, 260, has come a cropper during the war. Note the Bisto advert on the rear which at one time adorned almost every PMT bus. The wartime camouflage of the upper deck contrasts somewhat bizarrely with the still pre-war lined out livery of the lower saloon, complete with white painted bumper. This was a typical accident when masked headlights gave the driver almost no help on unlit country roads. (STA)

This wartime picture of Longton Bus Station shows the multitude of bottle-shaped kilns and chimneys for which the area was once renowned. In the foreground a 1933 Leyland Titan with Brush 'dog's leg' front style of lowbridge body is on the stand for the route to Fenton and Hanley, via Victoria Road. In the middle-ground is one of last batch of SOS double-deckers to be purchased by PMT, carrying Short Bros 53-seat bodywork, new in 1934 about to depart for Meir on the southern extension of the 'Main Line'. Visible in the background are two of the Strachan Utility bodied 'unfrozen' Bristol K5Gs which came in 1942 but were transferred to North Western Road Car five years later. The black on white destination blinds were unusual on these vehicles. (JCC)

'They also Serve who Save' commemorating Victory in Europe and Victory over Japan in 1945 and publicising the National Savings Campaign; also demonstrating loyalty to the Crown! The vehicle was already in the new coach livery adopted in the postwar years but note the white-wall tyres. Leyland TS7-Burlingham 32-seat central entrance coach (222, BEH 951) is seen in this night time view in Stoke. (PMus)

PMT PERSONALITIES –
Charles Warwick Wroth

Mr CW Wroth began a long and distinguished career as General Manager in 1942, a position which he held until 1959 when he was succeeded by SJB Skyrme. 'CW', as he was often known at PMT, began his transport career as an apprentice at Tilling-Stevens before moving to the bus industry. His first major appointment was as Chief Engineer to the North Western Road Car Company in Stockport, a position he held until becoming Manager of Stockport Corporation in 1936. Warwick Wroth returned to the BET group in 1942 when he became General Manager of PMT, a position he held through the difficult years of the Second World War, and perhaps the even more difficult years rebuilding both the fleet and the company during the post-war period and throughout the nineteen-fifties. He 'retired' in 1959 but very soon was made General Manager of Trentham Estates Ltd which involved the daily running of Trentham Gardens, the Stoke-on-Trent leisure and garden complex. He remained at Trentham throughout the 'sixties when he was succeeded by one Gerald Bright, better known as 'Geraldo' of dance orchestra fame!

PMT and Trentham Gardens were well-known to each other, the Gardens featured prominently in the Tour Guides and were a popular – and local – destination. (AC)

Associated Bus Companies Ltd

The major wartime event, in 1944, was the merger with PMT of the Associated Bus Companies, adding about 65 vehicles and the garage and offices at Vale Place. Whilst technically a merger the effect of this was to end the 15 year life of the ABC and it brought about the removal of the largest of the independent operators. Of their vehicles, almost all were placed into PMT service though some were withdrawn very quickly. A number of others, including some of the new utility buses, were to remain for many years. During its short life ABC buses managed to carry no fewer than five different liveries, starting off in cream and green until a change to maroon and cream (or yellow) was introduced in 1937. This had become red and cream by 1940, changing to maroon in 1942 when red and grey began to appear, lasting until the merger but with wartime deliveries in a matt rust colour! Associated built up over the years until its route network and number of vehicles looked as if it might rival that of PMT. At its height some 24 operators were involved, some of which re-assumed a separate existence. The operators and routes involved in the Association were as shown in the table alongside:

PMT and Associated Bus Companies came together in what was technically a merger, but more like a take-over in 1944, PMT acquiring 65 vehicles. Typical of the single-deck fleet was this Leyland TS7 with Willowbrook body, posed before delivery at the Willowbrook works. In spite of the coach-like styling and livery style these were bus-seated saloons, albeit well finished and comfortable. EEH 995 (39,539 with PMT) was new in 1937 and was scrapped twelve years later. *(AC)*

Operator	Date of Joining The Association	Principal Routes
JT Stanier, Newchapel	December 1929	Tunstall-Chell Heath, Tunstall-Longton
GE Jenks, Smallthorne	December 1929	Tunstall-Longton
SV Caswall, Tunstall	December 1929	Tunstall-Fegg Hayes
R Fisher & S Plant, Hanley	June 1930	Hanley-Newcastle
FR McDonald, Etruria	September 1930	Hanley-Newcastle
T Tilstone Ltd, Tunstall	March 1931	Hanley-Newcastle
JE Pritchard, Stoke	November 1933	Tunstall-Longton
Grice and Greaves, Burslem	June 1934	Burslem-Bradley
DK Davies and ME Edwards	July 1934	Hanley-Riley Arms
H Whalley, Hanley	May 1935	Burslem-Great Chell
Bradley and Beech, Shelton	February 1936	Tunstall-Longton
Cooke Robinson & Co. Ltd, Burslem	March 1936	Tunstall-Longton
Hargreaves Motor Bus Co. Ltd Burslem	June 1937	Tunstall-Longton
North Staffordshire Motors	May 1939	Tunstall-Longton, Tunstall-Mow Cop
Tunstall (F Peake)		Tunstall-Sandbach Stoke-Newcastle, Hanley-Crewe
DW Reid & AE McMinn, Tunstall	July 1939	Tunstall-Longton
A McMinn, Burslem	July 1939	Tunstall-Longton
H and F Cartwright, Stoke	July 1939	Tunstall-Longton
Dana Motor Service (Barker), Newcastle	July 1939	Tunstall-Longton
S Hill & Sons, Hanley	July 1939	Tunstall-Longton
C and S Eaton, Longton	July 1939	Tunstall-Longton
Garbett and Bonnett, Silverdale	July 1939	Newcastle-Silverdale
W and E Kent, Stoke	July 1939	Tunstall-Longton
Basford Service, Basford	July 1939	Hanley-Basford-Newcastle

Two things become quite clear from the above list, first the amount of competition PMT was still facing on the Tunstall-Longton route, the old 'Main Line' of the tramway days, and secondly the number of operators to give up their independence in 1939, clearly seeing the coming of the dark days of war and feeling better able to survive within the consortium. They did not! An early result of the 'merger' came quickly when the Chell-Smallthorne-Hanley and the Hanley-Victoria Road-Longton routes were joined to provide a through service from Chell to Longton via Victoria Road. Chell (or Riley Arms) to Hanley had been an ABC route whilst Hanley-Longton was joint with Baxter who retained a share on the whole route.

One other operator gave up during the war years, JW Bradley of Harpfields with a route from Newcastle to Eccleshall. Four Tilling-Stevens buses came with the purchase, but were not operated by their new owners. This very rural district between Newcastle and Eccleshall including the villages of Swynnerton, Yarnfield and Slindon has always been difficult for bus operators being both sparsely populated and wealthy. It did, however, become a little easier during the war, and for 20 or so years after, caused by the building of seven staff hostels to house workers at Swynnerton ROF. These were all named after Navy Admirals and at least two still exist, one (Howard Hall) as a Telecom Training Centre and the other (Drake Hall) as a women's prison! Nelson Hall, which was for many years a Teacher Training College, has become a housing development and Raleigh Hall an industrial estate. Frobisher Hall still stands on the edge of Swynnerton Village. At various times the area has been the operating preserve of PMT, Austins, Bassetts, Stevensons, Matthews Handy Bus, Midland Red North, Petes Travel, D & G Buses and latterly of Bakers of Biddulph.

Stoke-on-Trent was not ravaged by bombing as many other towns and cities were but a great deal of rebuilding and redevelopment was still needed as the war came to an end. The 'Main Line' itself now required 60 buses to operate it of which PMT provided 40, three of the remaining independents providing the remainder. Much needed post-war housing would soon become a reality as people moved out from the old towns, and thought would have to be given to providing new services to the developing housing estates at such places as Chell Heath, Bucknall, Blurton, Clayton, Bradwell and Meir.

People began to want to get out and about more, not just to shop, but to go to local beauty spots and to visit places of interest and attractions further afield. Tours, excursions and private hire would all need to be expanded. Mr HR Smith was appointed Senior Traffic Assistant in 1947 from Midland Red, to oversee this expansion. By the end of the Second World War the

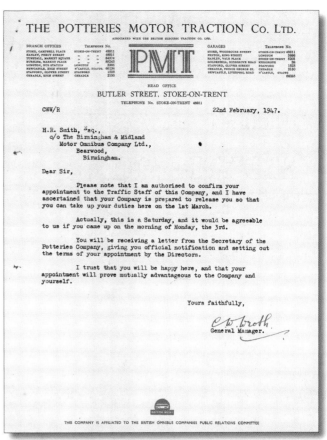

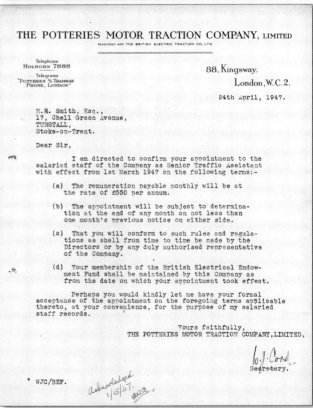

Letters from CW Wroth in Stoke and WJ Coad in London confirming the appointment of HR Smith, the writer's father, to the position of Senior Traffic Assistant in 1947. 'HR' became Tours and Excursions Manager, retiring in 1972. (AC)

PMT fleet had grown to 400 vehicles, but post-war recovery did not come quickly or easily to the Potteries company. Time expired buses remained in service long after they should have gone. Many of the better pre-war and wartime vehicles were refurbished in various ways, but that is a story to be told in a later chapter. The Second World War came to an end on 15th August 1945 with the defeat of Japan.

At the 1947 Annual General Meeting of the Company the Chairman was able to say:

'… by 1939 our fleet had grown to 270, and today we own 390 public service vehicles operating on 1,250 miles of route and carrying 300,000 passengers daily..

'… we can report that last year we carried nearly 103 million passengers. We should record a tribute to those early enthusiasts who made such a figure possible.

'The total staff is now 2,200 and the fleet consists of – 268 Single-deck omnibuses;122 Double-deck omnibuses a total of 390 omnibuses, with additional vehicles for servicing, engineering and traffic, for breakdowns, and for staff purposes.'

The Associated premises at Vale place in Hanley, in spite of the office accommodation being used by the Tour and Excursions and Private Hire Departments, were seen to be inadequate for their primary use as a bus garage. It was decided to replace these buildings with a new purpose-built garage on a site bought from the City Council in 1948 at Clough Street in Hanley moving the Tours, Excursion and Private Hire Departments to Burslem.

The garage was designed by the Company Architects Department headed by Bill Gott, for many years responsible for the design and construction of various premises within the BET group. Clough Street was a 'state of the art' bus garage consisting of three bays, each of 228ft in length with a span of 65ft. In addition to the garage itself the buildings comprised workshops, offices and a canteen as well as a large open parking space. Covering an area of 16,546 square yards it was designed to accommodate 120 30ft by 8ft buses.

The official opening was on 2nd February 1953 and the garage was brought into full use during March. Clough Street was to become PMTs third garage in Hanley. A move had been made to Vale Place in 1944 vacating the original garage in Buxton Street, Sneyd Green. This garage had come to PET in 1929 on the acquisition of Morton and Sons.

Number 352, JVT 610, was the last of ten Guy Arab II 5LWs with Northern Counties 56-seat highbridge bodies to be purchased by PMT. Though of smart appearance these were nevertheless relaxed utility bodies. Northern Counties was unique amongst wartime austerity bodybuilders in using metal-framed construction with window pans and so never took on the full austerity appearance of most of the other builders. *(PMus)*

The 'Big Five' and Wells – Glory Days

Crosville Motor Services Ltd of Crane Wharf in Chester had a small base in Newcastle-under-Lyme from which to operate their routes from Staffordshire into Cheshire and Shropshire. These included the trunk route from Newcastle to Crewe and Chester, a number of market day services, and two summertime express routes. Eight buses were housed in the end bay of the PMT Newcastle Garage. In the early post-war years the BTC Group were actively looking for expansion and saw possibilities in North Staffordshire and so carried out a feasibility study of what became known as 'The Big Five' independents in the Potteries and Newcastle. These were Browns of Tunstall, Thomas Tilstone of Burslem, Stoke-on-Trent Motors and Milton Bus Service, adding that Mainwaring Bros of Audley 'might be included in any purchase'. It was also decided to include Wells Motor Services at Biddulph. The report concluded that stage carriage receipts from all the companies were good and this should continue though 'no savings in mileage operated could be looked for on amalgamation, as nearly all services are run jointly with Potteries Motor Traction or other operators on a co-ordinated timetable' but management economies would be made.

The report went on to state that PMT was the main operator in the district 'and it may be possible for PMT to be awkward if it felt that way inclined' especially when it is realised that these were both area agreement companies. These area agreements had been negotiated between the Tilling and BET companies at various dates from 1921 with a clearly defined boundary between PMT and Crosville. However, the Road Transport Executive of the BTC (British Transport Commission) decided to press ahead with negotiations and placed the day-to-day dealings with the 'Stoke Group', as they called it, with Crosville where they became the responsibility of Ian Patey, Assistant General Manager, who in writing to FG Manning, who was Assistant Director of Acquisitions at BTC Headquarters, pointed out 'that any purchase that is made cannot be made in respect of one or two companies only: it might be possible to take Browns, Tilstones and Stoke Motors without taking Milton or Wells, but there is no doubt that Milton and Wells by themselves would be no good.' He further pointed out that 'Mr Crosland Taylor's (Crosville's General Manager) report of 16th March 1949 recommended that Mainwaring Bros Ltd might be included in any purchase. In a reply to Mr Patey in June 1950 FG Manning suggested that 'negotiations with the Stoke Group were nearing a successful conclusion'. One can only speculate now what would have been the subsequent history of bus operation in North Staffordshire if this had all come to a successful conclusion for the BTC Group. It was quite clear that they intended to put the Stoke Group under the control of Crosville, but in the event nothing came of it, the BTC 'messed about' and the independents lost interest. As previously mentioned, PMT was one of the few BET Group companies in which there was no railway shareholding, and so there was no BTC representation in the PMT Boardroom as there was in most BET companies after railway nationalisation on 1st January 1948.

Whilst all this was going on the 'Stoke Group' or 'Big Five' independents were busy replacing their aged fleets and large numbers of Leyland, AEC, Guy and a few Crossley buses were taken into stock. Two of the companies jointly acquired a small operator when Tilstones and Stoke Motors purchased the business of OW Gurney in 1947. This was to enable these two operators to start a new route from Bradwell to Blurton which ran over most of Gurney's service from Hanley to Longton via Heron Cross. Two vehicles were involved, a Dennis Lancet and a Leyland Tiger both with Willowbrook bodywork, the pre-war Dennis going to Tilstone and the post-war Leyland entering the fleet of Stoke Motors.

In the event all of the 'Stoke Group' duly sold out, not to Crosville as may have been expected but to PMT. The first, Mainwaring Bros of Audley – the 'also ran' of the group – sold on 2nd June 1951 and by the end of the month all of what became known as the 'Big Five' had become subsidiary companies of PMT and so remained until February 1952.

A brief summary of each of the companies may be appropriate, in the order of sale:

Mainwaring Brothers, Audley

The Mainwaring family of Bignall End, Audley were Coal Merchants and Undertakers who began operating a bus service from Bignall End to Newcastle and from Newcastle to Butt Lane in the early 1920s. In 1932 they acquired the Newcastle-Audley service of PET and in 1935 built a new garage in Audley. They also had licenses to operate Day Tours and Seasonal Express Services from their garage. The livery was red and maroon changing to blue and cream in 1946, though the writer remembers buses in the old livery almost to the date of the sale. The fleet included seven Leyland Titans, TD3s and TD5s, which were new to Leicester City Transport and three post-war Crossley double-deckers, two of which were lowbridge buses.

The single-deck buses consisted of four post-war Guy Arab III 5LWs and a number of Leylands including three post-war PS1s. Mainwarings premises became PMTs Audley Garage until being rebuilt some years later. At the date of purchase routes were operated from Newcastle to Audley, Chesterton and Butt Lane, Halmerend and Wereton.

Stoke-on-Trent Motors Ltd

Stoke-on-Trent Motors Ltd was at its formation an association of five companies, Heron Cross Motors, Blue Motors, P Prince, Pryor and Leese and LW Mitchell, to which two more, Hughes and Pointon and A Bloor, were added later, and one, Prince, left to resume independent operation! By this time the company had moved from the original premises in Whieldon Road, Heron Cross to a new garage and office in Vernon Road, Stoke. Mr JG Leese was Chairman of the Company, a position he held in tandem with a similar role at ABC Ltd Mr Smith of Blue Motors became Managing Director. The company had tours and excursions licenses from Stoke and Hanley. The livery of turquoise and cream with dark green relief was applied to a fleet consisting of a mixed-bag of elderly buses and a few post-war vehicles of AEC, Guy, Leyland and Morris-Commercial makes amounting to 30 in all. Half of these were placed into service by PMT, most having quite long lives, some after rebodying. At the time of take-over the main routes operated were:

Bradwell-Blurton (Joint with PMT and Tilstone)
Hanley-Heron Cross-Longton (Joint with PMT and Tilstone)
Longton-Tunstall (Main Line) (Joint with PMT, Tilstone and Baxter)
Hanley-Barlaston
Longton-Chaplin Road-Meir
and
Stoke-Leek Road-Milton

The author could not resist this splendid picture of an unidentified Stoke-on-Trent Motors vehicle out in the countryside on a Private Party booking with what looks like a group of young men about to attend a formal occasion – note the bow ties and the banjos! *(AC)*

Milton Bus Service Ltd, Milton

Milton Bus Service Ltd of Leek Road, Milton was founded on 13th September 1928 largely as a result of the acquisition of a number of smaller operators in the isolated Milton area of North Staffordshire by Mr EL Smith. Mr Smith was a 'pirate' operator in the true sense of the term having commenced his operations in 1921 over the PET Hanley to Milton route. Further competition came on the same route in 1923 from the Clews Brothers who were acquired in 1925 by Hardings 'Karrier Bus Service'. Harding already operated from Hanley to Ball Green and Bagnall, but in 1928 was bought out by F and N Bradley who acquired the Smith business in the same year. This business and Buckley and Cookson were bought in 1930 and in 1932 the PET Hanley to Milton route was acquired legitimately, a bit of David and Goliath here! Various premises had been used over the 28 year life of the company starting in Bath Street, Hanley, moving to Stoke Road, also in Hanley and finally, in 1938, to premises in Leek Road Milton. The Leek Road premises became PMT's Milton garage.

Milton Bus Service was always a drab looking fleet using, as it did, a livery which has variously been described as two shades of brown, caramel and mustard, nutmeg and chocolate, or even mud and ....! This was also a comparatively small fleet and always entirely single-deck. Twenty-one buses were operated in 1951 consisting of seven Guy Arab IIIs and 14 Leylands, all of post-war manufacture. The bodywork makes were a mixed bag consisting of three SEAS, three Pochin, two Burlingham, two Massey, two Metalcraft, seven Barnard and one each of Santus and Brush, all of very varied quality it must be said.

Routes operated, all from Hanley, were to Abbey Hulton, Bagnall, Ball Green, Greenfields, Milton, Stockton Brook and Stanley and from Leek to Milton and Leek to the North Staffordshire Royal Infirmary.

Above: Mainwaring had the distinction of having more pre-war double-deckers in its fleet than any of the 'Big Five', all purchased second-hand from Leicester City Transport in 1950. Number H9, JF 5882, having come to PMT in the following year, had its destination aperture rebuilt to standard PMT style and received a livery of all-over red, but was withdrawn in 1954. It is a Leyland TD3 with MCCW highbridge body new in 1934. Also in the picture is a 1946 Burlingham-bodied Daimler CVD6. *(STA)*

Centre: SN370, RRE 588 an ex-Mainwaring Leyland PS1 with Barnard body new in 1948, and in common with S372 (following picture) is in Stafford Street Hanley. Many of these saloons acquired from the 'Big Five' were sent to Milton Garage, hence many pictures of them were taken in this location where the Milton area routes terminated. The full canopy has been built on by PMT to accommodate the standard destination blind aperture. This bus retained its original body until withdrawn in 1963. *(JCC)*

Lower: An ex-Milton Bus Service Leyland PS1 with Pochin 37-seat body new in 1948 (S372, PRF 599). It is seen in Stafford Street Hanley with a former Birmingham City Transport Daimler-Weymann 8ft wide bus originally intended for Johannesburg in 1942 but now in service with Procter of Hanley. The Pochin body was scrapped in 1955 when the Leyland chassis received the Weymann body from OPD2 chassis SN445, NEH 445, thus remaining in service until 1962. *(JCC)*

Thomas Tilstone and Sons Ltd, Scotia Road, Burslem

Thomas Tilstone was much the oldest business, having been established in 1900 by Thomas Tilstone from premises in Audley Street, Tunstall as a haulage contractor using horse-drawn vans. Bus operation began in 1923 when a Vulcan was purchased and fitted with removable bus and van bodies. The first true bus arrived a year later, being a Guy BA which stayed with Tilstone for three years. Expansion was contemplated, unsuccessfully, in 1925 but a route from Burslem to Chesterton was started and a 'Crush Bus' license was acquired for the Hanley to Milton route. 'Crush Bus' was a wonderful term used by Potteries operators! When the writer's father first heard it he came home chortling over the term which simply meant 'Duplicate'.

Tilstone's offices moved in 1928 to Forster Street, still in Tunstall, and finally to Scotia Road in Burslem, premises which became a distribution depot for Tizer soft drinks when vacated by Tilstone. Some success was achieved with the operation of North Staffordshire's first weekly express service, a summer-only operation from Burslem to Blackpool. In 1928, the year the Limited Company was formed, Tilstone obtained a share on the 'Main Line' from Tunstall to Longton, buses frequently operating showing the unhelpful 'MAIN LINE' in the destination box. Tilstone's livery was maroon and cream, and buses always looked clean and smart. At the end 32 buses and coaches were operated, PMT retaining only 14 of them including two Bristol double-deckers. The remainder were post-war single-deckers of Leyland and AEC make, and a splendid AEC Regent III with Strachans lowbridge bodywork having the distinction of being the first 8ft wide double-deck bus in the Potteries and of being the last exposed radiator half-cab double-deck bus in the PMT fleet, lasting until 1963.

Main routes operated, in addition to those already listed under Stoke Motors, were at the time of take-over:

Newcastle-Basford-Hanley (Joint with PMT)
Newcastle-Garner Street-Hanley (Joint with PMT)
Hanley-Birches Head
Middleport-Burslem-Sneyd Green
Tunstall-Red Street-Chesterton
and
Tunstall-Milton Station

Browns (Tunstall) Limited, Scotia Road, Tunstall

In many ways the history of Browns Motor Company is quite different from that of the others of the 'Big Five'. Browns did not grow through acquisition, nor were they involved in any of the associations. The brothers Brown began business in 1919 with a very short route along Moorland Road between Burslem and Smallthorne, in direct competition with the PET trams. A second route from Brown Edge to Norton was commenced a year or two later and further expansion came until by 1931 seven stage-carriage services had been established covering the whole of the northern end of Stoke-on-Trent and beyond to Kidsgrove and Leek. Excursions and Tours licenses were held from Hanley, Burslem, Tunstall and Kidsgrove. Originally, buses were painted all white and the fleetname 'The White Fleet' was used, but soon dark brown was added in varying amounts. The final livery change came in the early 1930s when the dark chocolate brown gave way to a delicate 'milk chocolate' shade. With some 43 vehicles, Browns was the largest of the 'Big Five'. The fleet in pre-war days consisted of a mixture of AEC and Leyland vehicles. The last Leyland, an 'unfrozen' TS11 with Burlingham utility body, entered the PMT fleet together with twelve

Nineteen-sixty, when we had 'proper' snow and the buses kept running! This picture was taken in Trinity Street, Hanley but, perhaps regrettably, additional snow has been added by touching up the photograph in front of the 1948 Daimler CVD6 with Burlingham body, one of ten added to the fleet (417, LVT 698). Incidentally, all of the buses in this view were later exported to the Canary Islands. *(JCC)*

AECs, two of which were double-deck. Double-deck buses did not appear in the fleet until the war years when the two AECs were purchased second-hand from Davies of Pantyfynon. New buses began to arrive commencing with a collection of Bedford OWBs, all Mulliner-bodied known colloquially as 'Jeeps'. None entered the PMT fleet but all the wartime double-deckers did. These were ten Daimler CWA6s with Duple bodywork, all lowbridge.

Routes operated from Burslem went to Ball Green, Norton and Brown Edge, Lask Edge, Endon and Leek, Ridgeway and Sandbach, this latter joint with Tilstone. There was also a route from Newcastle to Radway Green via Alsager, and two interesting circular services. The first known as 'The Newcastle Circular' was from Newcastle to Talke-Pits, Butt Lane, Tunstall and thence back to Newcastle. The other was the 'High Lane Circular' covering Tunstall-Greenbank Road-Riley Arms-Chell-Pitshill-Tunstall. What made this route interesting is that it was a joint service with PMT, even though it only took one vehicle to operate it, PMT and Browns alternating early and late turns on a weekly rota.

Wells Motor Services Ltd, Congleton Road, Biddulph

But those, the 'Big five' of the Potteries independents, did not quite account for Crosville's 'Stoke Group'. There remained Wells Motor Services Ltd of Congleton Road, Biddulph. Could they remain independent? Would they even now join Crosville or follow Biddulph and District into the North Western fold? They were a reasonable distance out of Stoke-on-Trent, but relied

quite extensively on the City and North Staffordshire conurbation for their operating area. They were of reasonable size but with awful premises spoken of in the Crosville report as 'consisting of corrugated iron sheds' adding that 'the working conditions in these sheds and also in the offices would not be tolerated if the Company was owned by the British Transport Commission'. The answer came in early 1953 when Wells became a wholly-owned subsidiary company of PMT, remaining as such

Above: This Dennis Lancet with half-canopy Duple 35-seat coach body, C196, TRF 866, was the last new vehicle to be purchased by Wells Motor Services Ltd and came in 1950. In common with all post-war Dennis examples it remained in the Wells fleet during the years the company operated as a subsidiary of PMT (1953-59) briefly entering the PMT fleet proper after total absorption of Wells, but succumbing in September 1959 after the summer touring season. *(AC)*

Below: All of Wells pre-war vehicles were withdrawn in 1953, being replaced by PMT buses repainted into Wells green and cream livery. Seen in Wells Garage is S16, BEH 959, a 1935 Leyland TS7 with 1946 Brush body, the only one to receive a green roof. All other transferred buses were given a cream roof as on S97, EEH 134, a 1937 Leyland TS8 with 1949 Burlingham body, the only Burlingham-bodied bus to go to Wells. Both were withdrawn in 1957. *(AC)*

until March 1959 when it was fully absorbed. In 1952 their interesting fleet consisted almost entirely of buses and coaches of Dennis manufacture, 17 of them, 15 with Duple bodies. They varied in year of manufacture from 1933 to 1950. The two not to have Duple bodies carried coachwork by Weymann and Spicer. The 'odd men' in the fleet were a Bedford OB Duple coach, and a Bristol L5G with Beadle body purchased from Hants and Dorset in 1952.

None of these entered PMT service, though one or two of the more modern coaches carried PMT fleetnames and fleet numbers for a few weeks in 1959, and were used to cover 'Wakes Week' holiday requirements – Wells livery was green and cream.

During the time the business was operated as a subsidiary company a number of PMT Leyland Tigers were added to the Wells fleet to replace the older Dennis Lancets, and three new AEC Reliances with Willowbrook bodywork, diverted to PMT from City of Oxford, were placed into the Wells fleet.

Ernest Wells had commenced operations from a base in High Street, Biddulph in early 1914 becoming one of the earliest bus operators in North Staffordshire. The business expanded slowly in this very rural area and in the 1920s and early 1930s a number of other businesses were acquired including FE Goodwin, E Millward of Cobridge and finally, in 1948, the small business of Findlow of Timbersbrook. Services operated from Biddulph were to Tunstall (joint with PMT), Gillow Heath and Hanley (joint with PMT), and to the Stoke-on-Trent Hospitals. Routes from Congleton were to Biddulph Park, Crewe, Sandbach and Timbersbrook, from Hanley to Sandbach, Winsford and Over and from Tunstall to Chell Heath.

The second stage of the rebodying programme concerned the utility Guy Arabs, when 21 of them received these stylish, but heavy, Northern Counties lowbridge bodies; twelve of the Strachan bodies had already been refurbished by Bond of Wythenshawe. Number 331, JEH 564, is seen in its original all-over red livery outside the Evode Glue factory in Stafford in company with another rebodied vehicle, a Leyland TS7 with Burlingham body. (STA)

This splendid picture of High Street, Newcastle in about 1948 shows an almost new AEC Regal with a 34-seat Brush body. Behind is a new Leyland PD2 with lowbridge Northern Counties body emerging from Hassall Street with Tilstones 'unfrozen' Bristol in pursuit. Also visible further up the High Street is a Guy Arab with Northern Counties highbridge body and the rear of a pre-war English Electric-bodied saloon. *(AC)*

In 1949, 24 Leyland OPD2 buses arrived, with 35-seat Weymann bodywork in spite of being double-deck chassis to overseas specification. This was to prove useful to the Company when most of the bodies were used to replace worn out sub-standard coachwork on various Leyland and Guy chassis from the Big Five. The OPD2 chassis all acquired NCME double-deck bodies in three different varieties. In order for this to happen the chassis had to be shortened within the wheelbase to produce a 16ft 5in wheelbase. This 'cut-and-shut' operation was carried by out by Rubery Owen Ltd of Darlaston, Staffs. This is the only known photograph of number 466, NEH 466, before it received its NCME body in which form it was the first bus to be preserved by the POPS group. It was taken on Rigby Road, Blackpool coach park during Stoke Wakes fortnight where the author spent a number of happy Saturdays marshalling passengers in his vacation time with PMT. *(PMus)*

Parked up by the wall in Bowstead Street, Stoke outside No. 2 garage is Brush rebodied Leyland TS7 Number 67, BEH 967, new in 1935 one of 40 such, which marked the first stage of the post-war upgrading of the fleet. Behind it stands L262, JEH 564, a Northern Counties rebody of one of the Strachan-bodied Guy utilities of 1943. *(JCC)*

Developments in the 'fifties

B y the mid-nineteen-fifties, ever-increasing car ownership was significant, and beginning to take its toll on bus company revenues in two ways. Firstly by reducing the number of bus passengers, and secondly by creating traffic congestion which was already beginning to affect our towns and cities thus delaying buses resulting in a less reliable service. Add to this the ever-growing staff shortages and it was clear remedial action would be needed to both reduce operating costs and reduce staff requirements. Ever-rising wages and increases in fuel duty were also adding to costs. The obvious answer would seem to be one-man-operation (o-m-o) and ten AEC Reliance buses with Weymann Hermes bodies were purchased for this very purpose. They had been built with specially narrow entrance doors to prevent would-be passengers pushing past those paying the driver. However, the Trade Unions objected to the use of buses being used on stage carriage services without a conductor and after being stored for some months they eventually entered service in 1955 as fully crewed vehicles.

Certain economies in operating costs had been made in 1953 with a major service revision following the assimilation of the 'Big Five' into OMT. In order to improve timekeeping, and by all accounts theydid so for the Traffic Manager, Mr S Smith, was recorded only a month or so after their installation as saying, "I think it is true to say that for the first time in a number of years the services have been operating to anything like the schedule".

Lined up in Stoke is the first batch of AEC Reliances. These had the early style of Weymann Hermes body and were the first new buses to be painted in the red and ivory livery adopted in 1954. More importantly, they were built for one-man-operation, though only ever operated as fully-crewed buses. They had a special narrow entrance door and a full partition beside the driver to incorporate a 'pay point' with cash box and ticket machine. It will be noted that this was long before the low-floor era! (S4563-72, TVT 563-72). Below is a full view of S4568 behind the Weymann factory in Addlestone before leaving for Stoke – where the fleet number transfers would be applied. *(PMus; STA)*

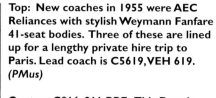

Top: New coaches in 1955 were AEC Reliances with stylish Weymann Fanfare 41-seat bodies. Three of these are lined up for a lengthy private hire trip to Paris. Lead coach is C5619, VEH 619. (PMus)

Centre: C816, 911 RRE. This Dennis Lancet UF with Plaxton 43-seat coach body was new in 1957 to Rowbotham of Harriseahead, the last new vehicle they purchased. It is seen in Stoke Garage, where during the summer months it was kept 'on call' to be able to quickly take over from a standard 41-seat touring coach that had become over-booked! (JCC)

Below left: Older coaches remained in service. This semi-chassisless Leyland-Beadle was one of ten, 'new' in 1951, and being built on running units provided by 1938 Leyland TS8s, remaining in the fleet until 1959. The front offside tyre is being changed by a fitter employed by the Michelin Tyre Co. Ltd who had a large factory in Campbell Road, Stoke. All tyre work was contracted out to Michelin at this time. (PMus)

Below right: C5623, VEH 623 was an odd man out when delivered in 1955 being a Beadle-Commer chassis with Beadle 41-seat coachwork. It would be joined by a further five examples in 1957, these later examples having echoes of the Weymann Fanfare in their frontal appearance. The roof-mounted radio aerial will be noted. (PMus)

Right: Another line up of new buses at Stoke, this time in 1956. The vehicles, Daimler CVG5s with lowbridge Northern Counties bodywork, were the last half-cab sunken-gangway lowbridge double-deckers to be purchased, (L6662-76, XVT 662-76). (STA)

Below: This splendid picture graphically illustrates the development over 15 years of the single-deck bus. Contrast Staniers Leyland PS1 with Lawton body new in 1948 with the 36-ft long AEC Reliance-Willowbrook of PMT, delivered new in 1963. PRE 545, the Staniers bus, was withdrawn by PMT on take-over in 1965. The 'Bogs Lane' destination of the PMT bus was used on a 4mm scale model by Corgi. The location is Greengate Street, Tunstall and the year 1963 when SN945, 945 XVT, was still quite new. (STA)

Facing page lower: Fluorescent lighting brought more than improved lighting to the interiors of buses. With it came the illuminated advertisement panel and demonstrating this is Leyland-Willowbrook H811, 811 JVT, originally ordered by Baxter as a lowbridge bus, but delivered to PMT with this highbridge body in 1960.

Clearly, the continuing modernisation of the fleet was helping with this as large numbers of Leyland Tiger Cub, AEC Reliance and, later, Albion Aberdonian underfloor-engined saloons were entering the fleet to replace many of the time-expired second hand double-deckers acquired only a few years earlier. New double-deck buses of AEC, Daimler and Leyland manufacture were also putting in an appearance, perhaps surprisingly,

the majority being of the highbridge type. In order to accommodate these, the roof of Stoke number 1 garage was jacked up en-masse at the end of 1952 to raise it by 18 inches. The opening of Clough Street garage in 1953 and the enlargement of the Burse garage did away with the office block that had been the headquarters of Browns. This ended the exile of the Tours and Private Hire Departments which were then rehoused in the main

offices at Stoke, a move made possible by the simple expedient of knocking down a few walls to create larger offices. Prior to the exile of these departments they had been billeted in the old ABC premises at Vale Place since their re-establishment after the war.

And then there were six

Two further small independent operators were acquired in 1954, both working the same route, and that joint with PMT, from Longton to Newcastle via Stoke with extensions to Poolfields and Clayton. These were GE Rowley of Bignall End and Davies Transport (Stoke) Ltd, the latter having also been in business as a haulage contractor until taken

into British Road Services on nationalisation in 1948. Amongst the vehicles taken over were two interesting early underfloor engined buses; both were AEC Regal Mk IVs, one with Lawton and one with Metalcraft body. A third take-over was that of Sutton Motors (Stoke) Ltd of Kidsgrove who sold out to PMT in 1954. There was one route, from Newcastle to Congleton, but this time no vehicles were involved.

By the end of 1955, it may be thought that there was little, if any, competition left for PMT to worry about, but a fascinating paragraph in the report produced for the Directors Visit in 1956 points out that there were still eleven small operators left. The report says:

'Despite the many past acquisitions by PMT, there remain eleven independent operators of stage services in the Stoke and Newcastle areas. Most of them also run tours and private hire (and some express services). …. The most important is undoubtedly Baxter, who is now our only co-operator on the 'main route' and on the route between Sandon Road and Chell via Longton, Victoria Road and Hanley. Recent housing developments have greatly increased the potential of such operators as Beckett and Stonier, each of whom shares with PMT in services to estates at Bentilee and Ubberley, Beckett serves Abbey Hulton also. Turner has the only direct service to Hanley from the districts of Brown Edge and Norton in which housing estates are expected to develop considerably over the next two years. Dawson and Duggins, although running only one vehicle each, are participants in important town routes from Newcastle. Duggins has shared with us a recent extension of service at Silverdale into the new Park Site estate (served also by diversions of certain journeys on Poole's Audley service). Berresford's method of conducting his business gives him

a nuisance value disproportionate to the intrinsic worth of the business.

Long-standing Traffic Manager Stanley Smith left the company in 1955 to take up a similar position with Maidstone and District Motor Services. His replacement, Robert Bailey, came from the Northern General Transport Company in Newcastle-on-Tyne. Three years later Walter Womar was appointed Chief Engineer from a perhaps less well-known BET Company, Eddison Plant Ltd and the following year C Warwick Wroth retired from his position as General Manager, a position he had held with distinction since 1942. Mr. Wroth went on to become General Manager at nearby Trentham Gardens, as mentioned elsewhere, and was replaced at PMT by JB Skyrme.

On taking up his appointment, Walter Womar described the amazing variety within his fleet. This consisted of 205 double-deckers, 249 single-deckers and 52 coaches on chassis which comprised 233 Leyland, 184 AEC, 71 Guy, 60 Daimler, 6 Commer, 4 Albion, 3 Crossley and one each of Maudslay and Morris Commercial.

To this would soon be added 3 Bedford, 2 Dennis and a Foden! Bodywork showed no less variety consisting of 37 Brush, 4 Barnard, 16 Beadle, 54 Burlingham, 3 Crossley, 7 Duple, 9 Lawton, 5 Leyland, 37 MCW, 7 Massey, 4 Metalcraft, 148 Northern Counties, 4 Park Royal, 9 Roe, 2 Strachans, 145 Weymann, 5 Willowbrook and 10 Windover.

As the Chief Engineer wryly remarked "not exactly a standardised fleet".

The next few years were to see a further reduction in the number of independent operators, commencing in 1958, as we shall now see.

'Charlie' Dawson was a great racing man and used his coach to operate, almost daily, to Race Meetings in many parts of the country. His final purchase was this Leyland Tiger Cub with Willowbrook Viking body in 1958 (C858, 136 EVT) two years before sale of the business to PMT where it joined five similar coaches on AEC Reliance chassis.

Baxter (Hanley) Ltd

Baxter (Hanley) Ltd was the company described in the PMT Directors' Report as being 'the most important'. The company began in Hanley in 1922 working at first on the Stoke to Trentham route. The Limited Company was formed in 1929. Much of its development came as a result of take-overs which included:

1927: L & C Buckley Ltd with shares in the 'main line' Tunstall-Longton route.

1930: Yoxall and Stanway, and also J Hawthorn on the Hanley-Victoria Road-Longton route. This was originally not approved by the licensing Authority but was after Baxter lodged an appeal.

1933: B & E Davies. Later in 1933 the shares on the Trentham route were incorporated into the Associated Trentham Omnibus Co. Ltd

1944: Baxters share in the Hanley-Victoria Road-Longton service was extended to include Great Chell, Smallthorne and Sneyd Green.

Much of Baxter's work consisted of tours and private hire. Only six vehicles were required for stage-carriage work. The livery was red with maroon and, usually, white relief. At take-over 15 vehicles were operated of which PMT retained 13 for further service. Amongst these were two remaining half-cab Leyland PS2s, both with Lawton bodies; one, NVT 678, PMT No. C504, remained in the fleet until 1963 becoming the last half-cab coach. After withdrawal it was sold to the Staffordshire County Police Central Sports Club and then onto a contractor in the Wolverhampton area by 1970. It was seen by the writer in 1973 and was known to exist at least three years after that, surely a gem lost to the preservation movement.

WS Rowbotham, Harriseahead

One further independent was to sell out during the 1950s. This happened on the first day of 1959 when large numbers of Rowbotham buses were paraded in PMTs Stoke Garage. The fleet consisted of 17 vehicles including two of the famous, if not entirely successful, Foden rear-engined vehicles, both with Lawton bodies but neither were operated by their new owner. One Foden did enter the PMT fleet, a PVD6 carrying a Massey highbridge double-deck body. Other interesting vehicles to come from Rowbothams included a Guy Arab II-Park Royal double-decker, new in 1944, which became the only ex-London Transport bus to be operated by PMT, and an unusual Dennis UF coach with Plaxton 43-seat body. It was the 43 seats which proved useful when on more than one occasion it was quickly substituted on a day tour for a standard PMT 41 seater which had, through some 'charting error' become overloaded!

Number 475, PEH 475, was one of ten Beadle-chassisless coaches purchased in 1951. In common with most BET and Tilling companies PMT were to update the coach fleet to accommodate the growing demand for longer distance travel. Ten pre-war Leyland TS8 chassis were sent to JC Beadle of Dartford in Kent who used the running units to build the integrally-constructed new vehicles. Never very lively performers, these smart looking and comfortable coaches performed a valiant service for seven years until withdrawn as a batch in 1958, mostly going on to further service with independent coach operators or contractors. (PMus)

Rowbotham's livery was blue and cream, sometimes with red relief. The business had been started in 1925 and grew gradually by the usual means of natural expansion and take-overs, most notably Swann of Smallthorne and after the war Kirkham of Mow-Cop. Mr WS Rowbotham assumed control of the company in July 1947. The garage was situated in High Street Newchapel and routes operated were:-

Mow Cop-Kidsgrove-Tunstall via Rookery and Mount Pleasant; Mow Cop-Astbury-Congleton; Mow Cop-Biddulph-Congleton and Newbold-Congleton and Whitehill-Sandbach.

The business of Wells Motor Services Ltd which had been operated a subsidiary Company since 1953 was finally absorbed into PMT in March 1959.

This decline in the number of independents was to continue into the 1960s, Beckett, Dawson and Stanier all selling before the decade was half over. First to succumb was CM Dawson trading as 'Reliance' who sold in April 1960.

The business had been founded in 1925 by Mr CM Dawson with one route, joint with PMT, from Tunstall to Newcastle. This was to remain his only stage-carriage service and took one bus, half his fleet, to operate it, but it was never the main core of his business. 'Charlie' Dawson was a great racing man and he took his 'regulars' to every possible Race Meeting using the extensive tours and excursion licence he held for this purpose. His second vehicle, always a modern coach, was kept for this purpose (see photograph on page 52). Dawson's headquarters were at Ash Bank quite conveniently situated for the Hanley starting point of the race-day excursions but less so for the Tunstall-Newcastle bus route. This livery was green and cream.

T Beckett and Sons Ltd, Bucknall

The business of T Beckett and Son Ltd of Bucknall was sold to PMT in March 1963, less than a year after it had become a Limited Company in May 1962. Beckett acquired the Hanley to Bucknall and Abbey Hulton routes in 1930 taking over from Evans and Finney of Bucknall. Beckett had purpose-built premises in Bucknall and expanded in the post-war years with the rapid expansion of population in that part of Stoke-on-Trent through the development of new housing estates. The livery changed frequently and in the early post-war years, when the writer first knew it, was fawn and green. By the early 'fifties it had become white and maroon, a livery which always looked peculiarly scruffy! Later it reverted to green, this time with cream relief. The reason for this latter welcome change was the purchase of a number of London Transport Country Area

Craven-bodied RTs which were not initially repainted by Beckett. Subsequent new and used vehicles were painted into this livery.

Only three of the 14 strong fleet passed to PMT. These were a Guy Arab LUF with Roe bus body, a Bedford-Yeates coach and an almost new Daimler Fleetline-Northern Counties double-decker which was always a bit of a nuisance to PMT being of the highbridge type, but looking almost the same as the standard PMT lowbridge buses from the same builders. It quickly found itself exiled to Cheadle where it remained until disposal in 1972.

Beckett's routes were:-
Hanley-Abbey Hulton via Eaves Lane
Hanley-Abbey Hulton via Newhouse Road
(both joint with PMT)
Ash Hall-Stoke and
Ash Hall-Hanley
Hanley-Bucknall (joint with PMT and Stonier

Staniers Ltd, Newchapel

This company was the last of the trio, in April 1965. Mr JT Stanier started in 1920 with routes from Tunstall to Harriseahead and Tunstall to Longton, competing with the trams. Eight years later, a third route, that from Tunstall to Chell Heath, had been started. Two of these, the routes to Longton and Chell Heath, were sold to Associated Bus Companies in 1929, the Tunstall-Chell Heath service later becoming the preserve of Wells Motor Services. The business of Adams of Newchapel was acquired in 1930 with a garage in High Street. This was redeveloped by Stanier, but the Head Office remained at The Kremlin in Biddulph. By 1939 the Harriseahead route had been transferred to Rowbotham and Stanier was well established on the Tunstall-Newchapel-Mow Cop route which came with the Adams business. Staniers routes were:-

Mow Cop-Kidsgrove-Butt Lane (Joint with PMT) and
Mow Cop-Newchapel-Tunstall.

The livery was red and cream with, in the earlier years, maroon, sometimes as the predominant colour. Of the twelve vehicles only five came to PMT. These were two Bedford coaches which lasted a couple of years, a Leyland Tiger Cub-Burlingham Seagull coach which PMT kept for seven years, though it was only ever used as a bus, an Albion with Duple Firefly body which remained a useful member of the coach fleet until 1973 and finally a Leyland PS2 single-decker with Lawton bus body, new in 1948.

As may be expected this latter acquisition did not enter passenger service with PMT, but was converted into a tow-bus and remained with the company for nearly ten years proving a useful addition to the fleet.

PMT PERSONALITIES
James Walter Womar
CHIEF ENGINEER and GENERAL MANAGER 1958-1962

Walter Womar spent a lifetime, wartime military service excepted, with the BET and its successor. Relatively few of these years were spent at PMT, but he left behind in Stoke his own legacy for good management and fine engineering which is remembered to this day.

He began his career, following in his father's footsteps, as an engineering apprentice at the age of 16 having spent two years as a tramway parcels boy. In 1934 he joined the staff of the North Western Road Car Co. where his father, Walter James Womar, was General Manager. This lasted until 1939 when he was called up for Military Service entering the Cheshire Regiment as a private and leaving as a major in the Royal Army Ordnance Corps on demobilisation at the end of the war.

In 1946 Walter returned to the bus industry entering the BET Management Training Scheme with Maidstone and District and on completion of this there came a spell at Northern General where he worked with Bob Bailey, a future PMT Traffic Manager. His next move was out of the bus industry, but still within the BET Group, going in 1951 to Eddison Plant Ltd and a move to live in Grantham.

Walter's days at Eddison came to an end in 1958 when he was appointed Chief Engineer of PMT, a boyhood dream had become fulfilled! His General Manager was Warwick Wroth, a man with whom, he said, he never achieved a good relationship going back to his time at North Western. The next General Manager was Jim Skyrme who, in some ways, 'thawed PMT out'. The writer, whilst working as a temporary traffic clerk, can still remember Jim and Walter taking their place in the lunchtime queue at the Staff Canteen in Stoke with traffic staff, engineering fitters, bus crew and other staff – there was no executive dining room in Stoke!

When Jim Skyrme moved to Southdown in 1962 Walter Womar became General Manager of PMT, only the second GM to have been promoted from within the company, the first being J Lindsay Wood who was appointed from his position as Traffic Manager. By this time the author had become a curate in Trentham and lived just around the corner from the Womars, whose bottle of sherry was always a welcome Christmas gift, and in 1964 the invitation to receive it in the General Manager's office was a real bonus! During his time at PMT Walter saw such buses as Albion Aberdonians, Leyland Atlanteans and Daimler Roadliners come, and, in large measure go! He saw PMT coaches win rallies at Brighton and Blackpool and enjoyed attending such events especially when invited to receive various trophies from judges or celebrities. He played a full life in the community, from attending Trentham church to playing an important role in the civic life of Stoke-on-Trent.

Walter Womar left PMT in 1966 to become Deputy General Manager of Midland Red before taking over as GM there a year later. In 1972 he was appointed to the Headquarters Staff of the National Bus Company, a company he referred to as being "no more than a normal merger between BET and Tilling Bus groups".

Below: Walter Womar finally realises that he did indeed make the right move by leaving Eddison Plant as he receives the *Coach of the Year Trophy* from actress Dora Bryan in Brighton in 1964 and takes the opportunity to explain the precise meaning of the engineering term 'kiss fit'. Driver Davies looks on approvingly. *(PMus)*

PMT PERSONALITIES
Driver Tom Cotterill & Conductor JT Harding

This remarkable pair worked together for many years. Both were originally employed by Browns and both came to PMT in 1951 remaining at the old Browns Depot which became PMT Burslem Garage.

What made them so remarkable was that they always worked together, both with Browns and PMT, which they did for almost 30 years and always on the same route! The route concerned was the Tunstall-High Lane circular, a joint service between PMT and Browns which took only one bus to operate it, except on Saturdays when two were needed. On Saturdays each operator contributed one bus, which went round and round in the same direction all day, swapping directions for the next Saturday. On weekdays the two operators swapped weekly between early and late turns, and each journey proceeded in the opposite direction to the previous one – just to stop the crew from going giddy! A full circle took just eighteen minutes, and operated every half-hour, increasing to every twenty minutes at peak times.

Messrs. Harding and Cotterill became known to almost everyone who used this route and would endeavour never to leave anyone behind. The writer, as a schoolboy, well remembers an early peak time evening journey when they loaded over 60 passengers onto a Bedford OWB, Browns usual steed, in spite of having to negotiate the something like one-in-five gradient of Greenbank Road. After Browns had gone PMT used Leyland TS8s and soon Leyland OPS1s, which in turn gave way to AEC Reliances and eventually Daimler Roadliners until the partnership came to an end when Tom Cotterill retired in 1968. The only change to the timetable throughout all these years was the change of service number from 65 to 116.

The picture was taken in Tunstall at the start of their final journey together with a Daimler Roadliner. *(AC)*

A slide in the snow. This Weymann-bodied AEC Reliance is believed to have been operating the Wednesday-only Stone to Uttoxeter service and to have made its unscheduled slide in the Milwich area during the hard winter of 1963. (SN6646, XVT 646 new in 1956.) Experiments with weight-saving measures had resulted in some vehicles being fitted with single rear tyres for a while, but judging by the detail of the skid track this was not one of them. Note the emergency rear exit has been used to evacuate passengers. *(PMus)*

More of the 'Sixties
– Halcyon Days

The 'fifties and 'sixties can only be described as momentous times, these were indeed halcyon days of consolidation and expansion for PMT but coming almost two decades later than for many other major operators. Though no night services as such had ever been operated it is interesting to realise that Works Services started at 3.30am and the final Colliery bus did not return to garage until 1.00am. By 1960 almost 700 miles of route were being operated with an annual number of passengers in the region of 130,000,000; this was achieved with a fleet of nearly 500 vehicles covering an annual mileage of over 37,500 for each bus and coach. Sixty years of public service, 1898-1958, were celebrated in June 1958; the PET as it then was, being founded on 28th June 1898. An exhibition was staged in a huge marquee in Hanley Park; each department of the company had its own stand, as did many other local businesses in both the engineering and pottery fields, and a number of buses were on show.

A commemorative booklet *PMT 1898-1958* subtitled *Wheels of Service* was written by the well-known historian J Wentworth Day and widely circulated. This received wide acclaim for its treatment of the tramway history of North Staffordshire, though the later history of PMT was dealt with in a somewhat more cursory manner.

Nineteen-fifty-eight was a fitting year indeed, to mark such an historic event in the annals of North Staffordshire history, for surely the post-war boom in public transport had now reached its peak. Indeed as more and more private cars were coming onto the roads there were fewer passengers to use the buses. No easy solutions were readily forthcoming. As the number of passengers decreased so the size of the buses began to grow. A palliative was found in reducing service frequencies whilst retaining the same number of seats. But longer gaps between journeys were not the only or even the most noticeable change in the timetables.

A far more important, and beneficial, change was in the offing, however. This was the development of a new breed of double-decker bus by Leyland, one where the engine was situated at the rear, leaving the whole of the body available for passengers. a revolutionary design that was to change the whole future of the double-decker bus. A somewhat ungainly-looking prototype vehicle was loaned to PMT and had many drawbacks which the extensive pre-production operating trials revealed, such as the dark and somewhat gloomy interior, the impracticality of the low ground clearance and roof mounted outlet for the exhaust system.

The production vehicles would be very different, and in one area proved to have taken a backward step when the drop-centre rear axle was replaced by a conventional one, meaning that a reversion to the unpopular lowbridge seating arrangement was necessary upstairs. Despite this, and the many design flaws, PMT found these 78-seaters ideal for their services, particularly those passing under low bridges and obtained a very creditable 20-year life from them.

In 1961 Daimler caught up with their equivalent Fleetline model, this having a drop-centre rear axle as standard, and PMT took examples between 1961 and 1965, later adding some single-deck examples.

Whilst Daimler had triumphed with the Fleetline, its next move proved to be a disaster perhaps only outclassed by the Guy Wulfrunian. A vertical rear-engined chassis – the Roadliner – was developed, partly with PMT and sadly turned out to be badly let down by its power plant.

Taking a step backwards, a new garage had been opened in August 1960, or rather a replacement for the old Wells premises at Biddulph. The Crosville Report of 1950 had commented that the old premises, consisting

An AEC Reliance-Alexander (SN875, 875 REH) negotiates its way past the dustcarts in Tipping Street, Stafford. This picture, taken by John Cooke when editor of the PMT House Magazine, was used in a series entitled 'Tight Corners'. Tipping Street is no longer used by buses, and is now one-way in the opposite direction. (JC)

largely of tin sheds and open parking for buses, would not offer acceptable conditions for its employees. PMT lost no time after Wells was fully integrated in producing plans for this new scheme which, from the start, was a joint venture with the North Western Road Car Company, who shared operations with PMT in the Biddulph area, giving the company two shared garages, Crosville still occupying a part of the premises at Newcastle. Another new garage was opened in Cheadle on 1st February 1963.

Plans were well advanced by this time for the introduction of the first one-man-operated (omo) buses. Four of the new Alexander-bodied Reliances were fitted with Setright Speed ticket machines and the soon to become familiar illuminated signs into the front panel. The buses were introduced on 4th April 1964, almost ten years after omo operation had first been considered, to operate three routes, viz. Newcastle-Eccleshall, Newcastle-Market Drayton, and Newport-Market Drayton, all of which have since been abandoned. By the end of 1967 the number of one-man buses had risen but slightly and was still less than a dozen, all Alexander-

bodied Reliances at Newcastle Garage. But the number of these buses began to grow rapidly the following year when some of the Leek and more of the Newcastle rural services were converted. By October the first one-manning from Hanley on services to Buxton, Crewe, Congleton, Lichfield and Sandbach had increased the number of one-man buses to 36. This did not prevent some quite drastic service cuts over the latter years of the decade.

First to be affected were Sunday services, then summer-only routes and soon market day services especially in the rural hinterland affecting towns such as Leek, Cheadle and Market Drayton. Then it was the turn of some of the main city services to suffer from reduced frequencies. The long-standing three minute headway on the 'Main Line' was reduced to a bus only every five minutes in October 1968 and ways and means of further reducing operating costs were being considered.

Johnson 'Fareboxes' were experimented with in 1969 on the short Stoke-Penkhull circular service and after three months were extended to the Longton-Blurton route. In both cases this, initially, proved successful and more 'farebox' buses made their appearance including

On the left is the second prototype Leyland Atlantean, 281 ATC, in service on the Longton-Stoke-Newcastle-Poolfields route on which it spent most of the time whilst on hire to PMT for evaluation. In the upper saloon front window may be seen the appraisal forms which invited comments from passengers offering hope of a reward for the most constructive comments. The writer received a prize of £2 for his contribution! This was a revolutionary design which was to change the whole future of the double-decker bus. However, the somewhat ungainly looking prototype had many drawbacks which the extensive operating trials would reveal.

The production vehicles above had much cleaner lines than the prototype and were really a development of the Weymann/MCW 'Orion' body which had proved so popular with operators throughout the land, the big drawback being the use of a more conventional rear axle requiring the rear four rows of seats in the upper-saloon to be the accepted 'lowbridge' side sunken gangway style. In spite of some initial operating problems these buses went on to lead long and useful lives, at least one example lasting for a quarter of a century.

Heading this line-up at Stoke Church prior to their Press and Civic launch, with advertisements already in place, is 773 EVT, L9773) while second in line is L9766, (766 EVT), now preserved by POPS (Potteries Omnibus Preservation Society). All this batch of 35 buses was new in 1959. (Both PMus)

Lower
Under the bus washer at Clough Street is SL1036 (AEH 136C), one of five AEC Reliances with Weymann dual-purpose body supplied in 1965. It was on this bus that the writer travelled to London one very wet August Wednesday to be interviewed at number 10 Downing Street by Colonel Salmon, the then Prime Minister's Ecclesiastical Secretary. He did not, however, accept the job he was offered as vicar of St Barnabas, Oldham. (PMus)

six double-deckers on the Hanley-Bentilee service in January 1971. This was later extended to include the cross-city Newcastle to Leek service. Contrasting with many other operators of farebox buses, no tickets were issued on PMT routes using them and it was possible (though not encouraged) to obtain change from the driver before placing the correct money into the farebox. By the end of 1969 there were 100 one-man-operated and farebox buses in operation.

The 20 year life of Longton Bus Station came to an end and the old tram depot at Fenton built in 1905 was closed on 1st December 1964 when Kingcross House became operational. This building, opened by Lord Stafford on 30th November, comprised a bus garage for 74 vehicles and a Bus Station with many of the bays for services terminating in Longton being under cover, the through routes being accommodated on two sides of the periphery of the building where outside parking facilities for vehicles on 'stand-over' were also provided. PMT extended their catering facilities with a snack bar, the *Chancery Grill* – a fully licensed restaurant – and a bowling alley known as the *Magnet Bowl*. The company became the first, and possibly the only, bus company to run a bowling alley, but this was a short-lived enterprise and through lack of support it was closed in October 1965 only to re-open as *The Jollies Night Club* which, for a few years, was a very successful enterprise.

The *Four in Hand* cafe at Newcastle Garage was now beginning to feel the draught from the opening of the M6; more and more express coach services were using the motorway and not calling at Newcastle for their refreshment halt. PMT had tendered for the franchise of the Keele Service Area on the M6, but were not successful in their bid. In 1966 the facility was losing money heavily and the cafeteria was leased to the Shearing-Pleasureway Group of Altrincham which had used Newcastle for many years as an interchange point for their holiday tours and for refreshment halts at week-ends. They modernised the premises and re-opened in May 1967 keeping the old name. The garage was, of course, retained by the PMT where a large operational unit continued to thrive. Yet in its day the *Four in Hand* had been a great success. Speaking at an Industry Conference only four years earlier, Jim Skyrme, PMTs General Manager, said of the *Four in Hand*:

'The premises acquired over 30 years ago on the main A34 route north of Newcastle … were converted to a snack bar, primarily for the benefit of coach services between Manchester and the north, Birmingham and London and remained open all night. In 1949 a cafeteria with two self-service counters, capable of serving over 1,000 people an hour, were added, and the snack bar converted into a café for quick service of lunches at reasonable charges. … The

PMT may have thought their problems in keeping up-to-date in the coach market were all behind them when these fine machines arrived – sadly they were to be proved right! C1097, KVT 197E poses at Swinnerton while engineering assistant, Peter Lanfranchi looks on. (JC)

character of the café was changed to that of a restaurant and at the end of 1961 a licence to sell alcohol with meals had been obtained. *The Four in Hand,* as the PMT establishment was named, provided parking space for up to 60 coaches and could handle their passengers.'

The Staffordshire section of the M6 had been opened in 1963, together with the mile long link-road to Hanford, nowadays the first section of the A500 'Potteries D Road'. The opportunity was taken to provide a limited-stop service from Newcastle to Stafford using both the link-road and the motorway. As compared with the normal time from Hanley to Stafford of 56 minutes the new service completed the journey in 34, a time which compared favourably with the Stoke-Stafford rail service, but service 80 was not a success and was withdrawn in 1964. An attempt was made to revive it under the name of 'INTERTOWN' in the 1980s but this service again only lasted a few months. Redevelopment of the main shopping centre of the City of Stoke-on-Trent, Hanley, geographically the centre of the 'Five Towns', had been going on apace. New shops, offices, and Hanley Mall, a small shopping precinct, had all been completed or were under construction; a new road which would enable a one-way system to be introduced was under construction, and, in 1967, there was the opening of the new Hanley Bus Station. For the first time all services terminating in Hanley would come to a central terminus and many cross-Hanley routes would pass close by, the only exceptions being the 'Main Line' and the Newcastle group of services. The Bus Station also included a snack bar and a new booking and enquiry office which opened in August 1968 after 50 years in the original office in Percy Street. A new Bus Station was opened in Uttoxeter on 6th September 1970. It replaced stands at various points in the town and, as well as providing a single terminal point for all bus services, it did much to relieve congestion in the town.

It must be admitted that the 'sixties had not been the happiest decade for the bus industry. It began, if not on the crest of a wave, then not very far over it! The growing popularity of the private car even for the daily journey to and from work was undoubtedly the major cause of the loss of bus passengers, yet it must be conceded that the industry had not always worked in its own best interests; in fact it had done little to help itself.

Cost cutting had become the mantra of almost all of the major operators which manifested itself in reduced frequencies on almost every route, justifying this by offering the same number of seats on larger and larger buses. The rear-engined double-deck was seating up to 78 passengers whilst the 36ft long saloon was carrying 53 seated passengers, or what a lowbridge double-deck had done ten years earlier. There was also the growing use of one-man-operation meaning passengers waiting longer, often in the cold and wet, to board

their bus. This was not all! The buses themselves were becoming less user-friendly; parcel racks disappeared from single-deckers, dual-door buses became the vogue and passengers, certainly in the Potteries, hated these with a passion and some would argue that buses were becoming less reliable. Add to this frequent fare increases and the use of the 24-hour clock in timetables when it was used nowhere else and the observer is drawn to the conclusion that this was the decade when the bus companies took their eye off the ball, lost the plot, and shot themselves in the foot!

Was this Commer 1500 Martin Walter 11-seater, 272 SEH, the first minibus in Britain? It was one of two purchased in 1961 for use by small parties requiring an evening out, but spent most of its time as a traffic department van, attached to the Tours Department. Both had gone by 1965. *(PMT)*

Plaxton Panorama coach, C916, 916 UVT, with driver Horace Davies wearing his traditional white coat, photographed by Norman Bennett, the company Claims Officer, when the coach was new. The occasion was a visit by a BET Publicity Film Unit to PMT to make a film about the procedure and method of operation of a Private Hire Department. *(PMus)*

Above. SN1000, 6000 EH was the prototype Daimler Roadliner with Marshall 50-seat low floor bodywork. It is shown undergoing a tilt test at the Chiswick Works of London Transport prior to its appearance at the 1964 Commercial Motor Show. Chiswick handled contract tilt-testing, a very specialised task, for several bodybuilders including Weymanns, and, as here, Marshalls.

The lower view was taken on the airfield at Cambridge, the home of Marshalls factory. *(STA both)*

Into the National Bus Company

What was then described as the most important day in the history of PMT took place in 1968, yet it was an event over which the company had no control. It was on 1st March that year that the British Electric Traction Co. Ltd agreed to sell its bus interests to the State. BET feared that the outcome of Government proposals for Conurbation Transport Authorities which became PTAs and PTEs would impinge on some urban areas of BET operation, the heart would be torn out of, for example Ribble, North Western and Crosville in Manchester and Liverpool, and perhaps even more significantly Midland Red in Birmingham and the Black Country. The last year of BET operation of PMT was 1967 when the company made a profit of £117,394 from a fleet of 495 vehicles, hardly a resounding success story. In accordance with the Transport Act of that year the National Bus Company was set up at the beginning 1969, PMT becoming one of the 41 operating companies within the 93 company NBC group which in the first year of operation :

Owned 21,000 vehicles,

Employed 81,000 people,

Carried 26 million passengers,

Earned a revenue of £148 million which produced an operating surplus of £7.5 million.

Was the largest bus company in the world.

The first direct evidence of NBC ownership of PMT came in 1972 with the first NBC publicity campaign which used the slogan 'Together we're Going Places'. PMT apparently was not! It carried on within its traditional operating boundaries of the North Staffordshire conurbation, now with very little threat from independent operators, there being only six left with a total between them of about 40 vehicles. Yet PMT was barely financially viable and in many of the NBC years it was making an operating loss.

More visible evidence of the arrival of NBC also came in 1972 with the application of NBC style fleetnames to all buses and coaches, sometimes without removing the traditional PMT ones! A year later the first new and repainted vehicles began to appear in the corporate image liveries of poppy red with a single white band by way of relief which was later removed from single-deckers. A few of the coaches appeared in the NBC white 'NATIONAL' coach livery whilst others acquired the half red half white local coach livery. PMT as a subsidiary of NBC was expected to operate a highly standardised fleet. Even in the 1950s and 1960s it had been quite standardised with 105 Leyland Atlantean double-deckers, 196 AEC Reliances and significant numbers of Daimlers and Albions and, of course, other Leylands, together with some considerable variety in the small numbers of vehicles acquired from the independent operators. Under NBC this standardisation was to be reinforced with the purchase of Bristol and Ford chassis and the Leyland National. There were also purchases of numerous second-hand vehicles, caused by the shortage of vehicles as a result of the Roadliner debacle. Leyland coaches came from Ribble, Standerwick and Southdown whilst five double-deck Daimler Fleetlines came from Midland Red together with nine Leyland single-deckers which had originated with Stratford Blue, and for Driver Training purposes, two Bristol Lodekka FS buses arrived from

Another Earls Court Show entry, this time in 1970, is Daimler Fleetline-Alexander W type dual-door bus, 141, 141 BEH. It is seen on the Daimler stand with a London Transport DMS and was very much a last minute entry into the show. In response to a phone call from Daimlers two weeks before the Show opened, this bus was taken out of service and prepared to 'new' condition in the PMT Workshops at Stoke. After this auspicious start the bus enjoyed but a short life with PMT, going in 1978 to end its days with East Kent as a 'Shuttle Bus' in the Port of Dover. (PMus)

This scene is by the Shropshire Union canal at Norbury Junction near Newport, Shropshire. The reason is PMT Publicity and a picture taken to advertise Private harter, as Private hire had become known by the early years of NBC. The coach, (40, XEH 140M) showing the new NBC logo, is a Ford R1014 with Duple Dominant 41-seat body new in 1973 and withdrawn in 1979. *(PMus)*

Southdown. Hired vehicles also came to brighten up the streets of the Potteries and create a feeling of nostalgia for the buses concerned were half-cab Leylands with Weymann 34-seat bodywork from Birmingham City Transport – though they were returned to the West Midlands PTE. Less glamorous were more traditional Leyland Tiger Cubs from East Midland in their sombre all-over dark red which were replaced by some rather more attractively liveried Tiger Cubs from Trent.

The reasons for this use of second-hand vehicles over the first half of the 1970s are legion; late delivery of new buses, unreliability of the Roadliners, lack of availability of spare parts for Leyland Group vehicles (most of the fleet) and the general parlous financial state of the company. This latter was not a new experience for PMT. In 1931 the Directors Report suggested that no dividends were paid out to shareholders, adding that no dividends had actually been paid since 1922! The PET had not, the directors admitted, been the unqualified financial success for which the founders could have longed. But it was a fact with which both PMT and NBC had to come to terms. In spite of being the most compact of the NBC operating areas, it had become known as an "outfit which is geared to make a loss from the outset. We need to make every economy to reduce the amount of that loss." said John Piper, the newly-appointed Chief Engineer. The effects of this financial position on vehicle maintenance were far reaching.

PMT was almost proud of having the least spare vehicle capacity of any NBC operator with the result that it was not easy to keep vehicles off the road for planned maintenance. In fact, a bus could have as many as eight

different crews or drivers during a single day. The buses were used so intensively that it was not uncommon for them to be out for the whole day, that is up to 18 hours running time. The unreliability of the Roadliners had the spin-off effect of the over use of the AEC Reliances which were being flogged to death, so much so that a number were purchased from Maidstone and District just to provide spare parts. The Reliances were used on motorway runs, often being sent out in batches, and all drivers would try to keep up with the best of the batch – with frequent detrimental mechanical results for the also-rans.

The writer once remembers, almost at the end of the Roadliner era, seeing one doing a turn on Hanley-Stafford, and finding it very hard to resist the temptation to travel on it just to see if it could get there and back without incident! However, time did not permit and he had to make do with a trip round the Tunstall-High Lane Circular on a Perkins engined vehicle. To make matters even worse, in 1974, a batch of nine Bristol VRTs intended for PMT were sent to Crosville to help with their vehicle shortage in Liverpool. Crosville clearly had more clout with NBC management than PMT. They finally arrived at PMT some eighteen months later to replace buses lost in a disastrous fire at Newcastle Garage. The Daimler Fleetlines, of which there were 77 including 20 single-deckers, were never popular with drivers because of their excessively heavy steering and so were doing far less mileage than the Leyland Atlanteans and Bristol VRTs. It was into this scenario that the Leyland National made its first appearance at the end of 1972.

PMT PERSONALITIES
Alf Fallows – Company Artist

Between the 1950s and 1970s Alf Fallows was the PMT Company artist, loosely attached to the Tours and Private Hire Departments. He was responsible for producing all the PMT publicity and many of the notices posted in the company Booking Offices of which there was one in each of the Potteries towns (except Fenton!) as well as Newcastle, Leek and Cheadle together with publicity for the bus stations in Hanley, Longton, Leek and Newcastle. The picture shows Alf admiring some of his own work on Leek Bus Station.

Alf was also a clever cartoonist producing a great deal of material for the PMT House Magazine as well as for similar magazines published by other BET companies including Midland Red and Ribble. He also worked part time as a freelance cartoonist selling his work to publications as varied as the Daily Sketch, Reveille, Picturegoer, TV Times and the Daily Mirror. He said that he became interested in cartooning during the 'thirties and by submitting some of his work to Cadbury's for a chocolate advertising campaign. Nothing was accepted but he was sent a block of chocolate for his efforts! During the war he produced cartoons for the North African and Eighth Army Newspapers and also for Tuniseree Liberee then under the control of one Hugh Cudlip. On demobilisation Alf joined PMT where he remained for the rest of his working life.

One popular way to make money and brighten the streets in those years was the ever growing popularity of the 'all-over advertising bus'. PMT made much use of these; the first three were Leyland Atlanteans, painted for The Heavy Steam Machine, a Hanley disco in a mainly purple livery, and two more restrained examples, one to celebrate 800 years of the Borough of Newcastle-under-Lyme and one for the London and Manchester Assurance Co. After these initial three all others appeared on Bristol VRTs and later Leyland Nationals. The first Bristol in 1975 was for the Britannia Building Society in a patriotic red white and blue scheme which was quickly followed by a multi-coloured effort for Regent Warehouses, a DIY Store which did not last as long as the bus. During the next few years many others followed, including Wrights Pies, Staffordshire Evening Sentinel, National Holidays, Wilsons Beers, Port Vale Football Club and Barclays Home Mortgage. Those on Leyland Nationals have included Focus DIY and Roberts Bakery. However, none of these buses had the windows painted out which seems to have become the latest 'fashion' with the present generation on all-over advertising buses. During those years no further independent operators were acquired by PMT, but the six became five when Stoniers of Goldenhill became a part of the Berresford Group, though continuing to operate as a separate company, but gradually its buses did receive Berresford's red and ivory livery, a definite improvement on Stoniers pink and burgundy. However, PMT did obtain one new route, that from Stafford to Uttoxeter and the Saturday working from Lichfield to Uttoxeter as a result of Midland Red taking over The Green Bus Service of Rugeley in 1973. These workings later passed to Stevensons of Uttoxeter, and later to Arriva Midlands North moving round in a full circle! Fares were now rising faster than ever before and passengers were voting with their feet, or their cars! Yet the industry still felt that it was performing a service which no-one could do without. Complacency reigned supreme and little effort was made to market its wares or attempt to keep its passengers, let alone attract new ones. The results were severe service cuts, fleet reductions and staff redundancies. This showed itself at PMT which in 1953 operated a fleet of 550 buses and coaches but by 1977 this had dropped to 410 vehicles – yet with more seats to offer would-be passengers!

The next few years would see a great deal of change, with even more staff and vehicle reductions. If in its first eight years NBC behaved as a sleeping giant, it was to change very considerably in the second-half of its existence. NBC became market-orientated, forward looking and considerably more adventurous. Hence, 1977 proved to be not only the mid-term year in the life of NBC, it was also the watershed which proved to be a turning point in the bus industry.

NBC – The Middle Years

1977 was the year of the Queens Silver Jubilee, and to celebrate the event Bristol VRT 652 was painted into a special silver-banded livery, and together with preserved Leyland OPD 466 and Bristol VRT 611, the Britannia Building Society all-over advertisement bus, took part in the Lord Mayor of Stoke-on-Trent's Gala Day and Parade on 13th August. Earlier in the year 652 and a number of other Bristol VRTs together with buses from other NBC subsidiary companies converged on Portsmouth for 'Operation Fleet Review' when, in her Silver Jubilee Year, Her Majesty the Queen reviewed her Fleet at Spithead. This involved one of the largest single bus operations ever undertaken, creating a vehicle requirement of over 100 double-deck buses for the period 25-28th June, most in Silver Jubilee livery.

But this was not to be a year of celebration for PMT and the year ended with the longest and arguably the most damaging strike in the history of the company, ostensibly about duty rosters and bonus payments but other more deeply-seated issues were at stake, possible redundancies not being the least of these. An unfortunate side-effect of the strike was to prevent the Britannia Building Society all-over advertising bus from appearing in the Lord Mayor of London's Annual Procession, the Building Society claiming substantial compensation from PMT and thus bringing an early end to the advertising contract.

Preserved Leyland OPD2 L466, NEH 466 with Northern Counties lightweight body dating from 1954 is seen with two Bristol VRTs, the leading one in PMT's variation of the Queen's Silver Jubilee livery, with the Britannia Building society all-over advertising bus at the rear. They are seen in College Road, Stoke at the start of the 1977 Lord Mayor's Gala Day Parade. (POPS)

However, there were celebrations in 1978 when the company commemorated the 80 year history of PET-PMT, this time Bristol VRT 677 was specially painted for the year reminding the people of North Staffordshire of the formation of PET, the Potteries Electric Traction Company Limited, on 28th June 1898, two years after the North Staffordshire Tramway Company had been acquired by BET. The major celebration took place in 1979 when several thousand people turned out on a week-end in early June to a Gala Day staged by PMT to celebrate 100 years of organised road passenger transport in the Potteries since the original horse tramway of George Francis Train. The oldest bus in the fleet, 766, the first of the original batch of Leyland Atlanteans to take to the road, was painted in a special livery, that used on the earliest double-deckers in the mid-thirties. After withdrawal this bus joined the fleet of POPS preserved vehicles still in this livery. This celebration was more than just a day out for those who came, there was a Rally of preserved vehicles organised by the Potteries Omnibus Preservation Society (POPS) and a commemorative booklet, entitled *A Century of Public Transport in North Staffordshire,* was published jointly by PMT and POPS. This was a photo-cavalcade of nostalgia for those with a love of Potteries buses and trams using mainly official PMT pictures.

The Stage Carriage operations belonging to Mrs Irene Belshaw's Princess Bus Service, between Newcastle, Knutton and Silverdale (Park Site Estate) were acquired in December 1978 though no vehicles were involved. Mrs Belshaw retained her contract-hire business. This firm, originally T Duggins Princess Bus Service, commenced operation from Louise Street, Burslem in 1923. Ownership passed to Mr S Duggins who transferred the business to premises in Clayton Road, Newcastle and thence to his daughter, Irene, who became Mrs Belshaw on her marriage. Only four independent operators then remained – namely Berresford of Cheddleton, Pooles Coachways of Alsagers Bank, Turner of Brown Edge and Proctors of Hanley. The final 'buy-out' in NBC days concerned none of these. It happened in April 1983 when the old established business of W Jeffreys & Sons (Goldenhill) Ltd ceased trading due to the compulsory purchase of the depot in Albert Street, Goldenhill and the near retirement age of the directors. Some of the contract work came to PMT though no stage-carriage services were operated and no vehicles were involved. Jeffreys' fleet was always quite small, carrying a livery of brown and off-white. The writer remembers Sunday School outings to Rhyl on Jeffreys' Bedford OB-Plaxton, this coach being a rebodied OWB, or a fine Maudslay with Metalcraft coachwork, not to mention a similar coach bodied by Yeates.

PMT held an Open Day and Trade Fair at Stoke in 1979 to commemorate 100 years of the company. In a corner of the Stoke No. I Garage is a Leyland National behind the Leyland Bison tow truck on the IRTE stand. *(PMus)*

Number 663, SKG 897S, was a 13ft 8in high Bristol VRT with ECW 74-seat body new to National Welsh in 1977. Following a low bridge accident on a school run in the Swansea area, National Welsh sought to acquire some fully low-height 13ft 5in buses.

This was just after Leyland had ceased production, so they came to PMT who exchanged three of their 13ft 5in buses. A similar exchange of two buses took place with Ribble in 1982. PMT quite happily ran all five on the 'Main Line' under the 13ft 10in Liverpool Road bridge in Stoke. However, this bus is seen by Stoke Church in Glebe Street. *(PMus)*

Three double-deck buses took part in operational testing programmes by PMT for the NBC in 1979/80. Two buses came new. On the left is Alexander-bodied Dennis Dominator 700 (XBF 700S) whilst on the right is 900 (WVT 900S), one of only six Northern Counties-bodied Foden 6LXBs built. In the centre is 686 (YBF 686S), a Bristol VRT already in the PMT fleet, re-numbered to 600 for the purpose of the tests. *(PMus)*

Market Analysis

MAP, the National Bus Company Market Analysis Project, came to North Staffordshire in 1978. The brief was to examine every part of PMT's operations and to determine the needs of the travelling public. Surveys were undertaken on every bus route as well as through house-to-house enquiries. Two members of the MAP team worked together on the buses, one handing out questionnaires to passengers (who had not yet been degraded by being referred to as 'customers') and collecting them back when the client alighted from the bus, whilst the other noted problems encountered on the journey such as traffic congestion,

boarding time and passenger loadings and monitored how such factors as journey times and therefore time-keeping were affected. When all the data had been collected it was checked and then processed through the NBC Computer Centre in Birmingham. Once the survey results became known the local authorities in Stoke-on-Trent and Staffordshire and – to a lesser extent where PMT was concerned – in South East Cheshire, South Derbyshire and North Shropshire became involved. County Councils had been given some responsibilities for Public Transport under the 1972 Local Government Act and this was, in the main, exercised by the granting of subsidies for uneconomic and socially necessary operations to the local NBC and independent bus operators. Operator and Council together worked out a viable network with an agreed level of subsidy, whilst paying due attention to the travelling needs of existing and potential passengers. This was then submitted to the Traffic Commissioners and, so far as the Potteries was concerned, a new, imaginative and far-reaching network of services was produced offering the bus user a wider variety of destinations than ever before, yet with a vastly reduced total mileage and fleet requirement. An anticipated loss of £1.25 million, in spite of £800,000 worth of local Council subsidies, had to be halted.

The operating territory was divided into six areas: the first rather grandiosely known as the Newcastle-Leek-Sheffield corridor was a joint project with Trent. The survey began on 9th September and the first area to be completed, Leek, found itself with a whole group of revised services, all with new service numbers, in November 1979. The remaining five districts had the rather more prosaic titles of City East instituted in June 1980, City South-West, City North-West, and West Staffordshire on 25th October 1980 and Kidsgrove and South Cheshire, this latter being carried out in conjunction with Crosville on 15th March 1980. Later in 1981 came some fairly major revisions to the City North-West and City South-West timetables in February, and 'new improved' Cross-City links were implemented on 31st October. The overall result being, in the writer's opinion, one of the most radical and exciting regroupings of services ever seen in North Staffordshire; the bus network had undergone a dramatic metamorphosis and in the end looked much better for it.

In 1957 the writer stood at Hartshill Church, having just taken his girl-friend, now his wife, back to the North Staffordshire Royal Infirmary where she was a student nurse, knowing that without a change of bus he could get no further than Longton, Poolfields, May Bank or Riley Arms; yet in 1980 from the same spot through buses became available to places as far distant as Shrewsbury and Sheffield! A journey in 1962 from Hartshill to Leek involved three buses; the same journey became possible on a single vehicle. In 1960 about ten buses an hour passed the PMT Burslem Garage in Scotia Road in each direction; in 1980 it was 14, the direct result of MAP. In 1950, from the writer's home in Chell he could travel on a single bus to four Potteries towns plus Chell Heath and Biddulph, yet 30 years later he could get to every Potteries town, Newcastle, Biddulph, Chell Heath, Hanford, Trentham, Mow Cop and Kidsgrove! This new bus network, the direct result of asking people what sort of a bus service they needed had produced in North Staffordshire an exciting and far reaching change, but at tremendous cost.

If the passenger had gained additional mobility from the new services the employees were to lose out badly. Staff reductions and redundancies were a

constant threat. The fears which brought about the 1977 strike had become an unpalatable reality. There was an air of gloom, anxiety and uncertainty amongst all the PMT staff; no one, it seemed, knew if his or her job was safe or for how long. No fewer than three of the eight garages were to close during 1980; Biddulph on 25th March, the Crosville vehicles housed there being shunted off to a piece of waste ground in Congleton, PMTs operations were transferred to Burslem; Milton on 27th June, operations going to Hanley, and on October 25th Stoke, though the premises were retained as the Engineering workshops and Head Offices, bus operations being transferred to Newcastle and Hanley. Only four operational garages remained: those at Burslem, Cheadle, Hanley and Newcastle. That year marked the end of all former BET type vehicles in the PMT fleet including AEC Reliances, Daimler Fleetlines and Leyland Atlanteans, and also saw the demise of the short-lived lightweight Fords together with the first withdrawals of Bristol single-deck buses.

In all 125 vehicles, amounting to one-third of the total fleet, were taken out of service, the direct result of the full implementation of MAP. The fleet strength now stood at about 275 vehicles, the lowest it had ever been since the PMT name was adopted in 1933. It seemed that the NBC had made its influence total at Stoke, and as if to emphasize the new image a new fleetname (or rather the resurrection of an old one) was adopted on publicity and on the buses. Towards the end of the year PMT gave way to 'POTTERIES' as vehicles were repainted, the first to be seen by the writer were numbers 249 and 259 on 17th December. This, however, proved to be a passing fancy and long before the whole fleet had gained the new nomenclature the old one returned and PMT again became the norm on buses, bus stops, and publicity. One spin off from this was that enthusiasts societies and various journals began to follow suit and began to refer to the company by its initials rather than 'POTTERIES'. PMT had always been the universally accepted handle to the company in North Staffordshire and surrounding areas.

MAP inspired services continued to be introduced, but in some cases it was not without a fight! People, it seems, want buses but not down the road in which they live. On no fewer than three instances, at Smallthorne, Packmoor and Clayton, groups of local residents formed small pressure groups to prevent them using certain estate roads which had not previously been served. After negotiations with the company and some compromise all three affected routes were introduced and soon settled down to fulfil a useful purpose.

A new stability in the services seemed to be reflected when a complete timetable book including all the routes in North Staffordshire was published in 1978, the last to date!

PMT PERSONALITIES
Wilfred Inskip – 'Mr PMT'
1932-1980

War service excepted, Wilf Inskip spent the whole 48 years of his working life with PMT. He joined the company only four years after the last tram ran and before the name change from PET, and continued into NBC days.

From his joining the company until he volunteered for War Service 'Inskip' was a clerk in the Traffic Office. He joined the Army in 1939 and on demobilisation in 1946 returned to his old job where he continued to acquire considerable administrative and operational experience in the road passenger transport industry.

His first promotion came quickly when he was appointed Traffic Assistant and Licensing Officer, a position he held until 1952 when he became Divisional Traffic Superintendent on the re-organisation of the Traffic Department following the take-over of the 'Big Five'.

With his fellow Divisional Traffic Superintendent, Philip Barnard, he continued to oversee the service changes and expansion into new housing developments during the later 'fifties and 'sixties under the Traffic Managership of Robert Bailey until 1964. On Bob Bailey's departure to Lancashire United as General Manager, Wilf became Assistant Traffic Manager, a position he held with distinction under difficult conditions within the company.

His final promotion came in 1970 when 'Mr PMT', as he had already become known, was appointed Traffic Manager. Inskip was ultimately responsible for the Market Analysis Project at PMT and the resultant drastic route changes. Wilf had many outside interests both within the industry and the local community, being an active member of the Institute of Transport and a lecturer in transport subjects at the North Staffs College of Commerce. He was also a member of the Stoke-on-Trent Hospital Welfare Committee, a keen sportsman, especially fishing and shooting, and a keen gardener. Inskip retired in 1980, his place being taken by one Trevor Smallwood.

Midland Red came to an end as an operating subsidiary of NBC on 5th September 1981, only the Central Works – the famous Carlyle Works in Birmingham – being retained by the original company. The operations were divided between five new subsidiaries which, for administrative, legal and accounting functions, were placed under the wing of a 'parent' NBC company. One of these, Midland Red North Ltd with its Head Offices in Cannock, Staffordshire became linked with PMT having its Registered Offices at Woodhouse Street, Stoke-on-Trent. This led, for a time, to Midland Red North buses being registered in Stoke and so carrying 'VT' and 'EH' index-letters. A new coaching unit was established at Stoke utilising the new Plaxton coaches and the latest Duple Dominants. These new 12-metre Plaxton coaches carried the new 'Paramount' bodywork which caused the coaching unit to adopt the name 'PARAMOUNT' Travel, an inspired piece of thinking this, and coaches used the fleetname 'PARAMOUNT' in blue with the letters P—M—T picked out in red. All the coaches were painted in variations of the National white livery with red and blue stripes, a livery which the then Assistant Chief Engineer, Julian Smith, son of one-time Traffic Manager Stanley Smith, claimed as being invented by PMT with the painting of two Duple Dominants into that livery. It was, he asserted, adopted nationally when a PMT coach in this livery appeared at London's Victoria Coach Station and inspired the powers that be, looking down upon it from their upstairs offices, to adopt it as the official NBC coach livery. And so, you can thank – or blame – PMT for all those stripey variations on National white that became a common sight up and down the land in the late 'eighties.

Julian Smith later took a post in Nairobi, his place at PMT being taken by Tony Marsh on promotion from within the company. Bert Boyes retired in 1982 after five years as General Manager to be succeeded by Mike Moors, a one-time Crosville Secretary, who in his first report to the company was able to say that in purely financial terms 1982 had been a good year for PMT, due in no small measure to the Staffordshire County Council subsidy; but the silver-lining surrounded a deep black cloud, the passenger loss was 7% over 1981. Making his Annual Report to the company a year later Mr Moors said:

'We shall need to continue to keep fare rises below the rate of inflation and to make more attempts to attract new passengers, not only with the introduction of more bulk purchasing tickets, but also by making efforts to improved advertising and publicity material and by continuing improvement to the appearance of buses and Bus Stations.' Adding comments about 'the importance of good time-keeping, smart uniforms and courteous staff.'

It all seemed to add up to just what running buses is all about – providing the right service in the best possible manner; had Mr Moors already got his eyes on future privatisation? He did not have long to wait, PMT was the fifth NBC operating subsidiary to be privatised. This came about on 15th December 1983 when the company was sold to its management who quickly introduced a new livery of bright red and yellow with a 'tear-round-the-dotted-line' stripe! This soon became known as blood and custard. After spending so much of its existence competing with, buying out independent operators, and complaining about their nuisance value, PMT itself became, for the first time in its history, an independent operator.

PMT PERSONALITIES
Bert Boyes, General Manager 1977-1981

Bert Boyes was a Liverpudlian by birth. He came to PMT from Crosville in 1977 succeeding WH Jelpke. The writer presented a copy of his first PMT book to Mr Boyes and so paid his second visit to the hallowed portals that were the GM's office in Stoke. Bert became the first President of POPS (Potteries Omnibus Preservation Society) taking a great interest in its activities until his retirement in 1981. On retirement he was presented with a model bus made by a POPS member from parts retrieved from old Setright Ticket Machines. This model was recently sold at a car boot sale in Hanley for an unknown sum to an unknown purchaser!

In 1982 PMT acquired four of the NBC order for Willowbrook-bodied coaches, only this one, 47-seater 22 (OEH 22W), (above) having the full National white coach livery. It lasted for a very short time, being withdrawn within four years, thanks, it must be said, to the Willowbrook bodywork which was far inferior to the parallel order for NBC from ECW. (PMus)

The bus on the right seen in the PMT training livery of pale blue and white, is ex-Baxter Leyland PD2 T679 (203 BEH) with Willowbrook body, the last new bus purchased by Baxter. It came to PMT in 1957 and in 1972 became a driver training bus, lasting until the late 'seventies. (PMus)

Minilink and PMT Engineering

"The moving life of the town was confined to the omnibus, which seemed to pass its entire time in going up and down between the town and the station, quite unembarrassed by any great weight of passengers."

Anthony Trollope, "Dr. Thorne", 1858

PMT claimed to be the first operator to use minibuses, a claim which goes back to 1961 when two Martin Walter-bodied Commer 1500 vehicles were purchased and used occasionally on private hire duties, but spent most of their lives as vans. The true beginning came twenty years later with the first 'Flexibuses'. These were in fact two London FL2 taxi-cabs which were quickly augmented with Mercedes 307 vehicles. The idea of 'Flexi' was different to that adopted in many parts of the country when small buses became popular. The concept originally was to have a fleet of flexible vehicles for a variety of uses. This grew in 1983 when PMT moved into the taxi trade with the acquisition of City Radio Cabs and by 1985 the resources of PMT Flexi and City Radio Cabs were combined bringing into being City Cabs-Flexi.

This operating unit was unique in offering a 24-hour service for 365 days a year available to convey from 1 to 21 passengers anywhere and at anytime. It also re-introduced the PMT parcel service, which had been scrapped in 1942 as an express packet service with a guaranteed 30 minute timed delivery service in Stoke-on-Trent and Newcastle-under-Lyme. At its height City-Cabs-Flexi had 40 cars and 15 mini-coaches.

The first true minibus service was that from Hanley to Bagnall and Stanley also in 1985. Others soon followed in the Abbey Hulton and Milton areas of the City, which became almost exclusively the preserve of Mercedes 19-seaters. Next to come were the Newcastle to Clayton and the Westlands group of routes, this time using Ford Transits. The day of the passenger-carrying bread van had truly arrived! Minilink appeared in such places as Weston Coyney, Barlaston and Blurton. In fact, PMT announced in the 1987 *Sentinel* advertising sheet that there would be 70 new Minilink services by September! This did not happen, but a fleet of over 200 minibuses was built up. They appeared like a nest of ants all over the City streets! All of these were operated as 'hail-stop' services everywhere outside the town centres offering, so it was claimed, convenient, high frequency, high quality bus travel! PMT Minilink would later extend to Red Rider routes in Cheshire and the West Midlands and so PMT became the most extensive user of minibuses in Britain.

As a result of the fleet reductions brought about by the Market Analysis Project, PMT found itself with spare engineering capacity so what should be done with it? The answer seemed to be to seek new business outside the company, so an engineering base was set up at the garage in Clough Street, Hanley. However, this soon proved to be inadequate for the amount of work being undertaken, and a move was made to a new base set up adjacent to the Central Workshops at Woodhouse Street in Stoke.

Early work amounted to the conversion of utility vehicles for Social Mobility purposes for Social Services,

PMT went into the taxi business in 1982 when these two Austin FL2 Carbodies vehicles, XRF1-2X, joined the fleet becoming the first 'Flexi' buses. They were used on a mixture of rural services and private hire jobs – but how many NBC companies operated taxis? On withdrawal the registration numbers were retained and used on other vehicles, eventually ending up on two Mercedes mini-coaches with Happy Days of Stafford. (PMus)

schools and voluntary organisations. A major project, however, was the sale and conversion of ten of PMT's own Bristol RE single-deck buses into mobile Works Units for Newcastle-under-Lyme Borough Council. The conversion involved dividing the vehicle into three sections, a living area with cooking and seating facilities, a washing area with washroom and toilet, and a working and storage area with racks and benches. A substantial roof mounted ladder rack completed the conversion.

Another aspect of the work was painting vehicles, a speciality being 'all-over- dvertisement' buses. The first of these was a BMMO D7-type double-decker advertising Severn Warehouses. Many of these were done for PMT themselves; Bristol VRTs to advertising Port Vale Football Club, National Holidays, Staffordshire Evening Sentinel, Wrights Pies and others. Leyland Nationals included a dark green scheme for Roberts Bakery and a basically white livery for Focus DIY.

This was the time when operators were beginning to realise that high capacity buses running infrequent headway services were not meeting the needs of the travelling public. So, from one extreme to the other! The era of the minibus had dawned and PMT was amongst the first to use this idea on high frequency city services. They had already converted a number of vans for the Flexi bus fleet, but now they were able to enter the van conversion business in a big way. Most of the work was carried out on Ford Transit, Fiat and Mercedes panel vans.

The company exhibited a Mercedes conversion at the 1985 *Bus and Coach Show* at the Birmingham NEC. Substantial orders came from other NBC subsidiaries, the largest being 64 Mercedes for Midland Red West for use on Worcester Town Services. These were 20-seaters with room for six standees. Other NBC orders came from Devon General, Cheltenham and Gloucester, Midland Red North for use in Wellington, Southdown, and Western National for use on the Dartmoor Pony Services, as well as, of course, PMT itself. These were a mixture of 18 to 20-seat Mercedes, and Ford Transits, which were usually 16-seaters. Outside orders were for users as diverse as the large Ulsterbus Company to small coach companies such as Wrays of Harrogate and Horsman of Reading.

PMT was producing van conversions of a high quality, being well-finished with full interior panelling, comfortable seating, power doors, built-in destination displays and excellent exterior painting. The next logical step was taken. This was to design and build bus bodywork from scratch and dispense with the panel vans. In this way a much more purpose-built vehicle could be achieved and at much the same cost. These used the now familiar Ford Transit and Mercedes chassis and running units, and also the long wheelbase Freight

Rover Sherpa and the Leyland Swift. Four types were built, the *Bursley*, the *Hanbridge*, the *Knype*, all names derived from the novels of Arnold Bennett that would not have meant much outside North Staffordshire, and finally the *Ami*. Many of these were for PMTs own use but orders did come from other sources.

The work began in 1987. The first design was the *Bursley* a rather angular 20-seater using the chassis of the Freight Rover Sherpa or Ford Transit, though it is doubtful if any of the latter were built. The *Hanbridge* was different, not only in being of a much more pleasing appearance, but also by being, technically, a van conversion using the Mercedes 609D running units and van framework. It was again a 20-seater. The *Knype* was an altogether different beast. The 1987 prototype, D333 EVT, was mounted on a Mercedes 814D chassis but most of the production units were on the Leyland Swift which was basically a commercial chassis (or should that be was a basic commercial chassis?). It featured coach seating for 29 passengers and plug-type entrance door, and was finished in a livery of red and silver, entering PMT service in May 1987. Production *Knypes* could seat as many as 39 passengers in bus form though PMT's own examples were 37-seat dual-purpose vehicles with jack-knife doors and, surprisingly, coach style destination displays with no provision for a service number. A second prototype, E342 NFA, was built, this time on a Leyland Swift chassis, and was followed by the production vehicles which entered service in 1988.

The final PMT body was the *Ami*, a midibus for mounting on Mercedes 811D chassis. The design had a simple uncluttered appearance, with a gently raked front and an almost 'utility' look suitable for either bus or coach applications. The all-steel body was available with a wide range of options but all featured an entrance door immediately behind the front axle and a deep single piece windscreen with the destination box mounted behind it. Depending on the level of luxury specified, seating could be provided for 25-33 passengers.

Paradoxically, PMT Engineering came to an end for two opposing reasons. First, large orders were being received which the company could not meet because the Stoke premises were too small, and expansion to a larger site was thought to be impractical. The second reason was that orders for panel van conversions had almost ceased. Orders to the present level could not last and a sustainable future clearly looked doubtful. The end could be seen not only for purpose-built van conversions but also for mini/midibuses as operators returned more and more to the use of full-size vehicles. Accordingly, the decision was taken in 1991 to phase out body production and return the premises to their original use as a PMT maintenance facility. In the event, even this was proved to be short-lived, as the whole Stoke complex was sold off in 1996.

The Midland Red D7 on the right was the first all-over advertisement livery to be painted by **PMT** Engineering. The basically all-white scheme had a yellow roof with the main lettering in blue. It was for the Severn Carpet Warehouse in Stourport. *(PMT)*

Below right. Looking more like a bus being prepared for an African Safari than a Council maintenance vehicle, is Bristol RESL PVT 203L after its conversion by **PMT** Engineering. The picture was taken before its hand-over to the Borough of Newcastle-under-Lyme. *(PMT)*

At the bottom right, work is progressing on the conversion of Mercedes panel vans into minibuses for Midland Red West in the **PMT** Engineering workshop at Stoke during 1985. *(GKS)*

Below and on the opposite page are examples of **PMT** promotional brochures publicising the different types of minibuses available. *(PMT)*

The Professionals PMT

EXPERIENCE

As a major stage and private hire operator PMT has amassed a great deal of practical experience in running a fleet of passenger carrying vehicles year in, year out. This experience has been utilised in the design and construction of the Company's range of Minibuses.

BODYSHOP

Minibus construction takes place in a specially equipped bodyshop where components are brought together for final assembly on a flow line basis. Many of these components, especially g.r.p. mouldings such as destination boxes, step wells, luggage racks and skirts are made elsewhere on the premises.

FINISHING

Finishing is carried out by skilled craftsmen operating in carefully controlled conditions whilst painting is undertaken in the Company's own lowbake spray booth. Specialist signwriters apply operators livery as required.

ENGINEERING

PMT Minibuses are constructed to conform to current transport regulations and have been developed and tested to meet the specifications demanded by operators in both rural and busy city centre networks.

FOR FURTHER INFORMATION CONTACT:—

P M T ENGINEERING

Woodhouse Street, Stoke-on-Trent, Staffordshire ST4 1EQ.
Telephone: (0782) 744744   Fax (0782) 744244

79

Privatisation and Diversification

The Transport Act of 1986, part of the Thatcher Government's privatisation policies, was to alter the whole face of public passenger transport yet again. It provided for the de-regulation of all bus services in England and Wales – coach services had been deregulated in 1980 – a substantial reduction in local authority subsidisation of loss making routes and the end of cross-subsidy whereby a profitable route could subsidise an unprofitable one. Most important of all was the provision for the sale of the National Bus Company, not as an entity, but by the sale of individual constituent companies as separate units. The first such sale was of National Holidays on 14th July 1986 to the Pleasurama Group and the last, the 72nd sale, was that of London Country Bus (North East) Ltd to Parkdale Holdings on 30th March 1988, so ending the 20-year life span of National Bus which had both witnessed, and been responsible for, a revolution in bus and coach travel in Britain. PMT Ltd, as it had by then become, was sold to a management team of four on 15th December 1986, the eighth company in the NBC Group to be sold.

A thousand staff and 300 vehicles were involved, with garages at Burslem, Cheadle, Hanley and Newcastle, a bus station complex in Longton and its Head Offices and Works at Stoke. The operating profit in 1986/7 was £236,000.

After spending so much of its long history competing with and buying out the independent opposition throughout North Staffordshire, PMT itself became, for the first time in its existence, a private operator. Perhaps it was because his father had been a 'company' man, spending the whole of his working life with BET and NBC, first with Midland Red and then with PMT, that the writer has always believed that 'big was best' and a large group company meant efficiency and doing the job properly. The small independent had never seemed to be 'professional' perhaps being more concerned with waiting for Mrs Jones at the cottage gate than maintaining a proper timetable!

Yet the ink was hardly dry on the buy-out documents before the company covered itself in glory for all the wrong reasons! It was all to do with the request for a subsidy from Staffordshire County Council to operate bus services over the Christmas and New Year period.

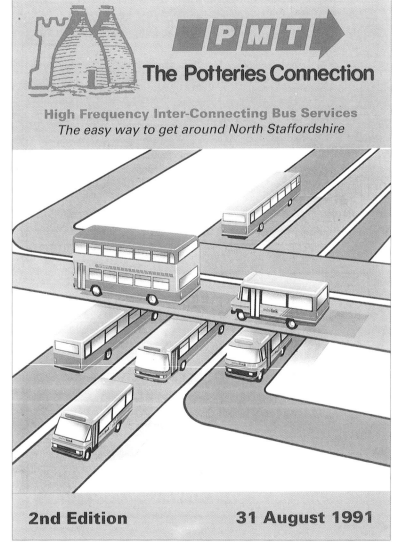

To summarise the whole argument, PMT said, "No subsidy, no buses". In reply the Council said it was the public duty of the company to run some buses, to which the PMT response was to threaten to withdraw all services from 25th December 1986 until 2nd January 1987, but the Council still refused to back down. The Government became involved when the Transport minister, David Mitchell, urged the County Council to dip into its 'petty cash' for the £9,000 for which PMT was asking, to which County Council leader Terry Dix said the Council would "evaluate" PMT's revised proposals. In the bitter end, after many column inches in the *Evening Sentinel*, PMT agreed to operate an 80% service without Council subsidy. The *Sentinel* further reported that services in Cheshire would not be affected as the County Council had agreed to a subsidy.

The first obvious change in the company came very shortly after privatisation. This was the new livery of bright red and even brighter yellow, soon to be known as 'blood and custard', complete with 'go faster' or 'tear round the dotted line' stripe. Though it was

perhaps better than some of the privatisation liveries this was garish and brash, giving the whole fleet a very down market image, especially when seen *en-masse* on Hanley or Newcastle Bus Stations. All buses had been repainted by the end of 1988.

At the end of the first year as an independent bus operator the Managing Director, Mike Moors, was able to announce a profit after tax of £1.1 million, significantly better than the company had ever achieved under NBC or even BET. The amazing thing was that this was achieved without any serious competition from small independents or 'invasion' by newly-privatised companies from outside the area that had become such a feature of bus operation in this freshly deregulated era. In fact, PMT reduced the competition to an all time low during 1987 and again in 1989 when three further small operators were purchased. There was the business of Samuel Turner of Brown Edge with the important route from Hanley to Brown Edge, followed by Berresford's of Cheddleton after the death of proprietor James Berresford. This was the operator referred to over 30

Opposite page. Representative of PMT publicity in the early post-deregulation era are these leaflets. On the left is a route map produced in 1990 whilst on the right is the second edition dating from 1991. *(AC)*

Upper right: Typical of the new full size buses to enter the fleet in the early privatisation years was SDC867 (N867 CEH), one of five Dennis Lance chassis which were given Plaxton Verde bodies with 45 semi-coach seats and were painted from new in 1995 in the sliver *Crewe-Alsager-Hanley* route-branded livery. The bus is seen heading out of Hanley on a bright spring day in 1998, three years after entering service. *(GKS)*

Lower right.: MCW Metrorider 29-seater 14 (F114 UEH) was the smallest vehicle to carry the Paramount Leisure livery. It was called *The Little Pullman* and entered service in 1989 in which year it poses beside the seaside. *(AC)*

years earlier as being of more 'nuisance value' than commercial threat. Two years later the Newcastle area bus services of Pooles Coachways were acquired but without the purchase of the business. This left Procters as the only 'original' independent which PMT had failed to acquire since the departure of the trams in 1928.

The business of Samuel Turner and Sons Ltd commenced in 1920 when Samuel Turner started his route from Brown Edge to Hanley, which continued to prosper as new housing developed along the route until its sale in 1987. There were also, at various times, colliery services and a couple of Leek Market Day routes. In the early years single-deck buses in a green livery were used but in post-war times a fleet of double-deck buses was built up, many purchased new, including half-cab Leylands with Massey bodywork which were followed by Daimler Fleetlines with Northern Counties bodywork in a chocolate and cream livery. The small coach fleet continued to use the green livery. After Samuel's death the business was taken over by his sons. The writer remembers talking to Edwin Turner, the engineer, about his Daimler Fleetlines. This was in the New Inn in Longsdon or the Black Horse in Endon where Edwin Turner used to meet his drinking pal Edwin Bloor, the writer's father-in-law. Edwin always said his Fleetlines were wonderful buses, but they were never on the road because he couldn't get parts for them out of Leyland. Unless you ran a fleet of 20 or 30 of them, he suggested, Leyland were not interested! In fact, he told me that he had to resort to PMT to obtain his spares. After acquisition PMT retained the Turner livery on a number of buses that were not always used on the Brown Edge route! This spoke volumes for the customer loyalty of Turners passengers and the professionalism with which the business was operated.

Mr Harold Berresford commenced his business in 1919 with a route from Hanley to Leek via Ash Bank and Cheddleton. He was later joined on that route by PET and F Procter and Son, the trio continuing to operate the route jointly until the end of Berresfords in 1987. A second, always marginal route, that from Longton to Leek, came with the part-purchase of EF Millward of Cobridge in 1930. A limited company was formed in 1938 with registered offices at 'Rosedale', Cheddleton. Services continued to expand, especially during the Second World War, but then no further expansion came until the late 1960s when Mr Harry Byrne sold out 'to his mate' Jim Berresford, who had some years earlier succeeded his father Harold as proprietor. Berresfords acquired the small Leek based coaching business of Byrne Brothers (Leek) Ltd, including the somewhat primitive Byrnes garage in Buxton Road. Sundry other bits and pieces were acquired but the largest expansion came in 1978 following the death of the Stonier brothers with the purchase of that company.

Stonier had started running buses from a base in Bryan Street, Hanley in 1919, the same year as Berresford, but no stage carriage licences were obtained until 1930 when a route was commenced from Kidsgrove to Meir covering – in the northern end of the city – much of the 'Main Line', but running through Ubberley and Bentilee in the south of the city rather than Stoke. During the 1950s Stoniers operations developed in the Bentilee area in close co-operation with PMT. Stoniers' livery was a very smart cream and green with red relief until the purchase of second-hand double-deckers from Ribble which may have 'inspired' the change to maroon and pink, but on acquisition by Berresfords, the Berresford livery of red and cream was adopted, though sometimes grey was used instead of cream. Berresford kept the Stonier name and garage premises at Goldenhill. Berresfords' livery of red and cream was generally applied to his vehicles, a motley collection of used double- and single-decker buses, and sometimes, new coaches. Former Stockport, St Helens and Accrington Corporation and PMT vehicles were operated in the livery of their previous owner, the whole fleet maintaining a generally run-down appearance epitomized by the garage premises at Cheddleton where withdrawn vehicles were usually dumped in a field and left to rot! Destination displays were always more of a 'declaration of intent' than a reality but passengers 'in the know' seemed to accept this!

On acquisition of the Berresford/Stonier business by PMT the key routes were:
  Hanley-Cheddleton-Leek
  Longton-Cheddleton-Leek
  Longton-Weston Coyney-Caverwall
  Kidsgrove-Meir
  Hanley-Bentilee
  and
  Stoke-Bentilee
together with various seasonal express services to coastal resorts and airports, excursions and tours licenses, school journeys and a significant private hire business.

Mrs Poole of Alsager Bank purchased a bus from another local operator, probably Mainwaring of Audley, in 1925 so as to link her village with Newcastle and so, more or less, the business remained virtually unchanged until 1989. The operation passed to her sons in 1937 becoming Poole Brothers until the limited company was formed in 1951. The small fleet, mostly purchased new, carried a livery of maroon, red and cream with ever decreasing amounts of maroon until it disappeared altogether in the 1970s. The small coaching side of the business went to McCready, a local haulage contractor. The take-over of Pooles became effective from 2nd August 1989 though the actual take-over under emergency control measures from Staffordshire County Council went through on 17th June.

Following the takeover of Turners, a number of PMT vehicles were outshopped with that operator's brown and cream livery, some in 'normal' Turner style and others, as in the upper photograph, in a reversed version. The location is Norton Green with PMT Leyland Olympian DOG740 (A740 GFA) operating Turner's main route from Brown Edge into Hanley. *(CB)*

After becoming a part of the PMT fleet, former Turner Leyland Leopard 80 (NED 433W) with Plaxton 53-seat bodywork new in 1981, found itself in Leeds as part of the CityRider fleet. Its rather strange overall white livery remains a mystery. It had been part of the small Turner coach fleet in which it would have carried a livery of light and dark green. *(AC)*

Scenes such as the one below will be, for many, the abiding memory of Berresfords Motors Ltd. This is the field at the rear of the Cheddleton premises which became the 'graveyard' for so many buses. Taken on a Model Bus Federation visit, this picture dates back to 25th January 1983. *(GKS)*

Butler Woodhouse Ltd

By now PMT Ltd had become *PMT Holdings Ltd* with three separate divisions, *PMT Buses, PMT Engineering* and *Paramount Leisure*. Paramount Leisure was responsible not only for the coaching operations of the company but also the National Express contracts and the chain of filling-stations which had been built up. Surprisingly, the Flexi-bus operation did not come under the Paramount Leisure umbrella but remained with PMT Buses. In 1989 the decision was taken to pull out of traditional tours, excursions and coastal express services. Private hire work continued successfully, using National Express, and sometimes PMT-liveried coaches and dual-purpose vehicles. The name of the holding company was changed to Butler-Woodhouse Ltd on 1st January 1989, named after the two streets, Butler St and Woodhouse St, in Stoke on which the PMT complex was situated. The fleet consisted of 30 coaches, 115 minibuses, 70 single and 140 double-deck buses, a fleet strength of 355 vehicles including the first four National Expressliners, the new standard coach for operation on the services of the National Express network, to be delivered to any operator.

If PMT had not been 'invaded' in North Staffordshire it certainly had predatory ambitions in areas outside its normal operating boundaries. The deregulation of bus services effectively meant the ending of all controls on routes, their fares and timetables, so that by giving six weeks notice to the Traffic Commissioners anyone with an operating licence could start a bus service which could either be a new route or one in direct competition to that of an established operator. By the closing date for initial registration of commercial services it became apparent that in some areas, or at certain times of day or at weekends, no operator had registered services. In these circumstances provision had been made in the Act for local authorities and PTEs to put services out to tender and to offer the successful bidder a subsidy in order to make the route viable.

PMT was to make full use of these provisions, first by moving into the largely prosperous Wirral peninsula where it calculated the use of minibuses would prove worthwhile. An operating base was established in Pasture Road, Moreton and both minibuses and full size vehicles moved in. Both types of operation commenced, *ie* commercial services competing with the established operator, Crosville, and, by successfully tendering, some non-commercial work. The operating name Red Rider was adopted. Concurrently with this PMT moved into Crewe with some serious competition on the town services, which had been the subject of considerable disruption caused by poor industrial relations and maintenance problems at Crosville under the short-lived ownership of ATL Holdings Ltd Having failed in

the tendering process, asset-stripped the company, and generally allowed bus operation in the area to fall to an all-time low, Crosville was again sold on, on 18th February 1989, this time to Drawlane of Salisbury who already owned North Western. This was not the old North Western Road Car Company of Stockport but the ex-Ribble operation on Merseyside. PMT opened their new depot in Crewe at Crewe Gates Farm Industrial Estate in 1990.

The Red Rider name next appeared in the West Midlands area, PMT successfully tendering for services in the Walsall, West Bromwich and Wolverhampton area, which started on 30th April 1989. A depot was opened in Ashmore Lane, Willenhall and a number of vehicles, mainly minibuses moved in, but a few full-size single- and double-deckers buses were also used. Willenhall depot seemed to be the dumping ground for vehicles which were unpopular with Potteries drivers, including two Dodge S56s with manual gear-boxes and second-hand Bristol VRTs from South Midland. More tendered routes were gained taking Red Rider into Birmingham and, for a time, as far south as Halesowen. Over time, tenders were won and lost, and some tendered routes became commercial services. A big setback occurred when the Birmingham tender was lost to Flights of Birmingham, and Stevensons of Uttoxeter entered the fray by registering as a commercial service a route which Red Rider had been operating under tender. However, PMT did not just throw in the towel! An agreement was reached with Stevensons whereby PMT would give up all its West Midlands operations in exchange for Stevensons depot and tendered routes in the Stockport area which could easily be incorporated into the Red Rider operations of PMT in that area as part of the unit set up largely to operate school contract services using double-deckers. This transfer took place on 26th September 1992.

Not content with an operating area stretching from Birmingham to Birkenhead, PMT tried a further expansion. This time the target was Leeds where a contract for services in Pudsey was gained. The title Cityline was used, there being legal reasons why the Red Rider name could not be used in Yorkshire. However, this operation was not successful and closed down due to loss of the contract in 1988 after just twelve months of operation. One of the reasons suggested for this was the unreliability of the Dodge minibuses that formed an important part of the operating fleet. PMT still had its sights set on a new minibus operation in the Leeds area but Yorkshire Rider set up Rider Cubs with the specific intention of preventing PMT re-entering the Leeds bus scene and no further attempts were made.

The coaching unit, Paramount Leisure, did its own bit of expansion by acquiring two geographically widely separated operations namely Landline and

Goldcrest coaches of Birkenhead which could probably have been run from the Moreton Red Rider depot but was sold off after only nine months and Linkline Coaches of Harlesden in West London, both in 1989. Paramount Leisure minuted that the big day of signing for Linkline went off like a damp-squib. Nevertheless, the business began to develop including Hypermarket trips to Calais and Boulogne, theatre trips, and some successful private hire work, some to the BBC who often required a coach at very short notice and even during the night! Negotiations took place to acquire a piece of land adjacent to the depot but this failed and the site was purchased by London Transport. Linkline was later sold to its management. Butler-Woodhouse Ltd acquired a 22.8% share in Rhondda Transport a year later. The privatisation of the bus industry was not to be confined to the sale of NBC; Local Authority-owned operations were also to be sold off. PMT bid to purchase Derby City Transport,but, together with Stevensons, Trent and Midland Fox, were unsuccessful, the winning bid coming from a consortium of employees jointly with the already employee-owned Luton and District company.

Whilst all this was going on competition was raising its head in North Staffordshire. New operators such as Moorland Rover, Scraggs Coaches, Mapleshore trading under the name of Stoniers, Matthews Handy Bus and Martin Hearson's Knotty Bus Company all appeared on tendered routes and niche market commercial services. Additionally, Stevensons came into the Potteries with the purchase of Crystal coaches of Newcastle and Drawlane, using their Midland Red North company, achieved some successful tendered operations mainly in the evenings and on Sundays.

PMT decided that new vehicles were needed for the Hanley-Crewe route and a batch of coach-seated Olympian double-deckers was bought for this route. These carried a special silver livery and were well received at a press launch gaining much welcome publicity for the company. It was decided to replace deckers on the Main Line with 20 new saloons, nine DAF SB220 and eleven Leyland Lynx were purchased for this. A quick look back over the history of the company shows the see-sawing between double and single-deck operation on the Main Line. During the 'twenties and 'thirties it had always been single-deck, double-deckers coming in the late 1940s only to be replaced by single-deckers in the 1950s. The 'sixties saw a return to double-deckers with mainly Atlantean operation. These gave way to 36ft long saloons in the 1960s and '70s and later to double-deck Bristol VRTs which in turn gave way to the Optare and Lynx buses to be followed by some use of minibuses and finally the return to double-deck operation with the Olympian.

PMT had confidently mounted an exciting and sustained advertising campaign in the Potteries. In addition to some well produced glossy leaflets there appeared roughly annually from 1985 through to 1995 a four-page advertising supplement in the *Staffordshire Evening Sentinel*. This included some news of the activities of the company together with photographs of vehicles and staff and a summary of services operated giving basic route details and frequency of operation. However, it has to be admitted that this was not always as helpful as it might have been, for example, in the 1985 edition for services between Hanley and Birches Head, potential passengers (or should they now be called 'customers'?) were treated to this:

HANLEY-BIRCHES HEAD Services 38 to 40
Service operates alternately via NORTHWOOD or TOWN ROAD to BIRCHES HEAD with some journeys continuing via SNEYD GREEN and BURSLEM to MIDDLEPORT
Monday to Saturday half-hourly service
HANLEY to BIRCHES HEAD 00 and 30 mins past
HANLEY to MIDDLEPORT 30 mins past
BIRCHES HEAD to HANLEY 07 and 40 mins past
MIDDLEPORT to HANLEY 17 mins past
Sundays No service

To add to the confusion this was also the time PMT began referring to Hanley as 'City Centre' and using it on destination blinds. Hanley has, of course, never been the City Centre of Stoke-on-Trent, that is Stoke; Hanley is the Shopping Centre. It also looked a bit odd when seen on a bus at Stafford Station. To which City Centre was it heading, Stoke-on-Trent, Lichfield or Wolverhampton?

In February 1995 a completely new network of bus routes was launched in North Staffordshire using the Title 'Network 95'. This introduced higher frequencies on many city services with new cross-city links and the extensive use of new service numbers. It was to last for just over three years!

PMT built up a chain of about a dozen filling-stations. This one is Stubbs Garage on Scotia Road, Burslem quite close to the original one at the PMT (ex-Browns) Burslem Garage. *(AC)*

Further Expansion – Crosville and Pennine

Perhaps the most unfortunate history of any NBC subsidiary company following the breaking up of the NBC belongs to the English part of the old Crosville Company. English Crosville had first been sold to ATL Holdings Ltd who, after cherry picking and asset stripping, sold it on Drawlane, later British Bus and now Arriva. This came about in early 1989 and left many wondering if the new owners would merge it with the Welsh Crosville Company which they already owned. However, this did not happen. Instead, parts of English Crosville were divided between other Drawlane owned English companies. Northwich, Runcorn and Warrington operations went to North Western whilst Crewe was handed on to Midland Red North. This left only Chester, Ellesmere Port and Rock Ferry to carry on the Crosville name in England. Nevertheless, Drawlane and especially these bits of Crosville, presented a number of problems to PMT and Red Rider operations by their extremely fierce tendering policies in both the Wirral and Crewe areas. Red Rider lost a number of tenders simply because they were won by Drawlane at a level of tendering which could never have been operationally viable.

Though these three remaining Crosville garages were potentially the cream of the English Crosville Company, they were not seen as being sufficiently large or lucrative as a stand-alone operation. Drawlane, therefore, took the decision to sell, PMT being the purchaser. The sale went through on 2nd February 1990. PMT had purchased three garages, Chester, Ellesmere Port and Rock Ferry, about 155 buses and coaches (not all of which entered PMT service), the Crosville name, and a whole host of problems. The take-over itself went very smoothly, almost, one might say, a seamless join, but PMT was the fourth owner in three years and morale was at a very low ebb. There had already been industrial unrest both at Crewe and on Merseyside and there was still considerable uncertainty over jobs and staffing levels. Additionally, the fleet was in a very poor state, compounded by an excess of 16-seat Sherpa minibuses, which were disliked by drivers, unpopular with passengers and too small to operate commercially. But further problems could be said to be of PMTs own making. There were major differences in the working conditions 'enjoyed' by the Crosville and Red Rider employees making it impossible to merge the two units. Both continued quite separately with the result that apparently no economies could be made. Yet, as ex-Crosville vehicles were repainted the only visible difference was the fleetname of Crosville or Red Rider with the occasional PMT fleetnamed bus turning up as inter garage transfers were quite common. All vehicles carried the same legal lettering, PMT Ltd Woodhouse Street, Stoke-on-Trent. Fleet repainting had

been completed by mid-992 when the once-famous green Crosville livery gave way to blood and custard. In parts of the Wirral, Crosville and Red Rider were competing against one anther, or to put it another way, PMT was competing with itself! Early operations were difficult also because of heavy competition from Crosville Wales and Merseybus. Mike Moors was forced to report that "1990 proved a very difficult year on almost all fronts".

One unfortunate by-product of the Crosville acquisitions was the decision by PMT to adopt the crazy fleet numbering system of Crosville which, surprisingly had survived since privatisation in both England and Wales. With this system the fleet number is preceded by a series of three letters, *ie* the first for the vehicle type such as double-decker or minibus; the second for the chassis maker or type and the third for the make of engine. So in the chassis listing V stood for Bristol (VRT) whilst B was Volvo (B10M). A was for DAF because D had been used for Dart, but in the engine listing A was for AEC so D had to be used for DAF. The Leyland Olympian became DOG (Double-deck-Olympian-Gardner), but fortunately SOD was not used for the Optare, this became SAD (Single-deck-DAF-DAF). Daft really, but SAD was quite an apt description for these sad looking buses with their drooping front-windscreen.

A group of redundant Greater Manchester drivers set up a company in 1990 under the title of United Provincial Services Ltd whose trading name was Pennine Blue. They were based in Dukinfield near Ashton-under-Lyne to operate services in competition with Greater Manchester buses in the south Manchester area. To do this they acquired a number of generally tired-looking double- and single-deck buses, a mixture of Leyland Atlantean, Daimler Fleetline and Bristol RE vehicles which, though tatty and run-down, looked no worse than many buses in these early de-regulation years.

In 1993 PMT purchased United Provisional Service Ltd which included the whole of the Pennine Blue operation and its vehicles. No buses survived more than a few days and replacements were sent out from Potteries area garages, and both buses and staff were moved from Red Rider in Stockport. The Stockport Red Rider base was closed for good in July 1996 and its remaining staff and vehicles were transferred to Dukinfield. Pennine was run as a completely self-contained subsidiary continuing to use the Pennine Blue fleetname though buses were painted in the PMT style, initially with blue instead of red, which seemed quite surprising when no attempt was made to use green instead of red on repainting of the Crosville fleet. However, this was short-lived and soon red and yellow was the norm. The fleetname became Pennine. Whilst Pennine was a PMT subsidiary, it did its own bit of acquisition with the purchase of a bus operator in the Potteries! This was Moorland Rover, a minibus operation that had sprung up in response to de-regulation.

Some 120 buses came from that part of the English Crosville company purchased by PMT. Almost half were Olympians including DOG161 (A161 VDM), a low-height ECW-bodied example pictured upper right on Lord Street, Southport on Saturday 6th June 1994, a few minutes into its lengthy journey to Chester via Liverpool. (GKS)

A number of second-hand buses entered the fleet in the late 1990s, some to replace dilapidated vehicles from Crosville. Amongst them was Duple Dominant bus-bodied Volvo B10M 865 (D499 NYS), one of three to come from Capital Citybus in 1999. When photographed on Crewe Bus Station (lower right) on Saturday 17th February 2001, it was working on a former Crosville service, though not many would have known that! (GKS)

At the time of the PMT acquisition of Pennine Blue, a fleet of somewhat run-down buses was operated. Many new operators with limited resources and similarly ancient vehicles came into being as a result of the ill-thought out privatisation Act, most of which did not stay in service for long. Below is one of three Leyland Atlanteans with Willowbrook bodies taking up service at Ashton-under-Lyne Bus Station in 1993. DCL888 (WWM 928W) was new to Merseyside PTE in 1981. (AC)

Moorland Rover was wound up but it did not seem to prevent it operating. Moorland Rover became Moorland Buses and carried on regardless, or so it seemed.

PMT was still on the lookout for further opportunities to expand by acquisition, and so purchased the business of C & M Travel of Birkenhead with 10 vehicles. This was in 1992 but the business was soon wound-up. Then, in 1993, the Wirral-based operator Toppings Coaches with over 20 vehicles and a number of useful contracts was acquired. When the business was totally absorbed in 1995 four Leyland Lynx vehicles came into the fleet.

Whilst all this was taking place other activities were concerning the company in Stoke-on-Trent. Two garages were closed, Clough Street in Hanley and Kingcross House in Longton, both relatively new premises. Clough Street had been opened in 1953 and Longton in 1964. Operations were transferred from both to new premises opened on 28th March 1993 at Adderley Green situated between Hanley and Longton, whilst the Flexi Minicoaches moved to Newcastle. Paramount Leisure moved briefly into Kingcross House before being sold later in 1993 to Leons of Stafford who took most of the coaches including the 'PL' registration letters used on many Paramount Leisure vehicles. These, however, were not perpetuated in the Leons fleet, Leons preferring their own 'LCT' registrations.

PMT made the National Press on 31st July 1993, this time for the right reasons! The story was the introduction of GPS satellite monitoring to bus route 24, Kidsgrove to Meir, and being the first UK bus company to introduce the Global Positional System for its buses, was deemed worthy of such press coverage. Mike Frewer, the Operations Director, suggested that the system would prevent bunching, buses would no longer suffer the 'banana bunch syndrome', unscheduled long service gaps would be a thing of the past and never again would a bus get lost on the Main Line! Another PMT bus appeared at a Motor Show in 1994 when a Dennis Lance with NCME Paladin saloon bodywork and bearing Crosville fleetnames was displayed at the Birmingham NEC Bus and Coach Show. A further small acquisition was that of Mapleshore who operated nine vehicles, midi and minibuses, and traded under the name of Stoniers using an all-over red livery resembling Ribble red. This was another of the post de-regulation operators and lived for about five years. It happened in 1995 just after PMT ceased to be an independent operator!

In 1993 Butler-Woodhouse was sold to Badgerline of Bristol headed by one time PMT Traffic Manager, Trevor Smallwood. The sale included over 500 vehicles operating in North Staffordshire, Cheshire, Merseyside and Greater Manchester using four fleetnames – PMT, Crosville, Red Rider and Pennine. The only noticeable changes so far as the travelling public was concerned were the dropping of the Minilink title and the appearance of a stylised black badger behind the rear wheel arch of buses. The Head Office moved from Stoke, following the closure of the Stoke complex which had been the headquarters of the company since the purchase of the Old Rectory in 1922. It was moved to Hobson Street, Burslem, into a property owned by Royal Doulton who found it surplus to their requirements.

Recession, rationalisation and retrenchment were affecting the pottery industry as well as the buses. What minimal maintenance facilities remained were transferred to Adderley Green but now rather than doing maintenance work for other people PMT were contracting out much of their own. Even before the whole fleet had gained its black badgers the Badgerline Group ceased to exist being merged into GRT (Grampian Regional Transport) to form FirstBus, which quickly became FirstGroup and later 'First' to better reflect the company activities in both buses, railways and Bristol Airport. Trevor Smallwood from Badgerline became Executive Chairman whilst Grampians' Moir Lockhead became Deputy Chairman and Chief Executive.

The merger created overnight the second largest transport group in the UK, only Stagecoach being bigger. The black badger soon gave way to the First 'f' logo stylised to represent a crossroads, the upstroke of the 'f' being a major road with the cross stroke a minor road – no hint of railways here! This was before the time of the First corporate livery, and one PMT bus, a Dennis Dart (956) was used as a guinea pig and paid a visit to the FirstBus Managing Directors' Conference in December decked out with logos in numerous colours of the rainbow. On the red rear and nearside it carried a yellow PMT and 'f' symbol, whilst the front and offside carried yellow PMT lettering with a grey 'f' logo. Additionally there was a red PMT with a grey 'f' on the yellow livery above the front side windows!

At the time of the setting-up of FirstBus, PMT operated 514 vehicles, 91 double-deckers, 193 saloons and midibuses, and 226 minibuses. These were operating a total of 19,000,000 miles and carrying almost 38,000,000 passengers throughout North Staffordshire, Cheshire and the North West. During the first three years of First ownership, 1996-9, PMT lost both PMT fleetnames, a matter of regret, and the Crosville style

of fleet numbering which reverted to a more sensible number-only system, which was not! Soon First would introduce its new national fleet numbering scheme which, they said, with no local fleetnames, would make inter-company vehicle transfers easier. PMT had become truly a part of a national bus company!

PMT celebrated its centenary for the second time in 20 years in 1998! On this second occasion they celebrated 100 years since the formation of the PET Co. in 1898 as the first ever subsidiary of BET. PMT painted a Leyland Lynx in the old PET livery to resemble a tram, which it did very well, and used it on the Main Line. Corgi painted their 4mm scale model of a Leyland Lynx into this livery, but managed to mis-spell 'Potteries' as 'POTTRIES'. The earlier centenary in 1979 had been to celebrate the 100th anniversary of the founding of the North Staffordshire Tramway Company.

It could justifiably be claimed that the years that PMT was an independent operator were the true heyday in the long history of an innovative and sometimes eccentric operator. The years of PMT Ltd, Butler-Woodhouse Ltd and Badgerline were all years of achievement. This was the time that the greatest expansion, certainly in terms of operating area, fleet size, new service networks and minibus operation, had been achieved. De-regulation had gone well in the Potteries without letting in much competition. The fleet had achieved a younger age profile than at almost any other time in its history, that is until the influx of the remnants of the Crosville fleet at which time the fleet size had reached over 500 vehicles, larger than at any time since the take-over of the Big Five 40 years earlier.

Company public relations had reached an all-time high due to the high profile publicity of bus routes and keeping the public informed of service changes, new vehicles, staff changes and sometimes company history through the extensive advertising space taken in the *Sentinel* and in the early 1990s by publishing its own newspaper which was distributed to over 160,000 North Staffordshire homes. In at least four different years, 1992, 1993, 1997 and 1998 the company even published an Official Fleet List which was made available to the general public. In spite of the unfortunate choice of canary yellow in the livery, the fleet had always been clean and smart and maintenance had been of a very good standard. But things were about to change.

Transforming Travel – First Ownership

At the turn of the century First PMT operated some 280 vehicles with a much reduced route network. New independents such as Wardles and D & G Coach and Bus were gaining in importance, whilst others were disappearing. Following the demise of Timeline, PMT took over the X1 Manchester-Macclesfield-Leek-Ashbourne-Derby service using two vehicles, one based at Pennine in Dukinfield and one at the out-station in Leek. Shortly after this the Pennine operation was transferred to First Manchester with X1 becoming a joint service between First Manchester and First PMT. This was from 1st February 2001. Further contraction came with the closure on 4th May 2002 of Burslem Garage, but an interesting new development was the 'First Student' operation established at Wrexham and operated by First PMT with eleven new Bluebird School buses.

As is usual with a change of ownership one of the first changes to be made is the change in fleetname and livery. At the start the First 'f' logo was applied to the PMT blood and custard livery, but this did not last long and the first 'Barbie' liveried buses soon appeared on the streets of North Staffordshire. The pink and blue on pale grey scheme soon became known as Barbie reflecting the similarity of the colours to the packaging of the famous American Barbie doll. This livery has been described as modern, crisp, professional and forward-looking but suggestions have been made that a sort of 'fog-grey' is not quite the wisest choice of colour for a bus. Then the now mercifully defunct Barbie 2 livery introduced a thunder cloud on the roof! Thoroughly depressing! As Barbie-liveried buses became established First adopted, in 2002, the previously mentioned national fleet numbering scheme, PMT being the first operating unit to use it, and with

the dropping of local fleet names the transformation from local bus operator to national conglomerate was complete. Would local route-branding save this? The Overground Network came and went until but few prestige routes carried any branding at all.

Following a widespread consultation on bus services which took place during April, to be followed by subsequent analysis, the 'Overgound Network' was introduced to the Wirral Peninsula on 4th June 2002. This was followed by a similar route branding exercise in North Staffordshire in August of the same year. However, PMT have never been good at keeping route-branded vehicles to their own routes and this proved to be no better, buses branded for route 6 Blythe Bridge-Biddulph and route 32 Hanley-Cheadle-Tean were often seen in Stafford on the 101 service between Stafford and Hanley, which route, incidentally, was put onto a twenty minute frequency having been every half-hour at least since the end of World War II!

During 1995, before the arrival of the FirstBus Barbie livery, the Badgerline logos were replaced with their FirstBus equivalent as illustrated above, together with the PMT fleetname. The combination can be seen on the left with the simplified deregulation livery applied after Badgerline dropped the 'zip' stripe. Photographed in Hanley Bus Station is IDC963 (M963 XVT) from the fourth batch of Plaxton Pointer Darts new in 1995, although this is a 9.8-metre vehicle with 36 bus seats as opposed to the more normal 9.5-metre version. *(AC)*

An event which passed by almost unnoticed was the ending of the Main Line route from Tunstall to Longton, through all the Potteries towns. A few years earlier the Hanley-Crewe service had been 'extended backwards' to commence from Longton but in 2002 this ceased and the Potteries terminus returned to Hanley. This left no through route through the Potteries on what had been the backbone of the tram system and the scene of much of the competition during the 1920s up to the 1930 Road Traffic Act when it had become properly regulated. Even in 1980 the frequency had been every 15 minutes, gradually reducing from the four-minute headway of 1950.

An inauspicious start to 2003 brought about in part by driver shortages in both Cheshire and the Potteries resulted in the resignation of three of the four First PMT directors when the Managing, Finance and Engineering Directors all left the company. The staff shortages hit the front page of the *Staffordshire Evening Sentinel* when the newspaper reported that drivers were being brought in from other FirstGroup companies. True or false adverse and often inaccurate reporting had brought relations with the local press to a new low, but traditionally they had not been very good until the Butler-Woodhouse period.

A new bus station in Longton opened on 25th May 2003, the third in 60 years and all of the town's bus services ran into it from the start. Leek outstation was closed at about this time, the drivers leaving the company rather than move to other depots and the original Red Rider depot at Moreton was closed in August. First, in common with other bus operators, made it clear that they would not operate unprofitable services without a proper Council subsidy and all operations would have to provide an adequate return on capital resources. If buses are not carrying enough passengers there is no point in running them! New Directors Julie Roy, Managing and Chris Hull, Engineering, were appointed, Julie Roy becoming the first female MD in the FirstGroup of companies.

An unfortunate accident involving two First PMT buses brought in vehicle inspectors who arrived in October. This resulted in serious inadequacies in maintenance being revealed and 58 buses, or 49% of vehicles inspected, were put off the road with problems which included faulty brakes, shock absorbers, oil leaks and defective exhausts. Fifty buses were rapidly drafted in from other FirstGroup companies notably Manchester and some 94-seat Scanias from Hull, these being the

Optare Solos made their appearance with PMT in 1999 and so were painted in Barbie livery from the start. However, 95 (X295 FFA) was painted in a special livery during 2002 to follow the Queen's Golden Jubilee baton for the nationwide tour to publicise the 17th Commonwealth Games held in Manchester. It is seen here with suitable police escort at Grotton near Oldham on the 24th July. The writer well remembers walking sedately out of Haughton Church leading a funeral cortege just as the 'circus' was passing along the A 518. The Rector wished he had a camera as one of the police motorcycle outriders apparently being totally confused at what to do when confronted by a funeral fell off his bike! Reg Sayer, whose funeral it was, would have been highly amused! Thirty-two of these vehicles came to First PMT, this one becoming 40025. Above the side windows of the Cadbury sponsorship inspired livery is the legend *First – Transforming Travel!* These buses were still at Adderley Green garage in late 2009. (AC)

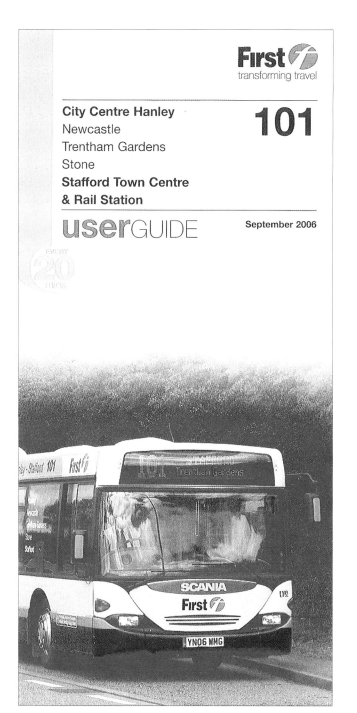

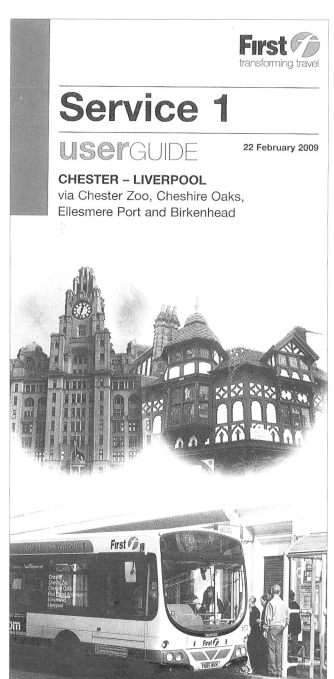

Timetable leaflets for two of First Potteries' 'prestige' routes. Service 101 from Hanley to Stafford via Newcastle dating from 2006 and Service 1 from Chester to Liverpool via Birkenhead and the Mersey Tunnel dating from 2009. Both routes operate on a main day 20-minute frequency. *(AC)*

highest capacity buses ever to run in the Potteries. The headline in the *Evening Sentinel* read 'First for Profit and Last for Service'. The Traffic Commissioner, David Dixon, described the maintenance regime as a 'dismal failure'! The operating licence was cut to 160 vehicles from 324, this with a fleet of 218 and a maximum vehicle requirement of 178.

Further, the Traffic Commissioner closed off the transfer of vehicles from other FirstGroup subsidiaries, preferring other operators to take over the routes, D & G being a considerable gainer from this, although they also had not been entirely free of censure for maintenance

difficulties from the Traffic Commissioner! Soon after promises were made that new vehicles would be provided but what turned up were 'nearly new' buses cascaded from the Rail Replacement Unit at Trafford Park in Manchester.

Regrettably, increased FirstGroup profits had not been reflected in the Potteries and Cheshire where service levels continued to be poor and routes were still being lost to smaller independent operators. This was happening even on some 'core' services due in part to poor maintenance and driver shortages leading to 'lost' journeys and passenger unrest.

No new vehicles had been delivered to the Potteries Company, apart from the Wrexham School buses, since 2000, the area having to make do with buses cascaded from other parts of the FirstGroup empire. The Flexi unit, by now renamed 'FirstGroup Coach Hire' closed and at the start of 2004 even more services were de-registered. Cheadle Garage closed as did the Head Office in Hobson Street, Burslem and the building was offered for sale. This closure would result in various management staff being made redundant. Unrest amongst staff was still rife and drivers held a strike ballot to register dissatisfaction over uniform codes, holiday arrangements and longer shifts. The projected closure of Newcastle Garage was announced, its garage Superintendent being made redundant, but the closure did not happen. The newly appointed directors Julie Roy and Chris Hull both left the company after just eight months in post.

Elsewhere in the Potteries, Moorland buses ceased to trade, services going to an ever-growing D & G and to Scraggs, thus bringing to an end the operation of Freight Rover Sherpa minibuses in Stoke-on-Trent. Morale within FirstPMT was at an all-time low amongst both staff and passengers, a situation which was not improved when the company was placed under the management of First Manchester. Remember that 20 years earlier the management of Midland Red North was placed in the hands of PMT.

However, this proved to be quite short lived and local management was restored to Stoke-on-Trent and based at the company garage at Adderley Green. Reasons for the low morale included the continuing use of small buses such as Metroriders and Mercedes Varios on trunk routes resulting in overcrowding and leaving behind would-be passengers on the busiest sections of route; not good when trying to use the bus to get to work or keep an appointment. In spite of this First announced further investment in new rolling stock for several areas including Manchester and Glasgow, but again nothing for the Potteries.

However, new managers did arrive in Stoke-on-Trent; new Managing Director Bob Hamilton came from First Bradford with Operations Director Christopher Blyth from First Edinburgh, Peter Iddon as Commercial Director from First Manchester and Paul de Santis as the new Engineering Director who joined FirstGroup from Stagecoach North East. In spite of the hoped-for new buses, this necessary boost to the new management was not forthcoming and further cascaded vehicles arrived from Manchester and Glasgow. The driver shortage was alleviated with East European drivers who started work at Crewe, but further service cuts saw FirstPMT cease to operate to Shrewsbury and Sheffield and resulted in the closure of the outstation at Ellesmere Port. Replacement services were provided

by Arriva in Cheshire and Scraggs, Wardle and D & G in North Staffordshire. FirstPMT were left with just five operational garages throughout Cheshire and North Staffordshire at Adderley Green, Birkenhead (Rock Ferry), Crewe, Chester and Newcastle. The final vehicles to operate the Sheffield service were the remaining two Volvo B10M coaches, one of which broke down in Baslow on the penultimate day of operation.

Threatened industrial action hit FirstPMT at all garages on 22nd and 24th October 2005 and again on some days in the following week and on 7th November. At Crewe, on the first day of the strike, Polish drivers wanted to take buses out, not to operate on service, but to blockade the town's main industrial estate in furtherance of the dispute! ACAS (the Arbitration and Conciliation Service) were called in during November. This resulted in a revised offer being put to all drivers which the union recommended they accept, and further planned strikes were called off. The strike action was inevitably followed by a fare rise in North Staffordshire, the third that year. The standing of the company with the bus-using public had never been worse, and a promise to improve services during 2006 was not helped by coming, as it did, just four days before more cuts in services.

However, amid the usual collection of mid-life and frankly elderly buses cascaded into the FirstPMT fleet during 2005, 16 new buses arrived, all Scanias, nine with Wright Access bodies and seven Omnicities. Ten more Omnicities came in 2006, eight of which were route branded for the prestige route 101 from Hanley to Stafford. Surprisingly, for PMT, they are used exclusively on this service! The previous buses which had included a couple in Chester 'Park & Ride' livery were moved across North Staffordshire for use on other routes including the 32 Hanley to Cheadle and Uttoxeter service.

This was a time when much Rail Replacement work was taking place in connection with modernisation of the West Coast main line, part of which was the introduction of a second service between Hanley and Stafford funded jointly by Railtrack and Staffordshire University and operated by Bakers of Biddulph. Both routes continue and appear to complement each other by taking a different route between the two towns. Further discussions took place regarding the future of Newcastle Garage, but again it was reprieved and continues as an operational depot.

Perhaps it was the appearance of some new and almost new buses, with the ever increasing number of routes operated with low-floor vehicles, or the gradual disappearance of the indescribably drab Barbie 2 livery, but things did seem to be settling down a bit by mid-2006. Service cuts were at least slowing down and staff morale seemed to be improving.

A new Managing Director was appointed in July of that year, a man described by the Wolverhampton *Express & Star* as a 'life-long busman'. Ken Poole came to the Potteries from a previous career at Travel West Midlands where he had been area director for the Black Country. More than that, Mr Poole is a local man living in Stafford. He was joined at FirstPMT by a new Engineering Director, Michael Branigan, whose previous career had been 22 years of military service with the Royal Electrical and Mechanical Engineers (REME), which he continues to serve as a Warrant Officer with the Territorial Army. Mr Poole, on arrival in the Potteries, set out his aims and objectives for his time at FirstPMT.

> "As a management team we are building on the hard work that has already been completed. It is business as usual. We have not lost our focus on maintaining the flow of service improvements that we know our customers are noticing."

May 17th 2007 was an auspicious date – it was the writer's 70 birthday and also the day that FirstPMT changed its name to First Potteries. It is worth noting that the Potteries fleet name was dropped in the 1930s in favour of PMT, that during NBC days the fleetname POTTERIES was re-introduced to replace PMT, but it did not last. Now that the letters PMT have, perhaps, other connotations and the use of local fleetnames by First has been dropped, it may just be that this attempt to use the Potteries title will be more successful than previous ones.

Finally, about that date, the sale occurred of Leyland Olympian G736 XRE, the first from the final batch purchased by PMT to be withdrawn. This was also the last batch of double-deck buses to be bought new by the company. So, with that snippet this story comes to an end, but before it does it may be of interest to note that when, in 1977, Transport Publishing Company produced *PMT – A National Bus Company* the bus company operated 194 bus routes in North Staffordshire either wholly or in part and independent operators provided just eleven. In 2007 in the traditional PMT operating area of North Staffordshire, First Potteries ran some 40 bus routes and D & G Coach and Bus, now the largest of the North Staffordshire independents, and unheard of three decades ago, has around 35.

First Potteries and its predecessors served the people of the Potteries and surrounding areas for nearly 150 years, but in July 2010 the Chester and Birkenhead garages, the remnants of the old Crosville company, together with the Wrexham school buses, were transferred to First Manchester. It is also proposed to transfer the Potteries operation, including Crewe, to First Midlands based at Worcester.

This will bring to an end the history of PET/PMT/Potteries and their predecessors, a sad but perhaps inevitable end to the PMT story.

First Potteries in Chester. In this picture consecutively numbered Marshall-bodied Dennis Darts 41073 (V373 KLG) and 41074 (V374 KLG) work local services on Tuesday 5th May 2009. *(GKS)*

Changing times. Here the churchyard wall opposite Stoke number 1 garage, once lined with parked buses, has become the car park for **PMT** staff in this 1993 view. The premises have since been sold.
(GKS)

Part 2 – The PMT Fleet

Early Buses and a tram

The first attempt to operate motor-buses on the streets of the Potteries occurred in 1901 when two Straker-Squire steam buses were acquired by PET at a cost of £690 each. The company spent a further £175 on each machine adapting them for its own purposes. The buses, which were built at the Vulcan Ironworks at Fishponds in Bristol, possibly had bodywork constructed by Brush. On entering service they became the first ever motor buses to be run by a BET associated company, even though only for experimental purposes. They were not a success and were sold within a year.

After one early attempt at bus operation in 1901 a second attempt was made, and further buses were purchased in 1904 being three Mutel-engined Brush bodied vehicles (EH1, 2 & 4) which were no more successful than their predecessors. These Brush-Mutel vehicles were interesting in a number of ways. They were petrol-engined 30 horse-power vehicles with a top speed of 14mph, though one wonders why they were allowed to operate at all! Two of the buses (EH 1 and 2) were double-deckers with a front entrance and nearside staircase which severely restricted the drivers' nearside

view. They also had automatically operated fare-boxes! The third bus, EH 4 was a single-deck bus which may have been bodied by Brush. It remained with PET long after the two double-deckers had been sold in 1906, becoming a tower wagon for the tramway system until 1919. In the early years this tower wagon body was interchangeable with a charabanc body!

No further efforts were made to operate buses until 1913 when four CD-type Daimler buses were acquired, to be followed by four more in 1914. All of these buses were acquired by the War Department in 1915, and other vehicles were purchased to keep alive bus operation for the duration of the war. Additionally, two Daimler CD charabancs were acquired from the Sheerness Tramways branch of BET in 1916, and a further Daimler and a Tilling-Stevens TTA2 came from Wrexham in 1918.

But motor bus operation began in earnest in 1920 with the return of the Daimlers and the purchase of twelve Tilling-Stevens petrol-electric vehicles constructed by the Birmingham and Midland Motor Omnibus Co. Ltd from ex-War Department lorries. During 1921 and 1922 further ex-War Department vehicles were purchased. These were AEC and Daimler Y-types carrying both Brush and Birch bus and charabanc bodywork, together with two small Garfords with Birch bodies. By the end of 1922 some 40 buses and charas were in service. The fleet further increased during 1924 with the arrival of seven more Daimlers and five Tilling-Stevens machines. They represented the zenith of the bus fleet before the abandonment of the trams.

Following the purchase of the vestibuled car which became number 125 (illustrated on page 28) the decision was taken to rebuild two cars from the existing fleet, providing similar improvement. Car 50, shown here, was further converted to direct passengers to alight at the front, note the large lettering to that effect on the front dash panel. *(PMus)*

The note on the back of this photograph says EH 491, 12, and so this is one of the Daimler CD type machines purchased in 1913 as a rear entrance bus. It was requisitioned by the War Department but returned after the Armistice. Following its return to PET it was completely reconditioned at Stoke. Note that it now has a front entrance and many other bodywork differences after a complete rebuild or perhaps even a new body. *(JCC)*

Upper left: PET No. I (EH 489) stands in Newcastle-under-Lyme with the crew proudly posing for the photographer when the bus, a Brush-bodied Daimler CD-type, was new in 1913. This vehicle was requisitioned by the War Department two years later but returned after the war, continuing in service until 1929. (AC)

Lower left: EH 614, was one of six Daimler B-type buses, also bodied by Brush, new in 1914, and seen at Fenton. It is known that these buses were still owned in 1916 but little else has been discovered about their subsequent history. (AC)

Right.: Number 30 (EH 3228), was an ex-War Department Daimler Y-type with AEC radiator, new to PET in 1922. This 'birds eye' view of the Birch chara body shows the less common layout of these vehicles, with a centre gangway rather than the bench seats with a door into each row which was more usual. This body was replaced in 1929 with a bus body, the charabanc body going to North Western Road Car. Note that all three vehicles are fitted with solid tyres. (JCC)

SOS – Queens and Rolls Royce!

The Birmingham & Midland Motor Omnibus Co. Ltd, better known as Midland Red, had been operating Tilling-Stevens petrol-electric type buses similar to those operated by the Potteries company. Mr LG Wyndham-Shire, the Midland Red Chief Engineer, was not entirely satisfied with the performance or reliability of these vehicles and in 1923 he decided to design and build his own buses, soon producing the first prototype. The bus became known as the SOS, standing for 'Shires Own Specification', though others have suggested 'Superior Omnibus Specification'. Whichever, BMMO was confident enough in its own product to make it available for purchase by other BET group companies. In the event only three, PMT, Trent and Northern General, vailed themselves of the offer,

but SOS vehicles became the PET standard for almost ten years – throughout the tramway conversion period and beyond. An initial purchase of four S or Standard-type vehicles was made in 1924 for evaluation. These were normal control buses built onto Tilling-Stevens frames fitted with pneumatic tyres and carrying 31-seat Brush bodies. Seven more came in the same year and a further 31 true SOS chassis, but still of the S-type and again with Brush 31-seat bodywork, were purchased in 1925.

The first development of the SOS chassis was the FS standing for Forward Standard (though both Future Standard and Forward Steering have been posited). As the description suggests these were forward-control (or half-cab) buses seating 34 passengers. Only four of these came to the Potteries, all in 1926. The next development was the Q (Quality or Queen) type. This was a lighter and lower version of the FS with the front bulkhead moved as far forward as possible to permit 37 seats to be accommodated. The resultant bus, weighing only 4tons 4cwt 2qtrs was one of the lightest full-size buses ever built and PET bought ten in 1927. The next three years saw some of the largest single intakes of new buses ever for the Potteries company, exceeded only in the late 1950's. First to come were 50 SOS QL (Queen Low – not Quality Low!) type saloons again with Brush bodies seating 37. Smaller wheels were fitted to these machines to further lower the height off the ground, which, together with other detail improvements, produced a much more refined vehicle. They proved to be the ideal buses with which to compete against the independent operators following the withdrawal of the trams, being both fast and reliable. A further 16 QL's were added to the fleet in 1934. They had been acquired by Crosville of Chester with the business of Royal Blue Coaches of Llandudno and sold on to PMT, bringing the number of QL buses in service to 66.

Further large batches of SOS vehicles arrived in 1929/30. First to come were 25 M (for Madam) types. The seating capacity of these buses reverted to the 34 of the FS type, parcel racks were fitted down the full length of both sides of the bus, and again all were bodied by Brush. The type was conceived in an attempt to get more women passengers to travel by bus to do their weekly shop. Next came 21 COD class buses, again with 34-seat Brush bodies. These could almost have been described as dual-purpose vehicles being of a somewhat less functional appearance and offering superior interior fittings with more comfortable seating. As such they were ideally suited to the longer distance services from Hanley to Birmingham, Derby and Manchester and for the more recently introduced routes from Hanley to Lichfield via Stafford and, jointly with North Western Road Car, from Hanley to Buxton via Leek, as well as the growing private hire and day

excursion traffic. To encourage this latter type of work two QLC's (QL Coaches) and three RR (Rolls Royce) class vehicles were bought. All five incorporated many luxury features and six-cylinder engines which were both smoother and faster than the four-cylinder engine.

The IM4 (Improved Madam – 4-cylinder) came to the Potteries fleet in 1932 when six were delivered but much more significant was the next batch of buses, even though only four in number. These were of the REDD type (Rear Entrance Double-Deck) and caused quite a stir amongst the local populace being the first double-deckers to be purchased by PET since 1904! They carried 52-seat bodies by Brush with the typical 'dog's leg' slope on the front of the upper saloon and were amongst the very few lowbridge double-deck bodies (*ie* with a sunken side gangway on the upper saloon) ever to be placed on SOS chassis. The final SOS type buses came in 1934 when a further 15 lowbridge 56-seat REDDs were delivered. The first twelve had bodies by Short Bros whilst the final three were built by MCCW. A solitary LRR (Low Rolls Royce) type coach also came on which the writer remembers a splendid trip to New Brighton only a few days before the vehicle was withdrawn from service.

In total 174 buses and coaches of SOS manufacture had been purchased, the vast majority having Brush bodywork. The SOS was to remain a familiar sight on PMT routes during the war and for a few years afterwards. In 1940 a further 55 SOS vehicles of the RR, QLC and SRR types were hired from Midland Red; of these only a handful were ever returned to Midland Red and less than half-a-dozen saw further service with that company. SOS vehicles had served the company well, many lasting for 15 years before the last one, an MCCW-bodied double-decker, ran in 1949.

The change to other makes, which began with a single Leyland in 1934, became firmly established the following year.

Number 93 (EH 9012) was one of the SOS Q models with 37-seat Brush body. Ten of these buses came to PET in 1927 and all remained until 1935 or 1936. The Q was a development of the FS and the first of the high capacity saloons. Whilst quite basic inside there was a partition providing a smoking compartment at the rear. The registration number, on the back offside window, featured transparent lettering allowing the interior lighting to provide night-time illumination. *(STA)*

Number 224, VT 4524, is a bus with a story to tell! It was new to Midland Red, and was in fact built by them in 1929. An SOS XL (Excel) with a 30-seat Brush body, it was first registered HA 4989. In that year it came to PET on loan but was soon returned. It was rebuilt by BMMO into an RR (Rolls Royce) by the fitment of a 6-cylinder Rolls Royce petrol engine, together with a higher-geared rear axle and a new radiator, though the original body was retained. It came back to PET later in 1930 as 412, a new vehicle registered VT 4524. It was later joined by about 50 similar vehicles hired from BMMO in 1940 to help out with PMT's wartime commitments to Royal Ordnance factories. (AC)

A change of make – Leylands and Daimlers

It may have been the influence of the General Manager Mr James Lindsey-Wood that caused the first evidence of a new vehicle policy to be seen in 1933, when five new double-deck buses were bought. These carried the same lowbridge bodies by Brush as the earlier SOS buses, but were significant in that they were on Leyland TD3 chassis and together with a further single Leyland Titan in 1934 they were to be the start of an association with Leyland that would last for half-a-century. The reasons for this change of policy remains uncertain but could have been a result of the great advances in vehicle design being made by Leyland including the growing acceptance of the oil engine, or the experience gained with buses acquired from the independent operators, especially perhaps the Leyland PLSC Lions from Rogerson. Whatever the reasons, large batches were soon on order.

The influx began in 1935, with 35 Leyland Tigers. First to arrive were five coaches with 32-seat centre-entrance coachwork by Burlingham, mounted on TS7 chassis, and having petrol engines, still thought to be smoother and quieter for coach operation than an oil engine. These were the first true coaches to enter the fleet and set a very high standard of interior décor and finish. Additionally, they were the first vehicles to carry the initials 'PMT' on the side included as part of an elaborate motif which contained the full name of the company around the edge. Remaining deliveries that year were 30 oil-engined TS7 buses which split the

These five Leyland TD3 buses were delivered in 1933, followed by one more in 1934, all with petrol engines, which they were soon to lose to the new coaches which came in 1935. Brush 53-seat lowbridge bodywork was fitted to the same 'dog's leg' style as the earlier SOS REDDs, but they saw the end of the SOS era so far as PMT was concerned, and the change to other makes, predominantly Leyland. The wider driver's cab will readily be noticed. All remained in service until 1949. (STA)

Number 223 (BEH 952) is seen above in post-war livery picking up passengers on the outskirts of Manchester as it returns to Hanley on service X2 in 1949. This was one of five TS7s with Burlingham 32-seat centre-entrance bodies delivered with diesel engines in 1935, the diesel engines being swapped almost immediately for the smoother running petrol engines from the 1933 Titan double-deckers.

By any standards these Burlingham bodies were luxury coaches in the true sense of the term and were 'immortalised' in glass over the entrance to the Booking Office in Church Street, Stoke, which lasted until long after the coaches were withdrawn. Their demise happened in 1951 only a year after the fitting of oil engines and frontal rebuilding. *(STA)*

Number 96 (CVT 30) below was the first of five Burlingham-bodied 35-seat saloons new in 1936. Four of these were on Leyland TS7 chassis, but the fifth was an AEC Regal II. After receiving a new Brush body in 1946, number 96 became S48 in 1953, remaining in service until 1956. *(STA)*

body contract between Brush (20) and Weymann (10). They were unique to PMT in having a half-canopy style of body with a sliding entrance door.

Then, 1936 brought 23 more Leyland TS7s into the fleet, again with the body contract divided between Weymann (10), Brush (9) and Burlingham (5). All seated 35 passengers and began to develop the PMT style of half-cab single-deck bus with full canopy carrying a single name destination blind with twin track service number box. There was also a single coach, a Leyland TS7 again with petrol engine and Burlingham 32-seat centre entrance body but unique in that it carried a roof luggage rack and so earned the nickname 'The Camel'. An odd delivery was a single AEC Regal with Burlingham bus body. Of longer lasting significance was the arrival of a single Daimler COG5 saloon, with Weymann bodywork. The attraction of the Daimler may have been the already proven reliability of the Gardner engine, or the anticipated smoothness of the Wilson pre-selector gearbox, but whatever, this bus was quickly followed by a further four such vehicles. Eight more came in 1937 introducing yet another bodybuilder into the PMT fleet, this time English Electric. These buses, whilst maintaining the usual elements of PMT specification used the normal body shape of the builder.

Again the majority of new buses that year were from Leyland, another batch of 24 TS7s with the usual split of the body contract between Weymann (10), Brush (10)

and Burlingham (4) and 15 Leyland TD4s all carrying 56-seat lowbridge double-deck bodywork by Brush of a much more modern appearance than the previous batch. Fifty-six was then a high seating capacity for a lowbridge double-decker; 53 was more normal. This was achieved by adding two seats at the very rear of the upper saloon and one to the row immediately in front of that so as to seat three and moving all the rows forward.

By 1938 Leyland had moved on to the Titan TD5 and the Tiger TS8 models, both relatively conservative developments of the previous chassis. PMT took both, five double-deckers with the now-usual Brush lowbridge bodywork and 27 saloons bodied by Brush (20) and Weymann (7). However, Weymann bodied the next two batches of buses, all Daimler COG5s; seven were 35-seat saloons and the eighth a very stylish lowbridge double-deck machine seating 55 passengers to the same pattern as the Brush bodies. More Daimlers arrived in 1939, five double-deckers, still lowbridge, but reverting to construction by Brush, and ten single-deckers with Weymann coachwork. Yet again, however, the bulk of the years new buses were Leyland, 25 TS8s and yet again the bodywork contract was divided between Brush (10), English Electric (10) and Weymann (5).

The majority of new buses in 1940 were Daimlers. This was a large order for 15 double-deck COG5s with 53-seat lowbridge bodywork by Weymann and ten saloons with English Electric bodies. The final order to be delivered, before the outbreak of war stopped normal bus production, reverted to Leyland. A small batch of five TS8s again sprang a surprise with the choice of coachbuilder, this being Willowbrook. These bodies were built to a very similar style to that operated by many of the larger independents, but still with the PMT full canopy and destination display and having a sliding type entrance door.

This Daimler COG5 single-decker, number 113 (FEH 833), one of seven, was exhibited at the 1937 Motor Show. The centre window proclaimed it to be a '35 seat Omnibus body in Weymann Patented Flexible Construction'. This was the method of bodybuilding which Charles Weymann had developed and patented for his motor cars and which was continued for some saloons until the Second World War brought it to an end. All-leather seats on a sloping floor replaced the moquette trim and stepped floor of the earlier Weymann saloons, though later ones reverted to moquette seating. They remained in service until 1949/50. (STA)

Number 169 (GVT 134) was one of a batch of ten 1939-built Leyland TS8s with English Electric bodywork. In spite of being only five years old it looks decidedly run-down in this wartime picture on Longton Bus Station. The only route information is service number 4C which suggests that the two ladies about to board are on their way to the prosperous suburb of Trentham whilst the bus would continue on its circuitous route to Stoke via Hanford. The bus was withdrawn in 1952 and so played no part in the post-war rebodying programme. *(AC)*

The war came to Seighford when the RAF Station opened in September 1942, some ten years before number 171 (GVT136), seen centre, was about to set out for the Staffordshire village from a bus stand in Eastgate Street, Stafford, outside the Shakespeare pub, where there is still a bus shelter, though now only an unloading stop for terminating town services. The route to Seighford passed to Austins sometime in the 1950s and later to Arriva who now provide a minimal service as part of the Stafford-Eccleshall route. The bus is a Weymann-bodied Leyland TS8 35-seat saloon, new in 1939 and remaining with PMT until 1952, then sold to a Showman who used it for at least another twelve years. *(AC Abcross picture)*

Number 213 (HVT 278) was one of a batch of 15 Daimler COG5s with Weymann 56-seat lowbridge bodies new in 1940. They surely represent the pinnacle of pre-war bus design and demonstrate the better proportions of a lowbridge double-decker when compared to its highbridge counterpart! The superb gold lined livery was matched by an equally splendid interior specification. Moquette seating on the lower saloon, with leather upstairs, made for a very comfortable ride wherever you sat. These buses were firm favourites of the author following his 1947 move from Birmingham to the Potteries – was it something to do with the wonderful sounds made by the Daimler engine coupled to the Wilson pre-selector gearbox so well known to him from Birmingham Corporation buses? Half of the batch remained in service until 1952, whereas the remainder carried on until 1955. *(STA)*

Wartime & early post-war Buses

The operating requirements of bus companies made it increasingly obvious that some new vehicles were going to have to be provided during the war years. In order to provide some relief to operators, manufacturers whose production had been turned over to more obvious war work were allowed to build up buses from the already manufactured parts they had in stock. These 'unfrozen' buses as they were called were allocated in accordance with operators needs by the Ministry of Supply. PMT received ten such vehicles, all with utility bodywork. There were six Bristol K5Gs with Strachan lowbridge 55-seat bodies and four single-deckers, two Dennis Lancets with Strachan bodywork and a couple of Leyland TS11s carrying Willowbrook coachwork, if that word can be used to describe wartime products! Another way of releasing new vehicles was by the supply of frustrated overseas orders to British companies. Again, PMT benefited from this, first with seven more Daimler COG5s with Weymann bodywork, but very different from those previously taken into the fleet. They were 39-seaters, with a number of features that would have made them unlawful on British roads without Ministry dispensation to operate them. They were 30ft long and 8ft wide and had no proper emergency door, the rear window being a drop down flap. Known

as 'Battleships' they were part of a batch destined for Salisbury in Southern Rhodesia – the eighth bus went to the West Mon Omnibus Board. At the opposite extreme were four tiny Tilling-Stevens buses with Willowbrook 30-seat bodywork intended for the China General Omnibus Company. All of these vehicles were petrol-engined except for the two Dennis Lancets which had oil engines, and they all had upholstered seats, the days of slatted wooden seating had not yet dawned! Finally ,in 1942 there came the first two Guy Arabs for PMT and the only Arab Is, both having Gardner 5-cylinder engines with Strachan lowbridge bodies.

The Government quickly realised that these stop-gap measures would not be sufficient to keep even essential bus services going for the duration of the war. As a result a specification was drawn up for 'utility' bodywork which included the provision of only one opening window on each side of each saloon, slatted wooden seats, and no double-curvature exterior panelling. Initially, Guy Motors of Wolverhampton were tasked with building the double-deck chassis, later to be joined by Daimler. Bodywork was constructed by many of the established builders including, amongst others, Weymann, Park Royal, Brush, Roe and Strachans. Buses were allocated by the Ministry as companies could justify the need for them. PMT were to receive 15 Guy Arab IIs, all but one with 5LW

The standard wartime utility bus for PMT was the Guy Arab with Strachan 55-seat lowbridge body. Number 307 (JEH 472) was one of only two Guy Arab Is with this body and was new in 1943, becoming L238 in 1953, three years before withdrawal in 1956. *(AC Roy Marshall)*

Wartime utility buses first arrived in the fleet in 1942 when three Duple-bodied Guy Arabs Is were delivered. The majority, however, came in 1943 and 1944 when 32 Guy Arab IIs arrived, all with Strachan lowbridge bodywork. This view depicts the first of the 1944 deliveries (324, JEH 557) in post-war livery, but still with its 'reduced' wartime destination display. *(PMus)*

The upper photograph, taken in Longton Bus Station, shows another of the more common Guy Arab II wartime model. Number 326 (JEH 559) was new in 1944, becoming L257 in 1953 after having its body rebuilt by Bond of Wythenshawe. In this guise it lasted until 1961. *(AC)*

Pictured below is one of three Guy Arab IIs delivered in 1945 carrying Roe 'relaxed utility' bodies, the only Roe bodies to be purchased new by PMT. Seen alongside the churchyard wall in Bowstead Street is number 342 (JEH 954), the last of the trio, in the early 1950s all over red livery, looking a bit sorry for itself but still lasting until 1959. *(STA)*

engines in 1943, and all with Strachan bodywork. There was also a Daimler with a 53-seat lowbridge Brush body. A further 16 vehicles arrived in 1944, again Guy Arabs with Strachan bodies, and three more to what became known as the relaxed utility standard in 1945, this time with Roe bodywork. Interestingly, no buses with Strachans or Roe bodywork had been purchased before or since. Single-deck wartime bus production was entrusted to Bedford. These small buses, known as OWBs, all had petrol engines which were deemed to be the most suitable for smaller fleets, especially in rural areas. No Bedford OWBs came to PMT but a number of the independents got a few, most notably Browns of Tunstall who received 13 together with 10 Daimler double-deckers, giving them the highest proportion of utility buses in any fleet in the district.

Peacetime eventually came. The first true post-war deliveries in 1946 were double-deckers on Guy Arab II 5LW chassis, a type which PMT had come to respect during the war years. These were rugged and reliable buses, even if not the most refined, and many had remarkably long lives lasting well into the 'sixties. This batch were groundbreaking in two ways. They were the first highbridge buses to be operated in North Staffordshire and they carried bodies by Northern Counties, the patronage of which company PMT were to continue until the National Bus Company forced the purchase of the Bristol-ECW marque. Whilst still to the so-called relaxed utility standard these buses benefited enormously from the smart curved lines of the Northern Counties metal framed body, thereby looking much more modern than the other 'utilities' and they had upholstered seats – luxury indeed! A second 1946 delivery was a one-off so far as the chassis were concerned, being a batch of twelve AEC Regals carrying Brush 34-seat bodies and re-establishing PMTs association with that company. Was it that both batches of 1946 buses happened to have the same size single aperture destination box, with the possibility of its being used in endless different ways, that persuaded PMT to make it their post-war standard? Or did PMT order them like that; in 1946 it could be anyone's guess.

No new buses came in 1947, the only vehicle changes being the exchange with North Western Road Car of the unfrozen Bristol K5Gs plus a similar vehicle which had come from Associated for five Guy Arab IIs with Roe bodywork and three Daimlers bodied by Brush. The next year, 1948, saw a return to the pre-war norm of Leyland chassis with a secondary order for Daimlers. The latter were a batch of 10 CVD6s with 35-seat Burlingham saloon bodywork which, in spite of moquette covered seats, were still rather spartan having single-skin panelling and, for the first time on a PMT single-deck bus, had side facing seats over the rear wheel arches. They were also surprisingly harsh-riding, but were utterly reliable and very economical and so often found themselves used on long distance tours and express services for which they were most

unsuitable! They would, however, be the last Daimlers for a number of years. The double-deckers were a batch of 24 Leyland PD2s with Northern Counties lowbridge 53-seat bodies of particularly pleasing proportions. All were destined to have long lives with PMT.

Nineteen-forty-nine was an entirely Leyland year. First came 20 more PD2s with Northern Counties bodies, this time of the highbridge type. These were followed by two batches of saloons to overseas specification and, the 'Battleships' apart, the first 8ft wide vehicles for the PMT fleet. First came eleven OPS1s with 35-seat Burlingham bodies no better specified than the earlier Daimlers. The OPS1 chassis was basically an export type TS11 with pre-war 8.6-litre diesel engine. The next batch was much more exotic! They carried extremely elegant Weymann bodywork, seating 35 passengers, all facing forward and they had luggage boots! The chassis was the Leyland OPD2, ie an export specification double-deck chassis, powerful and very rugged. The next year was again a Leyland one, but unusual with a small batch of five all-Leyland highbridge double-deckers thought to have been part of a cancelled order for South Africa. The single-deckers were standard PS2s with 34-seat Brush bodies. Neither Leyland nor Brush supplied any further bodywork to PMT before each ceased to produce vehicle coachwork.

A large influx of buses came in 1944 with the acquisition of the Associated Bus Company. This Leyland TS8 with Willowbrook 37-seat body, number 549 (GVT 691), was new in 1937 as part of a batch of four. Two of the batch were rebodied, one was converted to a 32-seat coach, but this one was withdrawn in original form in 1952. *(AC)*

Top: S434 ,(NEH 434) a 34-seat Leyland PS2, was one of 15 new in 1950. These were the last Brush-bodied buses to be purchased before that organisation ceased production of bus coachwork. They were amongst PMT's first 8ft wide buses and were to the BET Federation standard specification with centre back emergency door and pantry door type entrance porch. The unrelieved livery, without even an advertisement above the windows, looks particularly drab on a dull day in Buxton as the bus lays over awaiting its journey back to Hanley. *(STA)*

Centre.: A much more relaxed interpretation of the BET Federation specification was taken by Weymann, even to placing the emergency exit at the front of the offside instead of centre back, thereby gaining an extra seat. Although carrying a later registration number than the Brush vehicle above, number 451 (NEH 451) was one of 24 buses delivered in 1949, the result of blocks of registration numbers being pre-purchased in order to match the fleet number with registration number, a first for PMT. The major interest of these vehicles, however, was the chassis specification, for these were Leyland OPD2, *ie* double-decker chassis to overseas specification and all would receive double-deck bodies before they were very much older. This bus, photographed when new, is in Piccadilly, Hanley outside the SMC Shop *en route* for Stoke with a typical reduced destination blind display. On rebodying with the NCME highbridge body from CVT 4 in 1955, its own body was used to replace the inferior one on a Leyland PD2 from the 'Big Five'. *(AC)*

Bottom: A hasty purchase of five buses in 1950 resulted in registration and fleet numbers not being quite matched as illustrated here by this picture of all-Leyland PD2/3 highbridge bus number 489 (OEH 889) in Percy Street, Hanley on the 17 service to Clare Avenue, Dimsdale. It is believed these buses were part of an order for South Africa but shipping difficulties prevented their export. The, by this time, unusual half-drop windows would support this notion. They were fine buses and a welcome addition to the fleet. Withdrawal for this batch came in 1964. *(AC)*

Post-war reconstruction

By the end of the war the fleet was run-down and dilapidated. The hired Midland Red coaches were not even fit to return to their owners and most were scrapped. Some of the buses taken over with the acquired independents in the late 'thirties had only been operated to 'help out' during the years of wartime deprivation, and most were time-expired, as were the majority of the SOS types. New vehicles were still in short supply, but some kind of rebuilding of the fleet was essential. The Engineering Department was fully equipped to deal with most requirements and the various tradesmen, electricians, fitters and others, were already well used to repairing and overhauling buses. The Company was justly proud of its Central Workshops at Stoke where all of this work was carried out under the eagle eye of its Chief Engineer, Mr WAG Hall.

A programme of renovation, rebuilding and rebodying of vehicles was begun in 1946 and would continue for ten years. None of the pre-war Daimlers were ever rebodied, and it was the post-war Leyland single-deck buses which were the first to receive attention when 40 of the 1935/6 TS7s, including eight chassis from ABC, were rebodied by Brush with 'standard' BET style bodywork having 'pantry-door' type entrance porch and a rear emergency exit. In the next years 40 of the later TS7 and TS8 chassis were rebodied, 20 each by Burlingham and Weymann including four of the 1940 Willowbrook-bodied buses and five from the ABC fleet.

The small coach fleet was next to go through the mill. All six of the pre-war Leyland-Burlingham coaches were refurbished in the PMT bodyshops and fitted with oil engines. Six coaches were 'created' by a similar refurbishment to the best of the 1939 Willowbrook vehicles from the ABC fleet. But the demand for leisure travel was increasing rapidly in those days before mass car ownership. The need to further increase the number of coaches was becoming obvious. Accordingly, ten 'FEH' registered Leylands from 1938 were given new 8ft wide Windover coachwork seating 33 in 1949, then in 1950 a further ten coaches were created, this time by JC Beadle in Rochester using Leyland running units from 1939 chassis to the standard BET pattern of the day. The resultant vehicles were considered to be 'new' coaches and were re-registered as PEH 471-80. Other rebuilds were the Battleships, the 1942 Daimlers intended for shipment to Johannesburg. These were modified at Stoke by fitting them with a proper emergency door opposite the front-entrance but leaving the rear-emergency window in place. They also received standard PMT destination boxes and were partially re-seated though still remaining as 39-seaters. Unusually, these buses were re-registered in 1950 from HVT 816-22 to OEH 294-300. New AEC engines were fitted to six of them in 1953 whilst OEH 300 had received a Gardner 6LW unit a year earlier.

So far little had been done to upgrade the double-deck fleet except that in 1947 PMT got rid of the seven wartime Bristols in an exchange with North Western Road Car, PMT receiving five Guy Arabs with Roe bodywork and three Daimlers with Brush bodies. In 1951 the ten 'CVT' registered Leyland TD4s were sent to Northern Counties in Wigan and returned with very smart highbridge bodywork with platform-doors, upper-saloon air exchangers, semi-highbacked seats and generally a very high standard of finish. The five 'DVT' registered TD4s from the same year received similar lowbridge bodywork. Unfortunately, these buses were heavy, and underpowered, and so under-performed from the start, but the writer well remembers a leisurely trip to Derby on the icy and snowy New Year's Day of 1952 when the skill of the driver and the excessive weight of the bus coped admirably with the adverse weather conditions. However, in this form, these buses were destined for a very short life. Some of the old Brush bodies were used to rebody similar 'FEH' registered buses.

Forty pre-war Leyland Tiger chassis were rebodied in 1949, the contract being divided equally between Burlingham and Weymann. S197 (HVT 297), one of the former, is pictured in Gaol Road, Stafford passing an old Fordson van and with an Austin A30 travelling in the opposite direction. The chassis was a TS8, new in 1940, and originally carrying a Willowbrook body. These Burlingham bodies were somewhat spartan, having only single-skin panelling and, for the first time on a PMT bus, side facing seats over the rear-wheel arches. (JCC)

Left: Eight former ABC Willowbrook-bodied Leyland TS8s were rebuilt by PMT and converted to coaches. So proud was the company of its achievement that it took number 572 (HEH 816) to Trentham Gardens where it posed for this publicity shot which for many years, long after the coach had departed this world, was used on the front of PMT envelopes in a sepia tone print. The coach was withdrawn from service in 1952. *(AC)*

Above and below.: Ten more 1938 TS8 Tiger chassis were rebodied in 1950 with 33-seat coach bodies by Windover to provide a welcome addition to the express and touring fleet, one of which, number 494 (FEH 810) is shown in service whilst fellow 490 is shown in the works being tilt-tested before being certified as ready for service. These were wonderfully comfortable coaches with very plush interiors and heaters! They were to prove to be the last half-cab coaches delivered to PMT but the first 8ft wide ones. *(JCC)*

ANOTHER NEW BUS
for PMT
PRIVATE ENTERPRISE
8 FT. WIDE   EXTRA COMFORT   PRE-WAR FARES

Rebody, rebuild, buy used

1951 was the year of the greatest expansion ever for PMT as told in the PMT Story. Of the 155 buses taken over from the 'Big Five' many were in poor condition suffering from lack of maintenance and about 80, all single-deckers, were scrapped only to be replaced by a similar number of equally time-expired double-deckers. In 1952 the decision was taken to increase the amount of double-deck operation in the Potteries, especially on the 'Main Line' and in the Bucknall, Abbey Hulton and Newcastle areas, as being the easiest way to meet the growing demands of an expanding City. Most of the pre-war saloons from the 'Big Five' were scrapped, but the double-deckers all entered service including nine pre-war buses, two AEC Regals from Browns, and seven all-Leyland highbridge buses from Mainwaring which lasted for some considerable time.

But where could the Company get hold of serviceable, cheap and readily available double-deck vehicles quickly? The answer, it seems, was Messrs Cowley, the Salford-based dealer from whom over the next two or three years more than a hundred double-deck buses would be purchased. Some were operated as they were for a matter of weeks, others were repainted and put into service whilst yet others were cannibalised to build some tolerably respectable vehicles.

To begin with the lowbridge vehicles first, a batch of Leyland TD1s originating with Wilts and Dorset which lasted a matter of weeks, even days! Later arrivals had useful second lives with PMT, often after considerable rebuilding either by PMT or Metalcraft, including the marrying of ex-Ribble Leyland TD5 chassis with some bodies from Hants and Dorset vehicles, a mixture of bodywork by Beadle, Brush and ECW and one Leyland from a 1931 Titan, which when it had been heavily rebuilt and mated to a 1938 TD5 chassis from Ribble,

produced a splendidly unique all-Leyland bus. There were three Leyland TD2s with utility Willowbrook bodies originating with Southdown, seven AEC Regal-Park Royal vehicles from City of Oxford and, later in 1954, four Guy Arab 6LW buses all with Roe bodywork from Hebble. In all, over 70 vehicles, of which only 32 remained in service long enough to carry a fleet number!

Surprisingly, a significant number of highbridge buses arrived and even more surprisingly all were AECs. Eleven of these which originated from Glasgow Corporation were followed by 22 from Halifax Corporation. All 33 were new in 1938 and carried bodywork by Weymann from Glasgow and Park Royal from Halifax. 'Odd ones' were CUS 820 (H172) from Glasgow which had an English Electric body and JX 7054 (H163) a Weymann from Halifax. There were also five ex-Halifax buses with Roe bodywork.

In 1954 six further AECs, new in 1940, arrived from City of Oxford, again with a mixture of Weymann and Park Royal bodywork. Most were given minor attention including the fitting, where necessary, of standard PMT size destination boxes and a lick of red paint. In fact, during this time the PMT standard livery became all-over red to ease pressure on the paintshops at Stoke and Burslem, and to get buses on the road into revenue earning service as quickly as possible. They all played a vital part in the post-war development of the company when all operators were coping with inadequately maintained buses, a shortage of new ones and an unprecedented boom in trade as people were able to travel again after the deprivations of war.

Hired buses also put in an appearance during the spring of 1952 when ten assorted lowbridge Leyland Titan TD1 and 2 buses came from Crosville and twelve highbridge buses, AECs, came from Leicester City Transport. These latter seemed doomed from the start! One hit a lorry on the way from Leicester and never

Standing in Stafford Street, Hanley, about to depart for Ball Green, is S410 (RRE 731), an ex-Milton Bus Service Guy Arab III looking slightly odd with its black painted radiator. It has a Barnard 37-seat body and was one of a pair bought in 1949.
Behind S410 are a PMT Leyland Titan with new Northern Counties body and Berresfords 1947 Leyland-Willowbrook, both on the stand for route 16 Hanley to Leek via Wetley Rocks.
In 1955 S410 received the Weymann body from SN447 whose chassis then received the Northern Counties body from the bus behind! *(STA)*

Mainwarings had three all-Crossley double-deck buses, two lowbridge and this highbridge vehicle H419 (TRE 23). New in 1949 they all departed the fleet relatively early in 1960 in spite of having being fitted with Leyland 8.6-litre engines. During its time with **PMT** this bus spent much of its time at Burslem Garage being a regular performer on the short routes between that town and Oxford and Chell Heath. *(AC/Robert Mack)*

Below: Number 148 (FEH 823) was new in 1938 with a Weymann body. This Leyland TS8 received a new body, also from Weymann, in 1949, seating 33. The smart appearance is apparent in this manufacturer's picture. Similar bodies were supplied to other operators, most notably North Western, Yorkshire Traction and Devon General – and London Transport on AEC chassis. *(STA)*

arrived in the Potteries, another hit the garage wall in Newcastle, and a third lost its roof under Longton railway bridge. Very soon after this incident and another bus becoming topless under Glebe Street railway bridge in Stoke whilst operating a Football Special, PMT decided to colour code the steering wheel of all its buses: White for highbridge double-deckers, black for lowbridge, red for single-deckers and coaches.

Whilst all of this was going on most of the wartime utility Guy and Daimler buses came in for attention in three batches. First, in 1952, twelve of the 1943/4 Guy Arabs were despatched to Bonds of Wythenshawe in Manchester to have their Strachan bodywork refurbished and updated by the fitting of upholstered seats (from scrapped pre-war PMT buses) and more opening windows. At about the same time a further 20 Guy chassis went to Wigan to receive Northern Counties lowbridge 8ft wide open-platform bodies to the now expected high standards from this bodybuilder. Thirty further chassis made up the last group. These made the journey to Northern Counties in 1954 to receive lightweight lowbridge bodywork of a simple yet pleasing design. Tenx chassis were Guy Arabs including two of the ex-North Western buses and one from the ABC. Ten Daimlers came next, eight of the chassis coming from the Browns fleet; the remaining two were from ABC. These 20 all had 7ft 6in wide bodies with a straight slope to the front of the upper saloon. The final ten were 8ft wide and had a modified and much improved frontal aspect. These were for ten of the Leyland OPS2 chassis new in 1949 with Weymann single-deck bodywork. The remainder of these chassis received the heavy NCME bodies from the 'CVT' and 'DVT' TD5 chassis which were scrapped. The

last NCME body, a highbridge bus, was placed on a PS2 chassis which came from Davies Motors of Stoke with a very sub-standard Hassall Coachcraft body, in the very year when a Leyland TS7 with Burlingham double-deck body was scrapped.

This left the way open for the final phase of the rebodying programme and it concerned the Weymann bodies released from the OPD2 chassis. The bodies were refurbished by PMT, the majority being lengthened to seat 39 passengers and were placed on post-war chassis of Leyland, AEC and Guy manufacture, most coming from the 'Big Five' independents with bodywork by Pochin, SEAS, Barnard, and one each from Massey, Santus, Willowbrook and Lawton. Fourteen of the bodies were mounted on Leyland chassis, all but one seating 39, and six were mounted on Guy Arab II chassis, only one becoming a 39-seater. One is tempted to ask the question, was the 35-seat body placed on a Leyland chassis intended for the Guy Arab chassis whose 39-seat body should have gone to the 35-seat Leyland? Finally, the 1946 AEC Regals received attention, five of the Brush bodies were lengthened to become 38-seaters, three remained as 34-seat buses and four of the Brush bodies were scrapped. The chassis from these received Weymann bodies lengthened to seat 39.

In all 140 single- and 100 double-deck buses were involved in this rebodying programme. A further 42 had their existing bodies extensively rebuilt either by PMT, Bond or Metalcraft. Additionally, nearly 70 second-hand buses were placed into service with varying amounts of refurbishment, and all were repainted. It affected almost half the fleet and was by any standards a massive project. Surely these were the glory days of PMT!

L225 (JEH 113) is seen here in Longton Bus Station *en route* to Talke on an extension to the 'Main Line' brought about by the integration of the Browns Hanley-Talke Pits service into a revised 'Main Line' service which came about in 1953. This Guy Arab I, new in 1942 with a Duple body, is in the second stage of its existence having received a lightweight Northern Counties body in 1954 and also the new red and ivory livery which it would have received on first repaint. It was sold to Lewis, a breaker, in Hanley during 1962. *(AC)*

L286 (KEH 269) was new to Browns of Tunstall in 1946 with a Duple relaxed-utility body. This replacement Northern Counties lightweight body of 7ft 6in width was fitted in 1954 and painted into the all-over red livery, one of ten Daimlers so treated. Withdrawal came in 1963, a life for the chassis of 19 years, although this required two bodies! *(PMus)*

S332 (MRF 349) was a Guy Arab 5LW new to Milton Bus Service in 1947 with a SEAS 37-seat body. In this form it gave a few years service but the rebodying of the OPDs released 24 Weymann bodies which were used to replace 20 inferior bodies on Guy and Leyland chassis from the 'Big Five', and four of the AEC Regal chassis new to PMT in 1946. This Weymann body from SN463 retained the original fleet number of the chassis and remained in service as a 35-seater until 1959. *(AC)*

To complete the post-war reconstruction and the absorption of the 'Big Five', a hundred or so used double-deckers were purchased from 1951 to 1954 to replace saloons from the 'Big Five' unfit for further service. Leyland TD1 UF 7427, fitted by a previous owner with a Covrad radiator, was new to Southdown in 1931, passing in 1939 to Wilts and Dorset who gave it this Brush utility body. In 1950 it went on extended loan to the Southern Vectis Omnibus Co. on the Isle of Wight. It entered PMT service in 1952 where it lasted a matter of weeks, operating in the green and cream livery of its previous owner and without either fleetname or fleet number. This did not, however, prevent it straying a long way from home where it was photographed on the parking ground at the back of Derby Bus Station before making the return journey to Hanley. *(AC)*

SN71 (CVT 684), shown in the upper picture in Tower Square, Tunstall, was one of the very few pre-war single-decker buses to be taken into the fleet with the acquisition of the 'Big Five' and one of the oldest. An AEC Regal with Duple 39-seat body, it came from Browns of Tunstall and was new in 1936. It speaks volumes for Browns standard of maintenance that no fewer than five similar vehicles were retained by PMT, albeit only until 1956. *(AC)*

On the acquisition of the 'Big Five' the majority of the vehicles taken into the PMT fleet were post-war saloons. The middle photo shows SN334 (LEH 448), a Guy Arab III 5LW with Duple C35F body which came from Stoke Motors. Though most would have considered it to be a coach, and it is seen here on a Private hire job performing as one, it was never accorded that status with PMT, carrying a 'SN' fleet number prefix signifying a single-deck bus with a luggage boot. This 1952 view shows it before even being given a fleet number and before it had received a PMT standard destination box with full canopy. Withdrawal came in 1959 *(STA)*

In the lower picture L288 (KEH 393) displays its original Duple relaxed-austerity body modified by PMT with the fitting of the standard destination blind aperture and sliding vent type opening windows to replace the original half-drops as it collects a goodly number of passengers outside the now demolished Pickens Outfitters shop in Stafford Street Hanley. One wonders what today's 'politically correct' generation would make of the destination 'Meir Council Houses'. Eight of Browns' ten Daimler CWA6s, including this one, received new Northern Counties bodies in 1954, continuing in service until 1962. *(AC)*

L129 (RN 8296) lasted a bit longer with PMT! The chassis was a Leyland TD5 new to Ribble in 1935 with Burlingham body. The Beadle body, which it carries in this picture, had come from Hants and Dorset, the component parts being mated by PMT in 1952. In spite of this the bus lasted only twelve months before being withdrawn in 1953. It is parked on waste ground at Longton Bus Station. What would operators have done without 'waste ground' in those less regulated days? (JCC)

L273 (JX 8456) was one of four Guy Arabs new to Hebble Motor Services in 1944, two with original and two with 1949 bodies, all built by Roe, which arrived in 1952 enjoying a somewhat longer time with PMT until withdrawal in 1959. This example, seen by the now-demolished Lewis's Arcade in Hanley, is one of the 1949-bodied buses. (STA)

This evocative Anthony Moyes picture of H527 (REH 527) clearly shows the white steering wheel fitted to all highbridge buses as it traverses the traffic island at the junction of The Brampton and Sandy Lane as the bus approaches Newcastle Town Centre carrying an almost full load on 9th October 1965. It is included here as this AEC Regent III is one of the chassis supposedly ordered jointly by Tilstone and Stoke Motors but delivered complete with these fine Northern Counties bodies to PMT in 1952, soon after the take-over of the 'Big Five'. Of the twelve, one, H529, departed the fleet following an accident in 1965. Another, H522, 'enjoyed' an extended life as a Mess room on Hanley Bus Station until 1969, but the remaining ten were scrapped between 1965 and 1967. (AC)

S678 (YVT 573) was one of a pair of AEC Reliance buses in the Baxter fleet with Burlingham 44-seat body new in 1956. It is seen operating route 7 to Longton via Stoke Station and Heron Cross, a route necessitating single-deckers because of the low bridge in Glebe Street, Stoke. This bus served PMT until 1970. (STA)

H715 (715 AEH), a Leyland PD3 with MCCW body new in 1957, is seen in the snow at Milton Garage a few days before withdrawal in 1972. This was not to be the end of its days in North Staffordshire as it was purchased from dealer Martins of Weaverham by Berresfords Motors of Cheddleton who ran it until August 1976 without repainting! They then used it as a store until 1981. These front-entrance buses, of which there were 15, were truly awful vehicles, being both hard riding and uncomfortable with very low backed plastic seats. The aluminium stair treads and platform floors were lethal when wet and not much better dry! They would not pass modern day vehicle or health and safety regulations. (PMus)

H7700 (700 AEH) is pictured at Smallthorne but with few would-be passengers. In fact, conductress Gwen Chambers appears to be standing on the back platform looking for them! This was the last rear entrance double-deck bus PMT bought new, and quite remarkably it was built without platform doors and never had them fitted. It was the first 30ft-long MCCW Orion and it was unique in having six bay construction. It had a Midland Red style Leyland 'tin front' and spent its whole life at Burslem Garage.
 The chassis, the prototype Leyland PD3 Titan, was actually rebuilt from an OPD2. It was exhibited at the 1956 Commercial Motor Show demonstrating yet again just how many prototype and show exhibits came to PMT. Two further points to note on the picture are again the white steering wheel and the 'METROPOLITAN-CAMMELL-WEYMANN LTD Designers and Builders of LIGHTWEIGHT Metal Omnibus Bodies' advertisement on its side. Originally built as a 74-seater it was soon down-seated to 68, losing four upper and two lower saloon seats to please the Transport and General Workers Union! In spite of some very unkind comments being passed about Orion bodies, most notably by a Baillie of the City of Edinburgh who described them as "ungainly, inelegant, monstrous masses of shivering tin!", they were often long lived and surely not that inelegant! This bus remained with PMT for 14 years until 1971. (PMus)

Royal Tigers, Reliances, and 'Jumpers'

A SOLITARY new double-decker arrived in 1952. It was an unregistered AEC demonstrator with Park Royal highbridge body which became 490 (PVT 936) in the PMT fleet and entered service in June, only to be taken out again in October to become a demonstration vehicle at the 1952 Earls Court Commercial Motor Show. Another 1952 show exhibit was 500 (REH 500) a Daimler CLD6 with the prototype MCW Orion bodywork – MCW being a pioneer of the lightweight double-decker. Despite the use of steel pillars and underframe, a ton was knocked off the weight of a standard body, 500 being the classic example. This 58-seat bus had a body weight of under two tons and a total unladen weight of 6 tons 2 cwt. It entered service early in 1953 but by the end of that year had become a Daimler CLG5, its original Daimler engine having been replaced with a Gardner unit. More unusual PMT double-deckers then arrived, 22 of them, all highbridge. First were twelve Northern Counties-bodied AEC Regent IIIs originally, so it is claimed, ordered by Stoke Motors and Tilstones, but the body order was almost certainly changed by PMT as there is no way that Stoke Motors or Tilstones would have had a requirement for highbridge double-deckers and there must be some considerable doubt as to their need for that number of double-deckers of any kind! These were followed by ten spartan Weymann Orion-bodied buses on Guy Arab IV 5LW chassis, an order diverted from Northern General Transport Company; six were delivered in the smart Northern maroon and ivory whilst the remaining four arrived in PMT light red livery.

Excitement came to the coach fleet when PMT's first underfloor-engined chassis arrived. These were ten Leyland Royal Tigers with the classically smart Burlingham Seagull coach body in its original 39-seat central-entrance form. These coaches proved to be real head-turners in the Potteries. Even though they were delivered after the take-over of the 'Big Five' it became obvious to the remaining independents that they could not compete with vehicles such as these. The excitement continued with delivery in 1953 and 1954 of 30 underfloor-engined single-deck buses. The chassis order was split, 20 Leyland Tiger Cub and ten AEC Reliance, but all were bodied with Weymann Hermes BET standard 44-seat bodies. The AEC Reliances marked more than one milestone. They were delivered in a light red and ivory livery, almost certainly inspired by the Northern General buses. They were the first vehicles specifically built for o-m-o operation, though because of Trade Union opposition were only ever operated with conductors, and they were the first batch of over 200

AEC Reliance vehicles the company was to purchase over the next 20 years. Not surprisingly then 1955 was an AEC Reliance year, with the delivery of 50 all with Weymann bodywork, 40 with Hermes bus bodywork to the later, and smarter, pattern, a beautifully finished interior and very comfortable semi-highbacked seating and ten with Weymann Fanfare 41-seat coach bodies. A further three came with quite austere Willowbrook bodies, redirected from City of Oxford Motor Services, and placed into the Wells fleet (WJO 742-4). Thirty more Weymann-bodied Reliances came in 1956/7 and a further ten with Willowbrook bodies of a quite different style to the earlier three. These were originally painted in PMT white coach livery, although in truth they were ordinary service buses, and seven went to the Wells fleet.

PMT was nothing if not idiosyncratic! Accordingly, Daimlers made a reappearance in 1956 when 30 new CVG5 double-deckers were placed into service. These were always known as 'Jumpers', their Daimler epicyclic gearboxes causing endless trouble to unwary drivers! Half had highbridge bodies of the now-standard MCW Orion type whilst half carried lowbridge bodies to a much smarter and better finished design by Northern Counties. These all had Birmingham style 'tin-fronts', the only such to be ordered new by PMT, and the Northern Counties buses were the last of the traditional upper-saloon side-gangway lowbridge vehicles to be delivered. Many of these buses acquired Gardner 6LW engines at various times during their lives.

A solitary Leyland did arrive that year, another prototype and another Commercial Motor Show bus, being exhibited in 1956. This was H7700 (700 AEH) a PD3/2 with MCW Orion 74-seat rear-entrance open platform body. Seventy-four seats were deemed to be too many for this type of bus and for 'health and safety' reasons, the Trade Unions had it reduced to 68 seats very early in its life. It must be said that this was a very impressive looking vehicle, its highbridge body, 30ft length, and six-bay construction all adding to its majestic presence on the road! This bus was followed by a further 15 PD3s with altogether more prosaic Orion 30ft bodies. They came in 1957 and were very different from the prototype firstly by having a front-entrance (technically known nowadays as a forward-entrance) and an exposed radiator as opposed to the BMMO style 'tin-front' of number 700. These were, possibly, the most unpleasant buses ever placed into service by PMT. The lowbacked plastic seats were uncomfortable and the aluminium floors and stairs were lethal when wet – so no mention will be made of the harsh ride and the rattling and banging that went on if they were anything but fully loaded!

Five more AECs with Willowbrook bodies came in 1958, this time carrying coach bodies of the Viking design. That year saw another PMT bus make an

A stylish coach in a capital location – a Leyland Royal Tiger with a Burlingham Seagull coach body, one of ten purchased in 1952 and the first underfloor-engined vehicles in the Potteries. The capital is London, the place The Wellington Arch. The label at the lower edge of the nearside windscreen reads 'Mrs Roberts Party'. *(PMus)*

appearance at the Earls Court Show, a Daimler CVD6-30 with 70-seat Northern Counties forward-entrance body, H8900 (900 EVT). This was to remain a PMT one-off, it originally came with an exhaust driven turbo-charger and was quite a lively machine. In common with most Daimler-engined PMT buses this engine was ditched in 1966 in favour of a Leyland 9.8-litre unit. Strangely enough, this bus entered service with 70 seats and kept them for the whole of its working life! The final batches of 30ft long AEC Reliances arrived in 1960 and 1961. First were ten dual-purpose vehicles with Weymann 41-seat bodies, the first true dual-purposes vehicles for PMT since the hired BMMO LRRs during the war.

They were known as the 'Jubilee Class' to celebrate Sixty Years of the PET/PMT. These were followed, in 1961, by 25 with bus bodywork by Alexander. Three other 'oddities' arrived, two Commer-Martin Walter 11-seaters originally for minibus work(!) but in the end used almost exclusively as vans, and a Leyland PD3 double-decker with Willowbrook highbridge bodywork originally ordered by Baxters, though one may assume that PMT changed the order from the lowbridge bus that Baxter would have required.

Other vehicles, of a far more controversial nature, were to appear before the 'fifties were out as will soon become apparent.

H500 (REH 500) a 'one off' double-decker was exhibited at the 1952 Commercial Motor Show, being the prototype MCCW Orion demonstration bus when it was a Daimler CLD6. It soon became a CLG5 when it lost its Daimler engine in favour of a Gardner 5LW unit. This prototype differed in many ways from the production Orion, most obviously in having upper and lower saloon windows of the same depth. Lightweight was the mantra of the day and this bus weighed in at a mere 6 tons 4 cwt achieved by an almost unacceptably spartan interior and total lack of exterior trim. Before entry into PMT service it went round the country on a demonstration tour and obviously offered many attractions to operators if the number of Orions subsequently sold is anything to go by. The bus is seen here at the end of its 15 year life setting out on its final journey for PMT. Did the school children it was to pick up know this? – or care! *(PMus)*

S5624 (WJO 742) seen here was the first of a trio of AEC Reliances with Willowbrook 45-seat bodies ordered by City of Oxford but delivered to PMT, and immediately allocated to the Wells fleet and painted into Wells green and cream livery. These buses had quite spartan interiors with hard unyielding plastic seats which made one feel rather sorry for passengers in Oxford if this was 'normal' Oxford fare. The bus is seen in Greengate Street, Tunstall about to depart for Biddulph on the one-time PMT and Wells joint service. It has been painted into standard PMT livery and is almost at the end of its life, which came in 1970. *(STA)*

The new coaches in 1956, in spite of their '7' fleet number prefix, were five Beadle-Commer TS3 *Rochester* type 41-seaters. These stylish and comfortable coaches were somewhat underpowered and noisy, this being especially evident on steep hills and motorways. The author remembers a somewhat 'scary' trip up the Horseshoe Pass in North Wales on Easter Monday 1957 on one of these, with driver Reg Johnson, who was never known for 'hanging about'! The picture of C7716 (716 AEH) is another PMT official shot taken outside Hanley Park Gates with driver Reg Brunt at the wheel. All five were withdrawn in 1968. *(PMus)*

The oldest vehicle in the Baxter fleet was this AEC Regent with Brush 53-seat lowbridge body, L501, DSG 167 new in 1942 to the Scottish Motor Traction Co. Ltd. Most of Baxter's stage carriage services, all shared with PMT, were operated with double-deckers, the two most important being the 'Main Line' on which this bus is seen and Chell to Meir. The Regent lasted until 1960 and is pictured in Parliament Row, Hanley still in Baxter's livery but with PMT fleetname and number. *(JCC)*

H8900 (900 EVT) was another 'one-off' so far as PMT was concerned and another Commercial Motor Show exhibit, appearing on the Daimler stand in 1958. Originally a Daimler CVD6-30 with Northern Counties 69-seat highbridge body, it lost its Daimler engine in 1964 when a Leyland 9.8-litre unit was fitted. Apart from the Leyland PD3 ordered by Baxter this was the last half-cab bus delivered to PMT. It was almost obsolete from its first outing, for these 30ft long half-cab 'Leviathans' were about to be brushed aside by the new breed of double-decker with the engine at the back, of which large numbers were soon to arrive in the Potteries. H8900 survived until 1972 before serving no fewer than three Scottish independents, including Rennies of Dunfermline. It was scrapped in 1974. *(PMus)*

Aberdonians Atlanteans and Roadliners – More unusual than usual!

The quest for economies with ever-lighter weight vehicles began in the mid-fifties with vehicles such as the Leyland Tiger Cub and the double-deck Weymann 'Orion', but this was to reach new 'heights', or should that be 'depths', a year or two later with the Albion Aberdonian. Four of these arrived in the PMT fleet in 1957 with the now-usual 44-seat Weymann bodywork. These were first used on the writer's local route, the 6 from Chell to Hanley, Longton and Sandon Road where they appeared to perform quite well on the basically level terrain of this route – until they were fully loaded that is, and then all hills were too much for them! Albion had been taken over by Leyland in 1951 so the Aberdonian was effectively a Leyland Tiger Cub, only lighter by almost half a ton! Walter Womar described the weight saving as "a slice too far" for the chassis design, and the brakes were not up to the strenuous and intensive bus work in the often hilly areas of North Staffordshire. But, before this was discovered, 30 more Aberdonians were on order, 15 from Weymanns and 15 with Willowbrook bodywork. These were first placed on the generally lightly trafficked Milton area services, but the hilly nature of the countryside proved too much for them and they were soon transferred to more leisurely pursuits around Stafford and Market Drayton.

An oddity in 1955 was C5623 (VEH 623) a Beadle-Commer TS3 41-seat coach. This was always a lively performer. The writer recalls a splendid run from Manchester to Hanley on it. The day was Whit Bank Holiday Monday, this coach was the 13th or 14th duplicate on the X2 service and I was its only passenger – the kind of coach journey never to be forgotten! It had a unique body style, plainer but smarter than the five standard Commer-Beadle *Rochester* coaches which came in 1957.

Another big advance in bus design was seen in 1959 when 35 Leyland PDR1 Atlanteans with Weymann low-height 73-seat bodywork were delivered. Over the next four years successive batches of these arrived until a fleet of 105 had been built up, to become the largest fleet of low-height PDR1s operated anywhere in Britain. Such a large fleet was built up because they suited PMT operating conditions and traffic requirements ideally. The prototype Atlantean, 281 ATC, had been trialled in the Potteries being used on a number of inter-urban routes and had proved its worth, but the production version proved to be a very different beast. Whilst a considerable amount of development work had been carried out after the building of 281 ATC and a number of its important features such as the transverse rear-engine and low floor within a total height of 13ft 5in appeared in the production model, it lacked the prototype's specially designed 'dropped' rear-axle. This loss in favour of a conventional rear-axle meant that the low-floor only extended to a point forward of the rear-axle requiring a traditional lowbridge type sunken gangway on the back four rows of upper saloon seating, resulting in an unsatisfactory compromise. In service these buses were not without their problems, mainly in the areas of the clutch and gearbox and overheating. One mechanic at Stoke said they required a new clutch just about every month! Yet they were comfortable enough buses to ride

The Atlantean featured a rear engine, housed in a detachable pod which could be easily removed for exchange or repair if necessary. An angled driveline went from the rear offside corner to the back axle. This is a bus from the first batch, photographed at Weymann's factory before delivery to Stoke. *(STA)*

Because of lack of headroom in the PDR1 Atlantean it was necessary to fit bench seats at the rear of the upper-saloon, as shown here. This was no longer necessary when the later drop-centre axled models were introduced, thereby catching up with the Daimler Fleetline. *(STA)*

on, the writer usually opting for one of the rows of raised seats on the upper-saloon, and many lasted in service for 20 years or more. But let PMT's then Chief Engineer, Walter Womar, speak of these buses:

'The early Atlantean soon became quite notorious for its mechanical failures, and it was evident that Leyland had not spent enough time confirming its reliability after what was quite an extensive redesign from the prototype. This was the first rear-engined model to go into large scale service with a variety of operators in Britain and everyone involved had a lot to learn'.

Single-deck deliveries reverted to a much more traditional pattern of AEC Reliances with some Leyland Leopards, but for the foreseeable future all would be to the newly permitted 36ft length. First to arrive in 1962 were 20 Willowbrook bodied 54-seat buses, ten on AEC Reliance and ten on Leyland Leopard chassis, and a further five Leopards carrying full coach bodywork by Plaxton, the first version of the famous Panorama design. This pattern was repeated in the following year when a further 20 Willowbrook-bodied buses arrived, this time with only 53 seats and to the later style introducing to PMT the standard BET windscreen. However, there were no more coaches and 1964 was all Reliances, except for the prototype Daimler Roadliner – but more of that later! – ten Marshall-bodied buses and five Duple Commander coaches. One of these, C989 4989 VT, carried a plaque throughout its life proclaiming that it was the 'Coach of the Year' at the Brighton coach Rally in April 1964 which was the first time PMT had ever entered!

Nine more Reliances arrived in 1965, five with Weymann dual-purpose bodywork which were amongst the most comfortable vehicles the writer has ever experienced which he did one very wet August day in 1965 on a day tour to London to be interviewed at No. 10 Downing Street by the Prime Minister's Ecclesiastical Secretary! He did not, however, take up the invitation to become Vicar of Greenfields in Oldham. The other four were 41-seated Plaxton Panorama coaches and again one, C1041 AEH 141C, achieved success at the Brighton Coach Rally, winning the Clacton Trophy in 1965. Unique to PMT on this type of Plaxton body was the narrow polished trim at the front with a band of red trim beneath giving a much greater unity to the styling.

The first of the Alexander Y-type dual-purpose vehicles came in 1967, a batch of four. Further small batches would follow until 1971 by which time a total of 15 had been accumulated, all of which had very hard working lives with PMT. Five full coaches with Duple Commander IV 49-seat bodies were delivered in 1969 and 1970 which, by contrast, were destined for a very short life in the Potteries. All five were sold in 1973 for economic reasons, four going to Ladvale Coaches of Cheltenham. Twenty more Leyland Leopards arrived in 1969, PSU4s with Marshall 43-seat bus bodies. These vehicles had 5-speed semi-automatic gearboxes, first gear being a crawler gear which enabled gradients of up to 1 in 4 to be climbed when fully laden – the lessons of the Abedonians had been learned. It must be admitted, however, that they were not required to climb many such gradients and were not often fully loaded in the rural areas of Uttoxeter, Cheadle and Stafford where they spent much of their lives.

After 1962, no more Leyland Atlanteans came, future double-deck requirements for the next twelve years, which were quite modest, were provided by the Daimler Fleetline, and all to the standard 13ft 5in low-height specification. The bus had the great advantage of a single drive-line and drop-centre rear axle giving a flat floor running the full length of the bus, and so allowing a central aisle throughout the upper saloon. At first one bus, L899 (899 UEH)was delivered. It renewed the long standing relationship with Northern Counties which proved to be short-lived. After a further batch of 15 in 1963, all further Fleetlines would be bodied by Alexander, two batches of double-deckers, 25 in 1964 and ten the following year. A batch of 20 single-deck Fleetline-Alexanders came to the fleet in 1970. These were dual-door standee type buses. One of them 141, (BEH 141H), was exhibited at the Commercial Motor Show of that year. Following a telephone call from Daimler this bus had to be taken out of service, smartened up and partly repainted to look like new, to make its appearance. However, these dual-door buses with their steeply raked floor and black and orange interior colours were extremely unpopular and were soon sold off, two went to East Kent for use inside Dover Docks whilst most of the remainder went to Northern Ireland where a significant number were blown up by the IRA!

The first PMT Fleetline (top picture) was Northen Counties bodied L899 (899 UEH) new in 1962. It was followed by a batch of 15 a year later, but more Fleetlines, of which there were 55, carried Alexander bodywork as seen on L1009 (5009 VT) (centre picture). After the simple clean lines of the elegant Northern Counties body these Alexander vehicles were not at all pretty with a frontal appearance quite out of character with the remainder of the vehicles. Further Fleetlines delivered in 1970 carried single-deck Alexander bodywork in which the rear window was that used for the front upper saloon screen of the double-deck design. Number 141 (BEH 141H) is seen in the lower picture, smartly turned out in preservation. It was the first of the batch which all had short lives with PMT, the steeply sloping floor and dual-door layout being unpopular with crews and passengers alike. *(PMus top and centre, STA bottom)*

But the real story of the second half this decade and the early 'seventies must be the saga of the Daimler Roadliner. Not many bus designs over the years have been disasters, though one could mention the AEC 'Q' from the 1930s, or Foden rear-engined chassis or even the Albion Nimbus of the 1950s, or supremely the Guy Wulfrunian which first saw the light of day in 1959. But more to the point so far as PMT is concerned was the Daimler Roadliner: a rear-engined low-floor single-deck chassis built by Daimlers with considerable development work by PMT and Metalastik. The then Chief Engineer of PMT was JD Mundella who, through time at Midland Red, had developed an interest in rubber suspension for passenger chassis. It had recently been introduced by Alec Issigonis on the famous BMC mini, and Jim Mundella had already used it on an AEC Reliance.

On paper the Roadliner looked good, and the prototype, SN1000 (6000 EH), looked equally good on completion. So confident were Daimler that they advertised 'only Daimler could make so outstanding a contribution to passenger transport'. It was a true low-floor bus with single-step entrance, almost flat floor, with the Cummins V6 engine mounted under the rear-seat. The Marshall body, to largely standard BET design, was well finished and comfortable.

Initially. it showed much promise; passengers liked it and the bus seemed to be quite reliable. Orders were placed for a further 50 with the body contract divided between Marshall and Plaxton, of the latter, three were coaches. Regrettably, as the buses entered service during 1966 and 1967 it became obvious that the early promise was not to be fulfilled. They were noisy, unreliable, and due to excessive off-road time due to breakdowns amounting to about 30% – expensive. It was said, almost seriously, that one of the coaches did once manage a trip to Great Yarmouth and back without breaking down. But when two of the buses broke their backs due to a combination of the long rear-overhang, chassis flexing and the heavy Cummins engine, matters became serious. Yet a further three Cummins-engined coaches were on order for 1968 delivery, this time with Duple Commander bodywork, and a batch of ten Plaxton-bodied dual-door buses for the following year. These final buses differed from earlier examples in having a lighter and less-powerful Perkins engine, but in reality they were little better. Only 230 Roadliners were built, from which total PMT bought 63, one of the Plaxton coaches actually winning the Brighton Coach Rally in 1967. The second largest customer was Black and White Motorways.

The root cause of the Roadliner problem according to Walter Womar, by then PMT's General Manager, was the Cummins V6 engine. He states in his autobiography:

> The Cummins V6 was an unhappy introduction of that engine maker, a much respected firm with a position in America quite similar to that of Gardner in Britain. Its problems were overheating, difficulty in starting when hot and smoke emission on stopping services.

All had short lives with PMT, none lasting more than eight years. The coaches went as early as 1972 and 1973, to be replaced by second-hand purchases. Six coaches came from Ribble, all Leyland Leopards, three with Harrington Cavalier and three with Duple Continental coachwork. Jim Mundella took all of this very badly and it is thought the worry and stress over the Roadliner contributed in no small way to his untimely death.

Despite the high expectations, and Daimler's considerable hype, the Roadliner was doomed to be consigned to the pages of 'disasters' in the history of bus design. In Daimler's defence it must be pointed out that this photograph shows exactly where the trouble lay, but that was scant confort to PMT when the troubles began. (PMus)

More of the classic Weymann Hermes bodies arrived in 1957, this time on the Albion Aberdonian chassis. An initial order for four was delivered and put to work on the relatively flat terrain of the Chell-Victoria Road-Meir service 6, where they performed adequately, especially if lightly laden! Thirty more such buses were ordered to be delivered later in 1957, vehicles which Walter Womar suggested were difficult to get going and even more difficult to stop, especially in the strenuous operating conditions of North Staffordshire. They were, in reality, a lightweight version of the Leyland Tiger Cub and to quote Walter Womar again "a step too far" in the quest to reduce operating costs.

As was frequently the case at **PMT** the body contract was divided, 15 having the splendid Weymann body enhanced by the red and ivory livery. The equally smart and well finished grey and maroon interior did not disappoint either. After an unsuccessful spell at Milton these buses were assigned to 'light duties' in the Stafford and Market Drayton areas and so enjoyed a respectable life span until 1971. SN8736 (734 CVT) is shown. *(STA)*

The other 15 arrived with Willowbrook bodywork and in spite of the '8' prefix to the fleet number all but seven were delivered in 1957, including **SN8759 (759 CVT)**, seen here with the destination blind set for the Penkhull circular service. The lop-sided look of the display followed the 1958 renumbering of routes when the 'old' service numbers were painted out pending the delivery of new blinds. The picture, taken in Campbell Place, Stoke, was for *Commercial Motor* who used it in a road test of the Aberdonian. This bus served until 1971 when it was sold via Cowley of Salford to Philips Coach Company of Shiptonthorpe, North Humberside, who purchased no fewer than 14 of PMT's 34 Aberdonians, most of which remained in service for a couple of years. *(PMus)*

Above: The spectacular background in this Anthony Moyes photograph is Mow Cop, the romantic folly on the Staffordshire-Cheshire border, with two weary walkers trudging towards their bus, one of the first twenty 36-foot long saloons bodied by Willowbrook and new in 1962. The seating capacity of 54 was one more than a standard lowbridge double-decker less than a decade earlier! The chassis makers were divided equally, the first ten being Leyland Leopards whilst the balance were AEC Reliances, of which this, SN933 (933 UVT), is one. Withdrawal came for all twenty in 1976/7 though 927, a Leyland, became a driver-trainer in 1977 being painted in the NBC bright yellow livery adopted for such vehicles. (STA)

Coaching never played a major part in the activities of PMT so it was something of a surprise when they began to enter coach rallies in the mid-sixties and even more of a surprise when they won! C989 (4989 VT) is seen in Brighton winning the British Coach Rally in April 1964. It carried a commemorative plaque for the rest of its working life proclaiming it 'Coach of the Year, 1964'. The driver at Brighton was the then top driver Horace Davies who also carried off all the driving trophies. This writer never had the privilege of riding on one of these vehicles, but by all accounts they were magnificent beasts, the best PMT ever had. Five were delivered, being AEC Reliances with Duple Commander coachwork seating 49. Withdrawal for all five came in 1973, passing to Everall, Wolverhampton and to independents in various parts of the Midlands. (STA)

C1041 (AEH 141C) was entered for the 11th British Coach Rally at Brighton in April 1965 and is seen, suitably garlanded, at Trentham Gardens after its return to the Potteries having won the Clacton trophy. This batch of four AEC Reliances carried Plaxton Panorama 41-seat bodies on which the unique-to-PMT narrow front end waist trim with red beneath is clearly seen. Withdrawal and sale to Everall came in 1973, this one ending up with Middleton of Rugeley. (STA)

Production Daimler Roadliners, of which there were 47, came in 1967 and differed from the prototype in having Metalastik suspension all round. Yet this was not the cause of the trouble; it was the Cummins engine that was considered the major weakness. All were low-floor 50-seaters with the bodywork contract divided between Plaxton (24) and Marshall (23). About to leave the perimeter road to Longton Bus Station after its conversion to Farebox operation is S1063 (KVT163E), a Plaxton-bodied example which remained in service until 1974. Only three lasted into 1980! (STA)

The last ten Roadliners, 130-39 (WEH 130-39) came in 1969 and differed in two important respects from the main batch. The Cummins engine was ditched in favour of a Perkins unit and they featured dual-door bodywork for 46 passengers by Plaxton. These Perkins buses were, if anything, even less reliable than the Cummins-engined vehicles and all had gone by 1976. Two of them were used as 'mobile' shops, 130 at Forton Services on the M6, and 133 at Farthing Corner on the M2. (PMus)

The short and problematic lives of the Roadliners contrasts with the 35 Weymann-bodied Leyland Atlantean PDR1s which had been delivered in 1959, the first of four batches – by the end of 1962 a total of 105 were being operated, the largest fleet of 'low-height' Atlanteans in the world.

Despite many problems with the Atlantean PDR1 chassis PMT persevered and made these into dependable front-line vehicles .

The true significance of this picture, however, is that it records the final journey of the last Atlantean in PMT service, and was taken by the *Staffordshire Evening Sentinel* to commemorate the passing of these long-lived and very good buses in October 1980 at the end of a 21 year life. (AC)

Fortunately not quite all of **PMT**'s eggs were in the Roadliner basket, and small numbers of **AEC Reliances** continued to be purchased, all with the iconic **Alexander Y-type** dual-purpose body. In all a fleet of 25 Reliance Y-types was built up by the time the final six arrived in 1971, of which 168 (**FEH 168J**) was one. Because of the unreliability of the Roadliners many of these vehicles built up tremendous mileages over relatively short periods of time on both bus and coach duties. This picture, taken at **Clough Street Garage** for the **PMT House Magazine**, shows the change in frontal appearance of the Alexander body. Number 168 was withdrawn in 1981 after a short but hard life, going on to work for **Calway Coaches** of **Washington, County Durham.** *(PMus)*

This trio of coaches, C911-3 (VVT 911-3G), AEC Reliances with Duple Northern Commander IV coachwork for 49 passengers, is seen at the Kings Hall, Stoke for the Keele University Degree Ceremony in 1970. This august beginning did not prevent these wonderful coaches from being withdrawn in 1973! An 'executive' decision taken at Stoke was to sell all the coaches irrespective of age, specification or condition and replace them with **NBC** standard Duple Dominants on Ford chassis! The lucky benefactors were Ladvale Coaches of Cheltenham. Ah, the benefits of Corporate Wisdom … ! *(PMus)*

NBC Standard Fare

During their short lives the Roadliners had proved themselves to be unreliable and very expensive to the company. But what was the alternative? PMT was to go along with what became standard NBC fare, and so the Bristol RE began to appear in the fleet. This chassis had not been available to PMT until the Transport Holding Company acquired control of BET's passenger transport interests on 1st March 1965. The first two batches were six RELLs with 48-seat dual-door bodies and 15 RESLs with 44-seat bodies. The following year saw the arrival of a further variation, the RELH6L, three with dual-purpose 49 seat bodywork; these were followed by a further four dual-door vehicles and finally 17 53-seater buses arrived making a total of 45 vehicles which just about replaced the Roadliners. It must be said that these buses were reliable work-horses beloved of drivers and engineers alike, but they were noisy, harsh riding, rattle boxes and with their unyielding plastic seats offered the passenger a thoroughly unpleasant experience.

Paradoxically, their Workington-built successors, the Leyland Nationals, in spite of their plastic seats, were more comfortable, quieter and smooth-riding and offered the passenger something to restore their faith in bus travel, but they were disliked by engineers and drivers alike! PMT's first Leyland Nationals, 15 '1152' 52-seaters came in 1972/3 to be followed by 15 short '1051' 41-seat buses in 1973/4; then 20 more 52-seaters '11351s' between 1974 and 1976 and a final two, again 52-seaters came in 1977. The only National 2s to come to PMT were five dual-purpose 47-seat vehicles which did not arrive until 1984. These buses all had their gearboxes modified before entering service on the Shrewsbury-Sheffield corridor and Hanley-Stafford. They were quite magnificent to ride in, in spite of the weak brackets holding up the parcel-racks – two were broken on one bus after less than four months on the road, but what a far cry from the Bristol RELH dual-purpose vehicles!

In total, PMT built up a fleet of almost 60 Leyland Nationals, and it must be said that they served the company well throughout the NBC years, proving themselves to be lively performers, being both reasonably reliable and economical to operate in spite of the relatively high fuel consumption. The last of PMT"s Nationals were not withdrawn until 1995 some lasting with second operators into the 21st century, in some cases a life of over 25 years.

Cost cutting, and lightweight buses, became fashionable again in the early 1970s. For this reason the Ford series of passenger chassis entered many NBC fleets including that of PMT. The first three were Plaxton-bodied R1114 53-seat coaches which entered

the fleet in 1972. All subsequent Fords, both R1014s and R1114s, were bodied by Duple with 41, 45, 49, 51 or 53 seats; in all a total of 20 were delivered over the period 1973 and 1974. Whilst these were all Dominant-bodied dual-purpose vehicles, some did acquire National white full coach livery for a time. These vehicles were seen by NBC as a short term measure and were expected to have a life span of seven years. As such they were useful in upgrading and modernising the fleet. All had, however, been withdrawn by PMT by the end of 1980 giving them the singular distinction of being even shorter-lived than the Daimler Roadliners!

The few full coaches to enter the fleet were all Leyland Leopards with Duple Dominant bodywork; four came in 1974, two in 1977 and one a year later which also saw the delivery of eleven more Leyland-Dominant coaches in dual-purpose livery, though only 49-seaters, to be followed by a further five 53-seaters and a final full coach, seating 46, in 1979. The last four Leopards came in the next decade, a full coach in 1981 and three dual-purpose vehicles in 1982 all with Willowbrook coachwork. Latter years of NBC ownership saw delivery of twelve Leyland Tigers all with Plaxton Paramount coach bodies, four in each of the years 1984-6. These years also introduced the minibus from both Ford and Mercedes-Benz, but that is another story!

Double-deck vehicles, at least in the early days of NBC. were Bristol VRTs, of which PMT built up a sizeable fleet. Nine came in 1974, which should have been 18, but the second nine were painted green and delivered directly to Crosville in Liverpool, not coming to the Potteries until the disastrous fire at Newcastle Garage in 1975 when 14 more VRTs came to Stoke. Larger orders followed; 24 in 1976, 10 in 1977, 28 in 1978 and 38 in 1979/80, adding up to 130 buses, the largest number of any type operated by the company, all were low-height vehicles and saw another return to the predominance of double-deckers in the fleet.

In the 1950s the single-deck AEC Reliance had been predominant, then the double-deck Leyland Atlantean reigned supreme in the 1960s, ably helped out by the Daimler Fleetline, only to see a return to saloons in the 1970s with the Daimler Roadliners, single-deck Fleetlines and the Alexander Y-type bodied AEC Reliances until the arrival of the VRT which again put the double-deck in charge throughout the late '70s and the 1980s.More interest came to the Potteries bus scene in 1978 when PMT was selected to undertake part of an Operational Testing Programme for NBC. Three buses were involved; No. 700 (XRF 700S) was an Alexander-bodied Dennis Dominator whilst 900 (WVT 900S) was a Foden 6LXB with Northern Counties bodywork, one of only nine built. These were teamed with an existing Bristol VRT 686 renumbered 600 (YBF 686S) and all three were closely monitored for performance, reliability, fuel-economy, passenger preference, and drivability (see also page 72).

All the testing was done from Newcastle Garage which offered the most variable and arduous operating conditions. The Dennis had been exhibited at the Scottish Motor Show of 1978 and all three were unveiled to the general public in the Market Square in Hanley on Thursday 28th September. The outcome of the operational testing programme became a bit academic as the Dennis Dominator was replaced by a later model, the Foden never went into full production and the Leyland Olympian succeeded the Bristol VRT.

For what it's worth, it may be said that the Foden was the favourite of the trio, with passengers finding it easier to get on and off, the Dennis was the drivers' choice being light and easy to handle whilst the Bristol was the engineers' bus. It was also the operators' bus being the most frugal in terms of fuel consumption – and also for tending to take fewer days off sick!

And so to the final type of bus to be purchased in the NBC years, the Leyland Olympian, 15 of which came to PMT in 1983/4. There would be no more until after privatisation when, in 1989, ten came with dual-purpose type seating, though all had moquette covered seats, what a pleasure after the many years of plastic style leather! They were initially used to upgrade the Hanley-Crewe service. Whereas the original buses had ECW bodywork, these had Leyland bodies. The then Senior Garage Superintendent at Hanley Garage described these as 'the best buses PMT ever operated'. Had we at last got a bus that satisfied engineers, drivers and passengers alike?

Perhaps the death-knoll of the traditional PMT/BET bus came with the first Eastern Coach Works-bodied Bristols in 1971. By the time they had all been delivered in four different varieties they effectively became the Roadliner replacement. The first to arrive in 1971 were four with the dreaded dual-door body, part of an order for ten, the remaining six coming the following year. Next, still in 1971, came eight RESLs with another eight in 1972. Number 185 (JEH 185K), below, was the second of these and is seen in Springfields in traditional PMT livery. Number 213 (PVT 213L), right, was the first bus to be delivered in NBC poppy red, in 1972, and is posed at Swynnerton to show it off. The appearance was not improved when an NBC edict demanded the removal of the white band. These buses benefited from having a rear-engine mounted under the floor, enabling them also to have a centre-back emergency exit. Number 213 was sold to Gastonia Coaches of Dovercourt who upseated it to 59! (PMus)

The Bristol VR was built in three heights by Eastern Coach Works and PMT took the lowest – 13ft 5in – version until it ceased production after which they had no option but to use the 13ft 8in mid-height body. The highest version was produced for use on the Leyland Atlantean chassis which never featured in the PMT fleet. Pictured is 674 (URF 674S), a 13ft 5in bus new in 1978 The classic lines of the ECW body are further enhanced by the NBC poppy red and white livery which always looked so much better than some of the drab reds used by BET in fleets such as East Midland, Ribble or even Midland Red. *(STA)*

1973 saw the replacement of PMTs 'top line' coaches with these Ford R1114s with Duple Dominant 53-seat bodywork, which many would describe as dual-purpose vehicles rather than coaches. They were the first 'benefits' of the Government's Bus Grant scheme to come to PMT. The first of them, number 25 (WVT 425L), is seen at *The Sheet Anchor* public house at Whitmore working an inward journey on the A53 road between Market Drayton and Newcastle on service 64 from Shrewsbury to Hanley run jointly with Midland Red with a running time of 2 hours. Midland Red's usual offering on this was a Plaxton-bodied Ford service bus. Eleven of these coaches were followed by a further two the following year, with only 51 seats and a luggage rack behind the driver. The whole batch left the fleet in 1980, at the end of a seven year life and many of them went on to further service. Numbers 25 and 28 went to Hants and Dorset and then back to Stafford with Happy Days Coaches while number 31 stayed even more locally working with Berresfords of Cheddleton for a couple of years. *(PMus)*

The interior of the NBC version of the Duple Dominant as bright and cheerful if not opulent, and reasonably practical for omo operation. *(PMus)*

Eight Ford R1104s with Duple Dominant Express bodies came in 1973/4. Half came in 1973 in local coach livery and the remainder the following year in **NBC** National Coach livery, the much despised 'all-white' scheme that is still basically unchanged today after nearly 40 years. The upper picture, posed against a background of bottle-ovens, shows number 41 (**OEH 41M**) of the 1974 batch at the Gladstone Pottery Museum in Longton whilst operating a City Tour. All were withdrawn in 1980, again providing reasonably modern coaches for independent operators, these being divided between Scotland and Wales! *(PMus)*

The first Leyland Tigers arrived in 1983, four of them, all with Plaxton Paramount coachwork, two 53- and two 57-seaters, of which number 24 (**ERF 24Y**) is one of the former. **PMT** used the ParaMounT name to good effect, using it for a time as the name of its coaching unit *Paramount Leisure*. The letters **PMT** were picked out in red with the others in blue – all in the spirit of **NBC**, if not the letter! In this view we are in Swynnerton again, but this time the coach is full of passengers enjoying a private hire outing and was photographed a couple of hundred yards further up the road than the more usual posed pictures. It could be returning to, or visiting, the British Telecom Training Centre at Yarnfield. In later life the coach was painted in blood and custard without the zip, remaining in service long enough to acquire a black badger behind the rear wheel-arch. By then it was a regular performer on the X64 carrying the fleet number STL24! It was withdrawn in 1996, so outliving Paramount Leisure which was sold to Leons of Stafford in 1993. *(PMus)*

Number 247 (**XEH 247M**) was one of 15 buses, the only batch of 10.3-metre Leyland Nationals for **PMT**, which came in 1973. The bus is pictured operating just the kind of rural service for which it was intended, and looking immaculate at Bagnall Church in April 1975. Withdrawal came in 1986. *(AC/Anthony Moyes)*

All Sorts of Strange Names
– The Minibuses

They were called *Bursley, Hanbridge, Dodge, Transit, Sherpa* and *Vario* but what was a minibus? This is a question with no definitive answer like the term lowbridge or low-height for double-deck buses. To the writer a low-height double-decker is anything that will pass under Liverpool Road railway bridge in Stoke! That is a bus with an overall height of 13ft 9in or less irrespective of the upper-saloon seating arrangement with or without sunken side gangway. A minibus is anything with 27 seats or fewer or any vehicle which PMT in their crazy 1993 fleet numbering system would have given an 'M' first letter, but like Topsy, over the years the minibus grew up!

Apart from a few small vehicles which joined the 'Flexi' fleet or City Radio Cabs the first true minibuses operated exclusively on public bus services came in 1984. As would be expected they were all panel van conversions by PMT. Two 15-seater 'coaches' on Mercedes 508B chassis were followed by a single 19-seater L608D 117 (B117 OBF). A second, but with 21 seats, 119 (B119 RRE) came in 1985 to be followed by the first Ford Transit, a 16-seater 118 (B118 RRE).

The first production batch comprised 40 20-seat Mercedes with PMT bodywork in 1985/6; then a couple of Mercedes with *Devon* conversion bodywork were acquired second-hand for the 'Flexi' fleet. Also

in 1986 the first 20-seat Freight Rover Sherpa 160 (D160 CRE) arrived. Apart from some used coaches 1986 was an entirely minibus year, and as such saw the only production batch of Ford Transits of which there were 16, all 16-seaters, eleven with PMT Engineering bodywork and five bodied by Robin Hood. This was the year with the largest influx of 'first generation' van conversions with the minibus fleet already up to 70.

PMT Engineering had been busy developing its own bodywork and these began to come on stream in 1987. Surprisingly, the Ford Transit was ditched in favour of the Freight Rover Sherpa; perhaps the longer wheelbase allowing four extra seats was the deciding factor. There were 31 of these all with PMT *Bursley* style bodies of which two were coach-seated. A further 14 Sherpas, this time with 16-seat Dormobile bodies ,came with the Crosville purchase in 1993. One further make of minibus entered the fleet, the Renault-Dodge S56, four with PMT 20-seat bodies coming in 1987/8 but the major batch of 28 came in 1988 with Alexander bodywork, 25 having 20-seat bodies and three seating 25. Opinions on these buses differ! Some liked the Alexander bodies but hated the Renault-Dodge chassis and drivers have been heard to suggest that they always hoped they would not start, because once they were running there was no knowing if they were ever going to stop! Does the minibus 'booby prize' go to the Dodge or the Sherpa? Whichever, the depths had been reached.

All future minibuses, until 1998, were to be Mercedes. Whatever Mercedes had failed to achieve in

Number 162 (C162 VRE) was one of two batches of Ford Transits. These were 16-seaters of a much more boxy appearance than the Mercedes vehicles as is evident from this picture taken on a wet October morning in 1985 in Newcastle Bus Station when the bus was new. Much of the fleet was still in full NBC livery as is the Bristol saloon in the background. *(GKS)*

the UK with full-size buses they undoubtedly reigned supreme where the minibus was concerned. Twenty-five 609Ds with PMT *Hanbridge* bodywork were added to the fleet, all 20-seaters. Next came a mixed bag of twelve in 1990 comprising 609D, 709D and 811Ds with bodies by PMT, Whittaker and Reeve Burgess. Ten were 20-seat buses, one a 25-seat bus and one a 20-seat coach. Three of these came as used vehicles. A further ten 608Ds arrived the following year with a variety of bodywork, Reeve Burgess, Alexander, PMT and Imperial, seating 19, 20 or 25 and all new in 1985 from Strathclyde buses.

The following year, 1992, was another Mercedes year, this time all purchased new. There were two with Autobus Classique bodies (not as exotic as their name might suggest!), two with Whittaker bodies and 17 with Plaxton Beaver 24-seat bodies. More used Mercedes vehicles arrived, all new in 1986, from Milton Keynes City Bus comprising twelve Alexander-bodied 20-seaters. Mercedes remained the favourite make for the next two years, twelve 709Ds with Dormobile bodies in 1993 being followed by eleven similar vehicles with Marshall bodies in the following year. Four more

Reeve-Burgess L608Ds came from Crosville together with eight 25-seat MCW Metroriders.

The first of the Plaxton Beaver-bodied buses with 24 seats, of which there were 19, came in 1992, with a further ten in 1994. Then 21 more, but with only 22 seats, arrived in 1995 and a further 25 of these vehicles in 1996. Mercedes deliveries came to end with 27 Varios carrying Plaxton Beaver 2 27-seat bodies in 1997 to be followed by a further twelve in 1998. Some of these vehicles are proving to have long lives and are still giving sterling service to the company. The final Mercedes of all were delivered in 1999 and comprised a small batch of five 614s with Frank Guy 14-seat bodies.

That almost brings to an end the PMT minibus era but some of the last to be delivered were to prove the most unusual. In 1998 five 9-seater Technobus-Gulliver electric vehicles MTE51-6 (S251-6 AFA) came to operate a service from the Woodside Ferry to the central shopping area of Birkenhead. But finally, mention must be made of one further oddity, the Peugeot-Talbot tri-axle 18-seater 449 (K449 XRF) which found a home in Dukinfield and served as a reminder that PMT had for many years championed the eccentric and idiosyncratic.

Number 503 (D503 ERE) was one of 30 Freight Rover Sherpas with PMT-designed-and-built *Bursley* bodywork. New in 1987 it had coach seating for 20 passengers and is pictured in the entrance to Clough Street Garage in blue and white 'Flexi' livery. Many of these buses were shunted off to Willenhall and Leeds for *Red Rider* and *City Rider* operations respectively. *(GKS)*

Parked on Hanley Bus Station with its back to the now-derelict multi-storey car park is number 453 (D453 ERE), one of 25 Mercedes with the *Hanbridge* style of body also seating 20, which entered service in 1987/8. During these early days of the privatisation era PMT loved to colour code buses for various purposes, this example being in green and yellow for the *Hospitalslink*. This provided services half-hourly or hourly from Newcastle, Hanley and Stoke to the North Staffs main hospital complex in Hartshill, including the City General Hospital on London Road, Newcastle and the North Staffs Maternity Hospital as well as Central Outpatients, the Orthopaedic Hospital and the North Staffordshire Royal Infirmary. *(GKS)*

Some would say it was an unfortunate change of chassis maker when the Renault-Dodge was introduced into the fleet in 1987. A batch of 30 arrived, all with bodywork by Alexander, six of which seated 25 including number 527 (E527 JRE) pictured above on route 6A from Meir Park to Biddulph. Unfortunate, because as at least one driver said, "They were difficult to get going but, if you did, they were almost impossible to stop!" *(GKS)*

The other Renaults had 20-seat bodywork to a less attractive style but still by Alexander. Hanley Bus Station is again the location for this view of number 519 (E819 HBF) about to leave for Longton on route 48 via Weston Coyney. *(GKS)*

MXU449 (K449 XRF) was the sole Peugeot-Talbot tri-axle 18-seater which was delivered in 1992, though three 9-seaters arrived in 1995 and a final pair with 22 seats also came in that year from Midland Red West, having been new in 1990. MXU449 is seen in Red Rider livery with *First* logo while operating from Moreton Garage. *(AC)*

The Mercedes Vario with Plaxton Beaver 27-seat bodywork became the standard second-generation minibus in the PMT fleet, of which 40 were delivered in 1997/8. These two pictures taken some eleven years apart are of the same bus, MMM232 (R232 ERE). The rear view shows it in Hanley, route branded for the 38 Birches Head-Hanley service when almost new in 1998, whilst the front view shows it in Chester Bus Station in full *First* livery and numbered 50022 on a drab day in May 2009. One of these vehicles in PMT livery but without route branding was the subject of a Corgi Original Omnibus Company 1:76 scale model. *(Both pictures GKS)*

Number 56 (S526 AFA), below, was the last of six of these strange Technobus Gulliver 9-seater electric buses built in Italy in 1998. They were used, not completely successfully, on a service between Woodside Ferry and Birkenhead Central Shopping area as part of the *Red Rider* operation. From the start of the minibus era the travelling public had become used to converted bread vans. It would seem they were now being asked to ride on passenger carrying milk floats, which the writer had thought were unique to Polperro in Cornwall! *(CB)*

Speeding ahead –
Swifts and Darts!

Following privatisation in 1985 and for the next four years all new vehicles were minibuses, most with bodywork constructed in Stoke. A few coaches were delivered to Paramount Leisure, including one Leyland Royal Tiger Doyen in 1987, which enjoyed a relatively short life with PMT but served for some considerable time in service with Bennetts at Cranberry. It had at least one owner between PMT and Bennetts, and during its 21-year life carried registration numbers E42 JRF, 2335 PL, E67 NVT and A20 BNT. Also to come were two Plaxton Paramount-bodied Leyland Tigers and two similar bodied Scania K112s. The following year saw second-hand coaches appear, including a Bova, a Scania and two Leylands, a Leopard and a Tiger, all except the Bova carrying Plaxton coachwork. More Bristol VRTs arrived in 1989, six coming from South Midland.

That year also saw the first new double-deck buses since privatisation, consisting of a batch of ten Leyland Olympians, seven of which were coach-seated and finished in a special livery to promote the Hanley-Crewe service. They had Leyland low-height bodies.

Leyland had never before been patronised by PMT for double-deck bodywork, save for the five diverted from South Africa in 1950, which they probably didn't have much choice about. These proved to be the last new double-deckers ever to be bought by PMT. The other 1989 vehicles were National Express coaches, four in number, being Volvo B10Ms with Plaxton Expressliner 46-seat coachwork, the first to be supplied to any operator, and a Metrorider 29-seat coach delivered in Paramount Leisure livery. It was 1990 before any new full-size single-deckers arrived. These came in two batches, nine DAF SB220s with Optare Delta bodywork and 11 Leyland-bodied Leyland Lynx, all with 48 seats. These were to be the last new Leylands and the only Deltas, though both types made reappearances later as second-hand purchases.

In 1988 a batch of ten Leyland Swifts entered the fleet. The Leyland Swift was an economy vehicle based on a commercial chassis, its small wheels giving it a slightly idiosyncratic appearance, which was emphasised by the 'different' styling of the PMT-built 37-seat *Knype* dual-purpose bodywork. Though nicely finished inside and with comfortable seating, these were nonetheless generally unpleasant vehicles to travel on due to their bouncy ride. They followed the original *Knype* body which was on a Mercedes 814 chassis,

Number 42 (E42 JRF) was the only Leyland Royal Tiger Doyen to join the PMT fleet. It came in 1987 and stayed for about five years before going on to enjoy a long life with at least two others operators, Daybird Coaches of Killamarsh in Derbyshire and Bennetts Travel of Cranberry, Staffordshire. This was a magnificent coach and if Leyland had properly developed the model it could have been a world-beater! Like so many potentially excellent British products it was allowed to fade away for want of foresight and investment. The highlighting of the PMT initials as part of the ParaMounT fleet name is well illustrated in this Hanley Bus Station picture. *(GKS)*

having 21 seats and an exterior finished in a very smart light red and silver livery. More Mercedes midibuses entered service in the years 1989 to 1991. They were bodied by PMT Engineering, with the last of the PMT design vehicles, the *AMI*. Delivered in three batches there were a total of 50 of these buses. Following the closure of PMT Engineering, the company had to look elsewhere for its midibuses. The decision was taken to buy three Optare Metroriders in 1993. Eight more of these vehicles came in the following year and a further six in 1997 before the arrival of the successor model, the Optare Solo, five of which were placed in the fleet before the end of the century.

For the next few years new buses were to come from Dennis, by now the oldest surviving British manufacturer. First to come, in 1991, was a batch of 18 Darts with Plaxton Pointer bodywork containing 35 dual-purpose seats, a second batch of 11 following in 1992 and a third batch of 5 in 1993. Then, 16 more came in 1994, 20 in 1995 having 36 bus seats, and a final four in 1997 making a total of 74. Two 'odd' ones came in 1993 with Marshall 36-seat bodywork and a dozen in 1999 with Alexander ALX200 37-seat bodywork. Further Dennis vehicles were delivered, this time the Dennis Lance. The first in 1993 carried a Northern Counties Paladin body seating 47. This was followed two years later by five with Plaxton Verde 45-seat

bodies and three more in 1997 with Northern Counties Paladin coachwork, the only Northern Counties saloons operated by PMT in spite of the connection with that bodybuilder going back 50 years to 1947.

New names came on the scene in 1997, the combination of Scania with Wright Access bodies, eight seating 50 were followed in the next year by six seating 40, the first new vehicles to be delivered in First's Barbie livery.

During this last decade of the twentieth century many fleet additions came as used vehicles, such as two Leyland National 1s from Rhondda Transport as early as 1992, two Leyland Lynx from Westbus of Ashford, Kent in 1993 and an Alexander TE-bodied Leyland Tiger from Brewer of Swansea in 1996, but most came following the acquisition of other operators. No fewer than six coaches came from Berresford whilst a further three arrived from Turner together with five Daimler Fleetline double-deckers. But by far the largest number, all typical NBC fare, came with acquisition of the remaining bits of the English Crosville Company. These included 50 Leyland Olympians, 36 Bristol VRTs, six Leyland Nationals, five Metroriders, and two Leyland Leopard-Duple Dominant coaches, amounting to some 118 vehicles. Eight further vehicles came from Pennine Blue, but none of these saw more than a few days service with PMT.

In 1988 PMT had another change of heart and decided to revert to single-deck operation of the Main Line, switching from the previous use of Bristol VRTs. Twenty new buses were ordered in two batches, nine Optare Deltas and eleven Leyland Lynx. Here the penultimate Optare Delta number 808 (H808 GRE) is seen in Piccadilly, Hanley when new and before being given either fleet name or fleet number. These sad looking buses with their drooping front windscreen were to have long lives with PMT who became the last outpost of the DAF SB220 within FirstGroup. Ironically, these buses would receive the fleet number prefix letters SAD! *(AC)*

Leyland Lynx number 858 (H856 GRE), is seen on Crewe Bus Station much later in life, looking decidedly down at heel. It is showing the completely inane destination display of 'Sorry, not in service'. It would, however, achieve Barbie livery before withdrawal. These buses entered service with the Optares in August 1990 and were the last Leylands to be purchased new. *(CB)*

Ten further Leyland Olympians were delivered in 1989 and were to be the last new double-deckers ever to enter the **PMT** fleet. Seven were coach-seated 72-seaters and carried this livery of red, black and yellow, on a silver background route-branded for route 320 Hanley-Alsager-Crewe. Number 759 (G759 XRE) is seen leaving Crewe Bus Station on a wet Saturday afternoon in February 1990. *(GKS)*

IFF105 (J328 RVT) was another second-hand purchase. New in 1991, it came to PMT two years later from a company rejoicing in the name of Rumplan of Newcastle-under-Lyme, trading as Roseville Taxis. It was an Iveco Daily with Reeve Burgess 29-seat coach body. At this time PMT experimented with various liveries, especially for the *Flexi* fleet, some of which, this one included, only saw the light of day on one vehicle. This coach, describing itself as *Flexi Ambassador*, is seen attending the **POPS** Rally in June 1993 held at what was then the National Mining Museum at Chatterley Whitfield Colliery, another worthwhile British venture which was allowed to flounder from lack of investment. *(GKS)*

Falling between 25 and 30 seats the distinction between a mini and a midi becomes blurred! Perhaps this, the prototype PMT *Knype* body on Mercedes 814 chassis, should be a mini, but it's not! Number 38 (D333 DVT) was a 29-seater coach new in 1987. The small wheels and curvy windscreen don't sit quite comfortably with the somewhat austere lines of the main body structure as demonstrated by this picture at a Mercedes vehicle demonstration beside the Blackpool seaside. *(AC)*

The Dennis Darts began to arrive in 1991. L941 LRF was from the second batch, new in 1994, with Plaxton Pointer 35-seat dual-purpose body. It was photographed in the early evening in Newcastle Bus Station when it was twelve years old and carrying its fourth fleet number. Its original 941 became IDC941 which later reverted to 941 becoming 40107 in the First national numbering scheme. The *Barbie 2* livery blends well with its gloomy surroundings. (GKS)

Four Lances carried these 43-seat Northern Counties *Paladin* bodies, the only Northern Counties single-deckers to be bought by PMT. They were new in 1997 but by the time this picture of SDC868 (P868 MBF) was taken in Crewe Bus Station in 2001 the Crewe-Hanley route had reverted to being No. 20. Route branding had ceased, the route had been extended to Coppenhall at the Crewe end and Longton at the Potteries end to provide the last vestiges of what had once been the prestigious 'Main Line' and the bus had acquired the *First* logo. (GKS)

Not much new

The opening years of the new century saw a mere handful of new buses coming into the Potteries Company. In 1999 three new Scania-Wright Access 43-seat saloons arrived and though this type was to prove the mainstay of the fleet most arrived as 'previously used' by other FirstGroup operators. It was 2003 before more arrived and in 2005 the almost new cascaded 'Rail Replacement' buses came. There were eight of these joined by the first five Scania Omnicity 42-seaters, some of which turned up in dealer white as did some Scania-Wright Access vehicles. Ten more Omnicity 42-seat buses came the following year, eight of which were route branded for service 101 Hanley-Stafford.

Eight more Optare Solos were delivered in 2000, seating 27 passengers and five more Dennis Darts came in 2001 with Alexander ALX200 37-seat bodies. The only new buses to arrive between 2001 and 2005 were the eleven 60-seat Bluebird School buses for use on school contract services in the Wrexham area.

Most of the cascaded buses were quite mundane, coming from First companies in Hampshire, Manchester, Glasgow, Essex, Leicester, Yorkshire, Bristol, London, Edinburgh, Northampton and Somerset and Avon! The most interesting, however, came from the Far East. Perhaps the most exotic bus came from Singapore Bus Services, a Volvo YH2 tri-axle vehicle with Alexander Royale body seating 84 passengers. Fittingly, recalling a previous high capacity bus, it was given fleet number 700 (K174 EUX). New in 1991 it arrived at PMT in 1994 and was sent off to Pennine at Dukinfield. The writer remembers riding on these impressive monsters in Singapore where they carried the legend 'Air-conditioned Bus'.

Ten further 'Asian' double-deckers arrived from New World Bus Services in Hong Kong in 2001. These were Leyland ON3R4s, again with Alexander Royale 84 seat bodywork, new in 1993. These, the most exotic buses ever to carry a PMT livery, never saw service in the Potteries, all going to Pennine and being transferred to First Manchester when control of Pennine moved north. Former New World FirstBus vehicles which did see service in the Potteries were much more ordinary being 1998 Dennis Darts with Plaxton Pointer 2 bodies distinguishable only by having air conditioning pods on the roof. Even these lasted a mere few months with PMT in 2001/2 before moving south to First Devon and Cornwall.

Various used double-deckers came to the North Staffordshire and Cheshire areas of PMT, almost

Northern Counties-bodied 74-seat Leyland Olympian DOG889 (F156 XYG) came to PMT in 1999 when it was already eleven years old, one of three from Yorkshire Rider. Attaining fleet livery before entering service, it was actually used in North Staffordshire and was operating service 18 from Hanley to Keele University when photographed. It was destined for a short life in the Potteries before transfer to First Manchester in 2001. *(CB)*

all Leyland Olympians with a variety of bodywork. Eight with Northern Counties coachwork from First Manchester in 2001 were followed in 2002 by two from First Bristol with Roe bodies and a further seven Northern Counties-bodied buses from First Manchester with six more in 2003. All were new between 1982 and 1986. Other double-deck deliveries were three East Lancs bodied Dennis Dominators new in 1988 which came from First Capitol in 2000. Then there were five Scania-Alexander 80-seaters new in 1992, again from First Manchester, and finally in 2005 three Volvos with 75 Alexander coach seats new in 1994 from First Glasgow. Most of these double-deckers were used in South Cheshire and the Wirral, few gracing the streets of Stoke-on-Trent and Newcastle-under-Lyme.

Single-deck deliveries included 16 DAF SB220s, twelve coming in 2000 from First Yorkshire, to be followed by four with Ikarus bodies from First Avon and Somerset, making PMT the only FirstGroup operator with DAF220s.

Over the years some 35 Dennis Dart SLFs have turned up from, so it seems, all corners of the First empire with a mixture of bodywork, Alexander, Plaxton and perhaps, most notably, twelve with Marshall B27F bodywork from Centrewest, London. The ubiquitous Wright -odied Scania has arrived from all quarters over the years until a total of 45 cascaded examples are in the fleet in addition to those bought new.

A few coaches have come to PMT. Two Plaxton-bodied Volvo B10M 55-seat former Green Line coaches arrived from First Beeline in 2002. These were initially used on the X1 Derby-Manchester service in full Green Line livery! Two similar coaches arrived from First Bristol the following year. One final Volvo was a dual-purpose Wright Endurance-bodied bus from First Manchester in 2001.

The Scania Omnicity buses of 2004 have come a long way from the Brush Mutel contraptions of 1904 and even further from the horse-drawn trams of George Francis Train almost a hundred and fifty years ago, but the purpose of efficiently transporting passengers across North Staffordshire and parts of Cheshire still continues whether in prestige new vehicles or the 'cast offs' of other FirstGroup companies. Long may it continue!

Confusion reigns supreme! This Leyland Olympian, DOG111 (KFM 111Y), was new to Crosville in 1984, coming to PMT some nine years later. It found its way into the First Manchester fleet after it left the Stockport-based *Red Rider* unit. After painting into the then current Manchester 'tomato soup' livery it was transferred to PMT's Newcastle Garage. The result is a Crosville bus in Manchester livery operating a traditional PMT route! This is Newcastle Bus Station in October 2000. The Hanley-Newcastle-Chesterton route has carried service number 34 for over 50 years and still does! *(CB)*

Number 60025 (J426 NCP) is seen 'loading' in Newcastle Bus Station with a typically informative destination display. The sticker at the base of the windscreen was offering 7 days unlimited travel for £10 whilst on the right-hand side of the screen is a hand written label with the destination display for the service from Keele to Bradeley via Hanley. By this time, 2002, PMT had become the repository for all DAF220s in the First fleet, this being one of six Ikarus-bodied 48-seaters to come from First Yorkshire who also supplied a further seven with Optare bodies. *(CB)*

Number 301 (S344 SUX) was numerically the first of nine almost standard Dennis Dart SLF-Plaxton Pointer 41-seaters to come from New World FirstBus in Hong Kong. Almost standard because they were fitted with air-conditioning, the 'pod' for which can just be seen on the roof. They were new in 1998 coming to the Potteries in 2001. Again, they stayed for a very short time before transfer to First Devon and Cornwall. It may have been thought the air-conditioning would be more useful on the Cornish Riviera! In the upper picture, taken in Longton in 2001, the full destination display will be noted. Perhaps there really was a 'class-distinction' between Barbie 1 and Barbie 2 liveried buses. *(CB)*

Maybe a certain nostalgia came to the Potteries in 2002 when 14 Marshall-bodied Dennis Darts, new in 1997, arrived from First London and entered service in London livery more akin to traditional **PMT** red and yellow. They later all received First livery and continued to grace the streets of the Potteries in 2009. Here 40177 (P128 NLW) is seen standing on Hanley Bus Station. *(CB)*

The London theme was continued when two of these Volvo B10M-Plaxton Premiere 51-seat Green Line coaches arrived from First Berkshire, having been new in 1997 to First Glasgow. They entered PMT service in full Green Line livery, again in 2002. One was used on the X64 Shrewsbury-Hanley service, as in this picture of 60130 (R346 GHS) in Newcastle Bus Station, whilst the other was the regular performer on the Derby-Ashbourne-Leek-Stockport-Manchester X1 route, which PMT operated for a short time in 2001-03. By 2007 this vehicle had gone to Colchester whilst its partner at Adderley Green had returned to Glasgow. *(CB)*

A number of Volvo B7s with Wright Eclipse Urban 43-seat bodies came to the First Potteries Chester Garage from First Manchester during 2008. Number 66851 (MX05 CHD) stands in the City Centre operating Park & Ride service 30 to Broughton Heath at 11:39 on 4th May 2009. Behind is a Leyland Olympian operating a City Tour, or rather, it would have been had it not been awaiting the arrival of the First breakdown truck which arrived a few minutes later. *(GKS)*

Ten Omnicities came in 2006, eight of which were route-branded for service 101 as shown in these views of 65037 (YN06 WMK) at Stafford Rail Station. It seems such a pity that it is felt necessary to route brand the windows especially on an 'intatown' service such as this where it may be expected that some passengers would be sightseeing. They would expect to see through the windows which, no matter what the official opinion is, contra-vision does not allow. *(GKS)*

COLOUR MISCELLANY

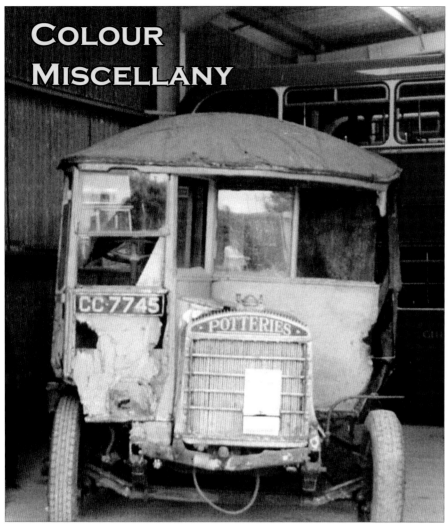

Left: Number 42 (CC 7745) was one of the QL type SOS machines acquired from Crosville in 1934. It had been new to Royal Blue of Llandudno , which company was purchased by Crosville in 1931. Finding these SOSs to be very non-standard in their fleet, Crosville soon disposed of them to PMT, where they joined 50 QLs purchased for the tram replacement programme in 1928. All had been withdrawn by 1937. It was pictured in need of complete restoration at the BaMMoT Transport Museum at Wythall, Birmingham in 1985, still with its POTTERIES radiator badge. Regrettably, no restoration has yet been carried out and the bus remains in the condition in which it is seen here. *(GKS)*

Below: This was the first colour picture ever taken by the writer! It was on a Kodak 620 roll film using a Box Brownie camera. In consequence, the early colour film and the passage of time have not improved the accuracy of the colour, but still it is a picture worth including! The bus, L229 (AJA 197), is one of the Roe-bodied Guy Arabs to come from North Western Road Car in 1947 and is seen at Stoke in 1953 after receiving its new fleet number (it had been 583) and some considerable attention in the body and paint shops, viz. the upper saloon sliding vent windows and 'PMT trademark' rounded ends to the lower deck windows. The classic lines of this simple livery may suggest that some of today's over elaborate schemes do nothing to promote the image of bus travel. *(GKS)*

Bill Hall, PMT's Chief Engineer, was heard to say, "No matter how these buses are painted they'll never look any good"! Nevertheless, these Leyland PD2-NCME lowbridge buses were splendid vehicles and gave years of reliable service in spite of the somewhat down at heel look of this one, L358 (LEH 766), seen in Newcastle Bus Station shortly before withdrawal in 1965. *(AC)*

The Milton area of North Staffordshire comprised a number of fairly rural services from the various villages into Hanley, which were both relatively lightly trafficked and hilly. After the take-over of the 'Big Five' a number of the acquired buses were shipped off to Milton Garage where they provided some wonderful variety as evidenced by one about to leave Stafford Street, Hanley for the very rural community of Stanley. SN415 (NEH 408) was an AEC Regal III, one of a pair new to Stoke Motors in 1949 with Lawton 35-seat bodywork. It remained in the fleet – and at Milton Garage – until 1963, so becoming one the last half-cab saloons in the fleet. It is in its final livery variation with a red roof and mudguards. *(JCC)*

This magnificent machine is another **AEC** with Lawton body, this time a Regal IV acquired with the business of **GE Rowley** of Bignall End. New in 1954, S494 (**XRE 235**) remained in the fleet until 1965, fortunately never suffering the disfigurement that the fitting of a standard **PMT** destination box would have inflicted. *(AC)*

A similar bus to the standard **PMT** Northern Counties-bodied Daimler Fleetlines came with the business of Thomas Beckett (no relation to the Archbishop of that name murdered in Canterbury Cathedral in 1170!) in March 1963 when it was only four months old. Though strictly not a full height bus, H992 (**83 XEH**) was nevertheless higher than the standard **PMT** vehicles and would not pass under a number of low bridges in the Potteries. For this reason it was given an 'H' fleet number prefix and became something of an embarrassment to **PMT**. It was soon exiled to Cheadle where it was photographed after being given a **PMT** standard destination box. Withdrawal came in 1972 when it joined the Godfrey Abbott Group. *(PMus)*

Celebrations

A century of public transport in North Staffordshire was celebrated in 1979 marking a hundred years since the formation of the North Staffordshire Tramways Company of Henry O'Hagan. In honour of the occasion, Leyland Atlantean L9766 (766 EVT) was painted in the livery of a 1930's double-decker. The scene here is Stoke Garage on 25th July 1979 when the bus was already 20 years old and a matter of months before it joined the 'fleet' of the Potteries Omnibus Preservation Society in whose ownership it remains, but regrettably not in this splendid livery. *(GKS)*

In 1998 Leyland Lynx SLC856 (H856 GRE) was chosen to revive the livery of an electric tram of almost a hundred years earlier. The celebration was the centenary of the founding of Potteries Electric Traction by the BET, an event which took place on 28th June 1898. Arguably, this was a year early as electrification of the tramway system was not completed until 1899. As mentioned in the text Corgi failed to cover themselves in glory when they produced a model of the bus with the fleet name misspelled as 'POTTRIES', spoiling an otherwise excellent rendition of the livery. *(CB)*

Preserved

Now preserved and in the ownership of Nigel Parkes, this PMT vehicle has won many trophies on its travels. Nigel brought it to show the writer whilst on his way to the POPS Rally in June 1993 when these pictures were taken opposite the rectory in Haughton, Stafford. The bus is one of the OPD2 chassis delivered with Weymann saloon bodies in 1949, receiving the Northern Counties lowbridge body shown in 1954 from the chassis of Leyland TD4 DVT 901. NEH 453 then gained the fleet number L453. In the pictures the quality of the Northern Counties body is wonderfully illustrated as is the high standard of the restoration. The figure standing in front of the bus is the present writer looking a bit older than when holding a ticket rack on the Prelim page! *(GKS)*

This **AEC Regent** with Park Royal 56-seat highbridge body was purchased as an unregistered demonstrator in June 1952, gaining the Stoke-on-Trent plate of **PVT 936** and fleet number **H490**. Later in the year it was temporally withdrawn to become a demonstration vehicle at the Commercial Motor Show of that year. It was unique in the fleet, never had a standard destination box, and disappeared without trace in 1965. *(AC)*

Newcastle (under-Lyme) Bus Station seems an appropriate place to see a bus diverted from Northern General, *ie* from Newcastle (on-Tyne). This **Guy Arab IV** with Weymann highbridge double-deck body, **H534 (SVT 934)** was one of ten to arrive in 1953. The picture shows the bus looking remarkably smart in 1967 with its **PMT** destination box and red roof and mudguards, about to take a full load to Tunstall just a week before its withdrawal. *(GKS)*

Both the vehicles above are AEC Reliances with Weymann bodywork. On the left is 'Jubilee' class SL804 (804 EVT), new in 1960 with a 41-seat dual-purpose body whilst on the right is SN5585 (VEH 585) of 1955, a 44-seat bus. The latter was withdrawn in 1968 but SL604 lasted until 1974 before becoming a driver trainer. Both are relaxing, in this view at Cheadle, where they spent many happy years! *(AC)*

Perhaps the most photographed bus in the PMT fleet was SN1000 (6000 EH), the prototype Daimler Roadliner with Marshall 50-seat body to BET Federation specification and new in 1964. It was used heavily for publicity purposes, and many pictures of it were taken by Daimler, Marshall and PMT. One such is this PMT picture showing the bus on publicity duties with blind display for the 'Main Line', a route on which it never operated! Initially, this proved to be an efficient vehicle well liked by passengers, especially for its low floor. Regrettably, faults began to develop, though these did not appear before a large order for further Roadliners had been placed. It was exhibited at the 1964 Commercial Motor Show before entering service for a mere eight years before being dismantled for spares in 1972. *(PMus)*

Standing in not too salubrious surroundings is C1102 (PVT 102F), the last of a trio of Daimler SRC6 Roadliner coaches with Duple Northern bodies having 49-seats, and new in 1968. To look at, they were magnificent coaches, but regrettably the promise was not fulfilled on the road and all had gone by 1972. This one found a second home with Greenhalgh and Pennington of Longton where it only lasted for a further year. *(AC)*

Driver Training Buses

Fulfilling its final role before preservation is **NEH 466** now with fleet number **T1**. It is a 1949 Leyland OPD2 with lightweight lowbridge body by Northern Counties. Becoming the first vehicle to be preserved by POPS, it is seen here in September 1993 on the muddy waste ground used as a parking space adjacent to the back of Stoke Garage. What ever became of muddy waste ground? *(GKS)*

Two of these Bristol FS6G ECW buses were acquired for driver-trainer duties from Southdown in 1976. New to Brighton Hove & District, the attraction of T1 (DPM 66C) was its fully manual transmission. At that time to receive a full licence drivers had to receive some of their instruction on a bus with a fully manual gearbox, even though the PMT fleet by then contained only semi-automatics. *(GKS)*

Yet another T1, this time AEH 135C, is seen during August 1984 taking a brisk trip down the A500 Potteries 'D' Road, so called because it leaves the M6 at junction 15 only to rejoin it a few miles further north at junction 16. The industrial landscape of Stoke-on-Trent 25 years ago has lost all the 'slag heaps' from coal mining and the 'bottle kilns' from the pot banks. The Daimler-Alexander bus had been taken out of passenger service in 1980 before spending something over five years in the training fleet which, at that time, usually consisted of just two or three buses. *(GKS)*

Not all driver-trainers received a special livery and 952 (952 **XVT**) was never a full-time training vehicle. After withdrawal this Leyland PSU3 with Willowbrook 53-seat body was used in connection with **MAP** (The Market Analysis Project). It is seen in Maclagan Street, Stoke-on-Trent on 1st May 1980, where the stone cladding will be seen to have done nothing to improve the look of the terrace of Victorian houses. *(GKS)*

In privatisation days this Bristol **VRT 605** (OEH 605M), from the first batch of such buses, had joined the **PSV Driver Training Unit** which had ceased to be purely for training **PMT** drivers as the advert on the side clearly indicates when the bus was pictured in Newcastle Bus Station in March 1989. *(AC)*

The AEC Reliance – Alexander Y-type dual-purpose vehicles had a hard life with **PMT** for reasons explained in the main text. On delivery 171 (**FEH 171J**), one of the final batch of six, had been painted in **PMT** dual-purpose livery but by the time of this scene in 1970 in Greengate Street, Tunstall it was resplendent in **NBC** poppy red having just arrived from Biddulph. *(AC)*

This Leyland Leopard with Duple Dominant I 49-seat 'grant door' coach body, 56 (**XBF 56S**), is adorned with the very patriotic red, white and blue livery for the unsuccessful '**INTATOWN**' motorway express services between Hanley and Crewe and Hanley and Stafford. Note the '**POTTERIES**' fleet name. *(PMT)*

The fleet on parade or at least representatives of it! From left to right, Austin taxi **XRF 2X**, then Mercedes L307D-Reeve Burgess 12-seater minibus, 112 (**YRE 472Y**), the second of a pair new in 1983. Next in line is Leyland Leopard-Duple Dominant coach, number 21 (**GRF 221V**), the only full luxury Dominant to come to PMT with just 46 seats, new in 1979. On the extreme right is 13ft 8in high Bristol VRT **NEH 730W** new in 1980, by which time these buses had gained moquette set coverings. All survived into privatisation. *(PMT)*

Six Leyland National 2 47-seat dual-purpose vehicles were delivered in 1984 in the always smart **NBC** local coach livery. They were used on the longer distance routes such as Hanley to Stafford and Newcastle to Shrewsbury for which their lively performance and comfortable seating was well suited. These were wonderful buses to ride on if not always the most reliable! *(PMus)*

This procession of buses moving along Piccadilly, Hanley in the direction of Burslem is about to pass the long-closed Bagnalls Model Shop. First to reach it will be Leyland Atlantean 903 (903 UVT) carrying an all-over advertisement for the London and Manchester Assurance Company. Fortunately, this was one of the more restrained of the 'all-over advertisers' as it was part of a long-lived contract with the London and Manchester covering a period of eight years and three buses. The first in 1972 had been Atlantean L9799 (799 EVT), followed in 1975 by this vehicle and finally in 1977 by Bristol VRT 620 (GBF 76N). *(AC)*

If you can advertise other people, why not advertise for yourself? This is exactly what **PMT** did using Leyland Olympian 745 (A745 JRE) in 1992. The promotion is for ideas for days out by bus and was sponsored jointly by the Countryside Commission, Signal Radio and PMT. The bus, newly shopped out, is in Newcastle Bus Station. *(AC)*

Eight Bristol VRTs intended for PMT in 1974 were diverted to Crosville to help out with a vehicle crisis in Liverpool. They returned to the Potteries in penny numbers in the following year and entered PMT service in green livery. Number 618 (REH 818M) was the last to return and kept its green paint until April 1976 when it was decorated for the Britannia Building Society. It took part in the Lord Mayor of Stoke-on-Trent's Gala Day in 1977 and should have gone to London to represent the Britannia Building Society in the Lord Mayor of London's Parade of that year. It was, however, prevented from doing this because of a strike by PMT drivers, an action which helped no one and brought this advertising contract to an abrupt and ignominious end. *(GKS)*

Not many single-deck buses found themselves in the roll of all over ad buses, but one that did was Leyland National 268 (GBF 71N) new in 1974. It was given this rather attractive look for the local Roberts Bakery when over ten years old in 1986. It is seen being reversed into a parking space on Hanley Bus Station where this livery looks a good deal smarter than many of the scrappy early privatisation schemes to be seen then. *(AC)*

Above: The 'Village Bus' was introduced in 1985 for the rural route from Hanley to Bagnall and Stanley using the first of PMT's panel-van conversions, Mercedes L608D 117 (B117 OBF). Could it be that the photographer of this PMT promotional picture taken at Bagnall Church was of the opinion that the best way to picture a passenger-carrying bread van was to hide it behind the trees? *(PMT)*

The 1978 Bristol VRT BRF 693T, on the left, briefly carried both fleet number 1493 and the yellow and blue version of the standard PMT livery for service with Pennine Blue. Note the midibus in the background carrying fleet number 1488 but in yellow and red and with Red Rider fleetname. *(CB)*

Thirteen Bristol RELL buses were acquired from Bristol Omnibus Company in 1983, eleven of which entered service in green livery. Two remained long enough to receive a coat of NBC poppy red, but only OHU 766F seen at Burslem Garage, survived long enough to receive blood and custard. New in 1968 this bus took fleet number 206, previously held by a Bristol RELL new to PMT in 1972 but used as one of the buses converted to a mobile workshop for Newcastle Borough Council in 1982. *(CB)*

Number 52 (URF 52S), one of the 1977 vehicles, a 49-seater, is in Stafford one morning whilst operating to Hanley which it would reach an hour later having travelled via Stone and Newcastle. The coach is seen in post privatisation blood and custard livery complete with 'go faster' stripe, later generally known as the 'zipped' livery. (GKS)

Few vehicles from the Berresford business were in a sufficiently good condition to remain in service with PMT. One that did was 203 (PCH 418L), a Bristol RELH6L with ECW 47-seat coach body and one of three which were effectively prototypes for this ECW body style and supplied new to Trent Motor Services of Derby in 1972. The one piece destination box without a service number blind distinguishes this vehicle from a dual-purpose bus with the same body style. The PMT red and yellow livery with go faster stripes looks particularly attractive on this coach and contrasts well with the coach behind in Paramount ex-NBC coach livery. The location is the forecourt of Clough Street Garage in Hanley. (GKS)

A number of fairly exotic buses came to PMT at the start of the 21st Century, not least being this tri-axle Leyland Olympian with 84-seat Alexander RH bodywork numbered 686 (K486 EUX), new in 1993 to New World in Hong Kong which arrived in 2001. A similarly bodied Volvo YN2, though a year newer, had come from Singapore Bus Services in 1999. The author actually travelled on these buses in both Singapore and Hong Kong during a once-in-a-lifetime holiday in 1994. They came to the Potteries and gained red and yellow livery and 'Shropshire' registration marks before being shipped off to Dukinfield. When Pennine closed they joined the First Manchester fleet. (CB)

There is a temptation in books of this nature to include too many pictures of one type of bus to illustrate different liveries or unusual locations. The writer may well be guilty of this by using this image of 759 (G759 XRE), a Leyland Olympian seen leaving Hanley Bus Station. No apology is made for its inclusion to demonstrate that even at this stage of its existence PMT could still be different, hence the PMT version of 'Barbie 2' livery with route branding for the X39 Hanley to Alton Towers service from which it seems to be earning a worthwhile revenue on the late Spring Bank Holiday of 2001. *(CB)*

This Volvo B10M with Plaxton Premiere coachwork, 61212 (L64 UOU), was used on the X1 service from Derby to Manchester but is seen at Newcastle Garage in the attractive First coach livery. One of a pair of 49-seaters new in 1994, it came to PMT in 2003 from First Wessex where it had operated for National Express. After a very short stay in the First Potteries fleet it became part of First Somerset at Weston-super-Mare. No further coaches have since been operated by First Potteries. *(CB)*

Acknowledgements

The author wishes to acknowledge his grateful thanks to numerous people who have made this publication possible. First of these must be John Senior and Venture Publishing for their willingness, not only to publish this book, but also for their constant patience and long-suffering and even acting on some of my suggestions. Colin Reeve took on the final daunting task of squeezing ever-more pictures into ever-decreasing numbers of pages and I record my appreciation of his forebearance for this; also that of my wife Margaret for her unending patience for living with 'the book' for so long. David and Mary Shaw, Venture's long-sitting proof readers, finally went through the finished result with meticulous care though any errors which may have slipped through are ours and not theirs. Thanks are expressed to Debbie Klemperer at the Potteries Museum and Art Gallery for so freely allowing access to the archive of PMT pictures now in the care of the museum. To Peter Jacques and the Kithead Trust for their kind reception and again for so readily permitting access to the various documents entrusted to their care. I am indebted to John Cooke for his readiness to share his photographic archive; as a past employee of PMT and one-time editor of the PMT House Magazine he is a mine of information. Where possible the photographs have been attributed to the original photographer, but as time moves, more and more frequently it becomes necessary to credit a picture to a collection. However I wish to place on record my thanks to Cliff Beeton for offering his valuable pictures from the last twenty-five or so years. The Newsletters of the Potteries Omnibus Preservation Society and the Staffordshire Bus Enthusiasts Group have proved a useful source of material again, especially for the last part of this story.

Photograph Credits

AC	Author's Collection		PMT	Potteries Motor Traction Company
CB	Cliff Beeton		PMus	Potteries Museum and Art Gallery
GKS	Geoffrey Smith		POPS	Potteries Omnibus Preservation Society
JAS	John A Senior		STA	Senior Transport Archive
JCC	John Cooke Collection			

Bibliography

PMT 1898-1958	J Wentworth Day (PMT1958)
A Sociological History of Stoke-on-Trent	EJD Warrilow FSA (Etruscan Publications 1960)
The Potteries Motor Traction Co Ltd	(PSV Circle/Omnibus Society 1967)
PMT – A National Bus Company	Geoffrey K Smith (TPC1977)
Midland Red, volume 1	P Gray, MR Keeley and JA Seale (TPC 1978)
PMT – A Century of Public Service	(POPS 1979)
The Potteries Motor Traction Co Ltd	
- part 2 1953-1982	(PSV Circle/Omnibus Society 1983)
The Leyland Bus Mk 2	Doug Jack (TPC1984)
Turning Points – a Lifetime in Transport	Walter Womar MinstT MIRTE (Venture 1995)
Independent Buses in Staffordshire	Neville Mercer (Venture 2009)
A Century of North Staffordshire Buses	John Cooke (Horizon Press 2009)

Various issues of: Bus and Coach; PMT House Magazine; POPS Newsletter; Staffs Bus Enthusiasts Group Newsletter

A criticism often levelled at bus books, especially from modellers, is that they rarely include rear views. PMT used to love photographing buses from the back, often to illustrate the properly sign-written advertisements. This typical shot is of 1949 Leyland OPD2 H445 (NEH 445) with the Northern Counties body it gained in 1954. *(PMT)*